Family Capitalism

Family businesses and family entrepreneurship represent, within most countries, between 50 to 90 per cent of all business entities. Families control 30 per cent of the Fortune 500 companies. These owners and their businesses are often an important part of the social fabric in local communities and, increasingly, the international economy. Despite this, *family capitalism*, or ownership, has been seen as synonymous with stagnation, conflict and crises. The authors focus on how family owners avoid these pitfalls, and how emotional resources develop strategizing capacities.

The book explores how successful family businesses innovate and create *visionary ownership,* and implement it. Two crucial leadership capacities are introduced: *leadership of paradox* and *distributed leadership*.

A renewed understanding of family capitalism shows how the family can generate unique strategic advantages in stewardship, succession, long-term thinking, risk management and building social capital. It offers a different perspective regarding value creation in the economy. The book provides new insights for family owners, advisers and leaders, as well as scholars.

The findings are from a *best practice research* project with cases from China, the USA, Germany, Colombia, Israel, Tanzania, France and Sweden. Applying *strategy-as-practice theory* demonstrates how families, across cultures and sectors, use generic ownership strategies and experiment, for example with cluster ownership and creating new ventures in successions.

Gry Osnes is a clinically trained and licensed psychotherapist and family therapist. She works with owners and entrepreneurs on succession processes, coaching of boards and interpersonal dynamics. She coaches and advises focusing on individuals and groups increasing their transitional and strategic capacity, using both system and modern psychoanalytic theory on transitions, authority and change. Her earlier research, and PhD publication, is on succession dynamics in different types of organization and entrepreneurship. She develops action research and collaborative research and was the academic leader of the research project leading to this book.

Family Capitalism

Best practices in ownership and leadership

Edited by Gry Osnes

Routledge
Taylor & Francis Group

LONDON AND NEW YORK

First published 2017
by Routledge
2 Park Square, Milton Park, Abingdon, Oxon OX14 4RN

and by Routledge
711 Third Avenue, New York, NY 10017

Routledge is an imprint of the Taylor & Francis Group, an informa business

British Library Cataloguing in Publication Data
A catalogue record for this book is available from the British Library

Library of Congress Cataloging in Publication Data
A catalog record for this book has been requested

ISBN: 978-1-138-21452-1 (hbk)
ISBN: 978-1-315-44420-8 (ebk)

Typeset in Bembo
by Saxon Graphics Ltd, Derby

Printed and bound by CPI Group (UK) Ltd, Croydon, CR0 4YY

For Agnes

Contents

Illustrations

Figures

Table

List of boxes

Contributors

Gry Osnes is a clinically trained and licensed psychotherapist and family therapist. She works with owners and entrepreneurs on succession processes, coaching of boards and/or interpersonal personal dynamics. She coaches and advises focusing on individuals and groups increasing their transitional and strategic capacity, using both system and modern psychoanalytic theory on transitions, authority and change. Her earlier research, and PhD publication, is on succession dynamics in different types of organization and entrepreneurship. She develops action research and collaborative research with different types of businesses and organizations and was the academic leader of the research project leading to this book. Email gry@family-capitalism.com

James Grady is a former leader of a private medical service, a senior member and practice manager for over 35 years. His interest in human behaviour, especially under stress, developed early in his career and he focuses on human motivation and behaviour in relation to business, practice and personnel management. In 2006 he and his daughter, Victoria Grady, started working together in investigating instability and behavioural reactions in employees as influenced by organizational culture and change. In 2010 they co-founded the family business PivotPoint Business Solutions with a focus on the relationship between leaders and employees, particularly within one-family businesses. Email james@family-capitalism.com

Victoria Grady is currently Assistant Professor in Management/Organizational Behavior in the School of Business at George Mason University. Her research, and PhD, focused on the behavioural implications (e.g. decreased performance, productivity and profitability) of organizational change. She continues to build on her original research and is actively investigating the unique role of the family business dynamic on her behavioural theory related to attachment, mourning, loss and the integration of the transitional object. She is co-author of *The Pivot Point: Success in Organizational Change*, Morgan-James Publishing, 2013. Email victoria@family-capitalism.com or, to learn more, please visit her website at www.pivotpnt.com or follow her on Twitter at @pivotpoint.

Mona Haug is a business coach and mentor working with CEOs, managers, project leaders and teams within family businesses. She has a special focus on leadership development and team coaching. Earlier research and publications are on team coaching, demonstrating the findings of the team and individual learning phases that strengthen the team and the individual team member alike. Her PhD research focuses on career development for female executives: what barriers as well as supporting circumstances affect women in top leadership positions. To learn more, please visit her website at www.monahaug.com or email mona@family-capitalism.com

Olive Yanli Hou is a communication adviser with expertise in promoting cultural exchange between Europe and Asia. She has a focus on creative industries, innovation and entrepreneurship and how one can learn from different cultures but also how cultural exchange can trigger new innovation. She develops complex communication strategies for major businesses and luxury brands in China and Europe and has worked with various companies and family owners. She has a special focus on social identity and cluster ownership in family ownership. She writes and contributes to the Chinese business publications such as *China Family Business Review*, *Economic Weekly* and *China Entrepreneur Magazine*. Email olive@family-capitalism.com or visit www.oliveschoice.com

Liv Hök is a clinically trained and licensed psychotherapist and family therapist. She has worked with individuals, families and groups over a period of 40 years. She works as an organization and role analyst and offers support and organizational psychological services to individuals, small workplaces and large companies. Furthermore, she teaches and trains other consultants in role analysis. Her group work also includes arranging and working as a member of staff on group relation conferences. Her latest publication is a book on role analysis and coaching drawing on psychodynamic and systemic thinking. Email liv@family-capitalism.com or visit www.livhok.nu/english

Angélica Uribe is the CEO of the family trust fund, which has developed urban and rural real estate projects in recent years. She is also executive director of a private education institution, Colegio San Patricio. She was trained as a corporate and financial lawyer with degrees from Universidad de los Andes and Georgetown University. Before she entered the role as leading owner on behalf of her family she worked in the public and private sectors in Bogotá, Colombia. Her work experience includes being a lawyer in the Ministry of Finance and legal counsel to several financial institutions. (angelicaug@gmail.com)

Acknowledgements

First of all, we would like to extend our thanks to the families whose inspirational stories comprise the central content of this book. All were tremendously generous with their time, and patient throughout the interviewing, writing and editing processes. Often, when we were stuck in an analysis, or needed more information, they would have to set aside further time so we could clarify questions that arose. The families were open with us in acknowledging the many difficult decisions that confront a business-owning family. They provided rich detail in how they dealt with these situations and how they learned from them. We hope it will be of guidance and inspiration to others. All are warm and compassionate people, in addition to being gifted entrepreneurs and business managers, and are a credit to the world of entrepreneurship and family ownership.

We would like to thank the Hexin Group and Mr He Shangqing, Mr He Bin and Ms He Xuefei for their generous support and openness during the Chinese case study. We would like to thank the Fox family and Fox Safari in Tanzania for being willing, when the editor of this book came across them on a holiday, to agree to taking part in several long interviews of the two founders of the business. Many thanks are due to Hani, Sami and Wedad from Jerusalem and their children and grandchildren for allowing us to interview family members, from all three generations still working in business, and the Managing Director, Steve. We are also grateful to the French family, the subject of the pilot study, whom the editor followed after the initial interviews over some years.

Many thanks go to the family and employees for opening the door to Sundström Safety AB and generously sharing the family and business story. In many of the case studies the families or employees agreed to partake in several interviews and set aside time for follow up conversations. In the Swedish case we needed extensive follow up on the in-depth details of their management and procedures for technological innovation. The same was true in the German case where, after interviewing family members end employees, we needed to come back for more information about the founding of the business. As with the others, we are grateful to the Foster family for the time they devoted and their feedback in follow up conversations.

We are also very grateful to other contributors who described their roles on specific issues. First, to Angélica Uribe from Colombia who contributed with her story to the extent that she became a co-author of the book and ventured into the role of author; second, to Nigel Farrow in the UK for contributing with his story about selling the business; and finally, to Eivind Reiten, in Norway, for his story about his role as Chair of the Board of several family businesses.

Ionna Psalti was indispensable in helping us with developing ethical guidelines, developing the information necessary to our research cases and aligning it with EU ethical standards for research. Furthermore, she gave us important support and encouragement. We thank our Routledge editor Kristina Abbotts, for her support, guidance and patience for the complexity of compiling a multi-author book, and to our editorial adviser Philip Whiteley for help in producing the final draft.

From Gry Osnes: Thanks to Professor Siv Boalt Boethius, University of Stockholm, and Professor Odd Arne Tjersland, University of Oslo for support, encouragement and advice; and to Xavier for patiently accepting all the time the research, writing and editing of the book took during weekends and holidays.

From James Grady: I wish to express my gratitude to my wife, Anne, my daughters, Tori and Jenni, and my grandchildren, Kendall, Grady, Anne Caroline (A.C.), and Reagan—you are my sunshine. And also to Johnnie T. Ferrell whose example, perhaps unknowingly, has rekindled in me the need for further self-reflection and contemplation in the service of personal growth.

From Victoria Grady: To Dr Jerry B Harvey, adviser and mentor, thank you for inspiring me to learn to write. May you rest in peace.

From Olive Yanli Hou: I would like to thank my parents Hou Xinrong and Wang Xiurong, my sister Hou Xiaoli and brother-in-law Luo Bin for their continuous support and tolerance. The strong family bond I am lucky enough to have was the main inspiration for this writing.

From Mona Haug: Thank you to my husband Michael and to our children Gabriel and Jessica. Thank you to my mother who inspired me to dream big and my father who taught me perseverance and stamina. Thank you to Nicola Leibinger-Kammüller who unknowingly has encouraged me to embark on this journey. My special thanks to Sarah Jones, who has patiently done all the proof-reading for me. Thank you so much.

From Liv Hök: Thank you to John Bazalgette for helpful discussions around organizational and role analysis; to my husband, Mats Wahl, author and scriptwriter, for helpful discussions on the art of writing; and to my translator, Cynthia Morissette, for helpful and immediate translations of my work.

Foreword

Denise Kenyon-Rouvinez

The contribution of family-owned businesses to economic development and society has been historically under-stated in economics and business literature, but in the past 20 years we have begun to see this imbalance redressed. A popular image may have been that the family firm is cautious, slow to adapt and hampered by nepotism – which is true for some – but recent research shows that family-owned businesses are also able to combine innovation with resilience, generating wealth for all stakeholders, and contributing to technological and economic development. The discipline and commitment of successful families to a longer-term perspective greatly aid economic resilience, encouraging wise investments and the capacity for strategic renewal. The philanthropic contributions of the most enlightened business-owning families have been transformational for many communities, while many family-owned firms commit themselves to the societies in which they have evolved, and to pursuing good social outcomes in the core business as well as in related charitable initiatives.

So I am delighted to welcome the publication of *Family Capitalism: Best practices in ownership and leadership*, an addition to the growing literature on family business governance and management. It is based on solid research, with relevant issues vividly brought to life in case studies from five continents of responsible and thriving enterprises.

Gry Osnes and her fellow contributors show that there is a flip-side for every perceived weakness of the family firm: that every challenge is also an opportunity, sometimes in disguise – and that some special individuals are ready to overcome them. They show how the issue of succession for a family firm, for example, can be used to turn the process into a form of strategic renewal. The case studies in this book, all described in accessible language with a helpful level of detail, show how entrepreneurship is often used as a tactic in succession; it is also used to build successions of higher-performing companies (ladder entrepreneurship) and clusters of innovative firms, similar to, and often forming a part of, larger regional clusters of business expertise. Such clusters create many opportunities, and they enable a group of linked family-owned enterprises to be flexible, adaptable and, where necessary, experimental. Such nimbleness is a huge asset at a time of rapid technological change and uncertainty in global economics and trade. We are likely to see this interesting type of business formation grow.

This book also shows how women often play a central role in family business development, including strategy and financial management, and not only in countries noted for their development of women's rights in legislature. The 'traditional' family firm, an inflexible patriarchal company with succession restricted to the eldest son, may hopefully gradually become much less predominant.

Family Capitalism: Best practices in ownership and leadership also offers a welcome focus on the importance of responsible ownership, and the disciplines and skills necessary. I have argued for some time that ownership should be seen as a professional discipline in its own right; in the past it has been overshadowed by the emphasis in business schools on executive management and on governance focusing on the business board. While it is true that owners should not interfere in day-to-day decisions, looking over the shoulder of the executive, this should not be interpreted as implying an approach of indifference or laissez-faire. Responsible ownership involves asking the right questions, being aware of major developments, holding management to account. It also involves maintaining the right culture – in this context, upholding the family's values. This means setting guidelines and principles on risk appetite, ethical conduct and investment strategy. Ownership also has an emotional element – again, an important dimension often neglected in conventional business education – relating to social impact, values and legacy. Ultimately, responsible ownership is a powerful role, not a passive one. The big decisions on strategic direction – which technologies to develop, which product areas to be in, which to shelve – lie with the owners.

There is clearly an awareness on the part of the contributors to *Family Capitalism* of the many different dimensions of the family business; an understanding not only of the roles of ownership, governance, management, employees and the wider community, but how each is a part of an interlocking whole. This comprehension is necessary, and is well illustrated in this thoroughly researched yet readable book.

One of the many achievements of Gry and her team is to combine theory and practice, in a manner in which the two nicely complement each other. This is a challenge for any author of a business book. Case studies without an accompanying theory can lack rigour, amounting to little more than anecdote, while theory without practical examples can result in material that is too abstract and difficult to implement for the busy manager or owner. This book selects case study examples that neatly illustrate a theoretical concept: stewardship, succession, entrepreneurship, cluster development, and so on, all backed by helpful reading lists of books and academic articles, for those who wish to access other research. Sections on attachment, loss and mourning are explored in Freudian depth, yet the writing style remains accessible.

The examples selected illustrate a wide range of types of firm, in different cultures and different sectors. Yet the lessons are generic and applicable to all, including the largest family-owned companies. Indeed, it is increasingly the case that many leaders at non-family businesses are also starting to study the practices at the most successful family-owned firms, particularly on the subject of responsible ownership.

As a book, *Family Capitalism* is a practical tool that families can use. They can ask the questions posed by the authors and apply them to their own situation. It is also backed by rigorous study, and is likely to be equally valuable to the student and researcher.

Denise Kenyon-Rouvinez, Wild Group Professor of Family Business and
Director of the IMD Global Family Business Center at IMD Business School,
Lausanne, Switzerland
March 2016

1 Introduction

Strategy practice in family ownership

Gry Osnes

This is a book about successful family owners and their businesses. It complements literature that has a focus on fault-lines, failures and problems seen as intrinsic to the family ownership of a business. Much of the literature on family-owned businesses has featured failed family ownership and enterprises and this should not be seen as synonymous with family ownership. An aspiration of this book is to describe the counterforces to these destructive dynamics. We describe and explore the resources and strategies families deploy as owners and leaders.

Family business or family capitalism

We differentiate between studying 'family capitalism' and 'family businesses'. The term 'family capitalism' captures both the family and its involvement inside the business, and the impact of leadership through ownership structures and governance. With this framework there is a wider perspective of what the family is doing with the 'object' (business). If one focuses on the business, and not the relationship between the family and business, one can fail to grasp the dynamic of how a family owner changes its ownership. It can be changing their use of governing structures; how they start and develop new ventures or use the proceeds from a sale of a business to develop a new business. Recent research shows that many families own several companies in a cluster (Tsabari, Labaki, and Zachary, 2014). Our technology excellence case was the only case where the family had owned only one company from its founding in the early twentieth century until 2016.

Jones and Rose (1993) question and refute a broader narrative of family businesses as a contributor to stagnation in the economy. We will build on these contributions and show how the family owners are renewing entrepreneurship, growing the business or developing new business, and by this contributing to economic growth. In addition many of the family owners and their businesses had other goals such as stewardship for a local community, building a wider social network of business communities, technological excellence and letting employees buy a company they owned. As such the family had impact beyond the financial aspect of their businesses. The USA family, risk averse and conservative, challenged themselves to expand and grow the assets they had over a period of thirty years. They sold businesses to former employees, who would continue to own and manage them successfully, so as to finance a bigger business. The Chinese business we describe had evolved a structure of a conglomerate with several interlinked companies which would be the driving force behind a business cluster in the region in China. This allowed them to continue to innovate and to cooperate on business activities and big contracts between different family-owned companies.

If only one in ten family-owned businesses have such a wide impact it would be significant, in addition to the economic contribution, for a local community or region. Academic literature has often ignored the influence of family ownership and family businesses in the economy, as the writers Heck and Stafford (2001) noted. Not only has there been a focus on dysfunction and family business failures in addition to a perspective that family businesses contribute to stagnation in the economy. More recent business history research challenges this notion (Jones and Rose, 1993). Our case study supports this perspective and emphasizes the crucial role of family as an entrepreneurial group as pivotal to value creation and innovation in an economy. The economic impact of family businesses and their ownership is formidable, and has probably been under-estimated. In addition to the economic aspect, our cases show how they are a part of the social fabric in the local community and increasingly an actor in their global markets. A major international study by the Boston Consulting Group reported in *Harvard Business Review* (Kachaner, Stalk and Bloch, 2012) found that family-owned firms tended to be more resilient and commercially successful than a comparator group, as a result of counter-cyclical investment, frugality, successful diversifications and long-term strategy-setting: 'When we looked across business cycles from 1997 to 2009, we found that the average long-term financial performance was higher for family businesses than for nonfamily businesses in every country we examined.'

There is a specialist research stream trying to quantify the economic impact of family-owned businesses. Numbers from The Family Firm Institute webpage, www.ffi.org, estimate that family firms to account for two-thirds, or 70–90 percent, of global GDP annually. Between 50–80 percent of jobs in the majority of countries worldwide are created by family businesses, 85 percent of start-up companies are established with family money. In most countries around the world, family businesses constitute between 70 and 95 percent of all business entities. Of the world's biggest companies (Global Fortune 500 Companies) 33 percent are family controlled.

The latest research shows that the individual heroic entrepreneur, often assumed to be a man, is rare compared to entrepreneurial groups. The latter accounts for 70 percent of newly founded businesses in the USA (Ruef, 2011). Entrepreneurship in groups does not only describe the founding of the business but also its renewal, in different ways, over the history of a successful business or ownership. We therefore focus on what the family as a group does, rather than on a single family member. It might appear that there is one person in control, but after looking under the surface a more complex dynamic often emerges. With more in-depth exploration, in all our cases, there was distribution of leadership and control to different family members within a generation. Furthermore, in all our cases there were three generations or more involved. Very rarely would the oldest generation retire, but instead would carve out innovative exit roles. In our cases it was always a couple that started the business and, contrary to the stereotype, the woman would often have financial control and veto power on investment. Of the younger generations emerging now, the sisters compete, and collaborate, with brothers or cousins.

Ownership and leadership

Members of an entrepreneurial, business-owning family are actors with drive, imagination and dreams that they seek to achieve and implement. These goals and dreams we regard as *visionary ownership* as described in Part I. It is about how one innovates a vision or dream and uses strategic practices to achieve them. We grouped three tasks that would be important for the vision: grasping and exploiting opportunities, entrepreneurship and consolidation, accumulating advantage for the family. A successful owner has to be able, over a long-term perspective, to manage these tasks.

In Part II we focus on two other important leadership strategies that we found these families used: the *leadership of paradox* (Ingram et al., 2016) and *distributed leadership* (Gronn, 2002). These leadership capacities are invoked when the family uses their emotional and social resources. The family and the business have needs and goals that are contradictory, resulting in paradoxes. An important part of family leadership is to be able to make priorities and create 'win-win' dynamics out of these paradoxes. Distributed leadership can happen in transfer of leadership between generations, among siblings and by creating clusters of ownership.

Strategy-as-practice theory

Our book describes best practices in how to optimize the outcome for a family and to maintain the business as competitive and financially profitable. These businesses were successful both in the short and the long term. The analytical approach applied builds on a strategy-as-practice approach, in which strategy is seen as a 'doing' activity (Whittington and Vaara, 2012). Different strategy practices that owners use are described in Part I: serial entrepreneurship, building social capital, creating cluster ownership and stewardship strategies. These strategy practice guides behavior and are macro strategies. At the micro-level praxes are creating and upholding these macro-strategy practices. Actions, or praxes, enable and implement the strategy practices (Ibid.). The difference is important as there is room for innovation and development when one executes praxis. At the praxis level one can slightly, or possibly dramatically, change the policy or procedure. In this way one can conceptualize how change can happen

OWNERSHIP STRATEGIES:
Enterpreneuring
Social capital
Cluster ownership   STRATEGY PRACTICE
Innovation
Stewardship
Succession

LEADERSHIP IN:
Role & autonomy
Loss & mourning
Power & authority
Gender
Choice of succession avenue

Figure 1.1 Strategy practices in family capitalism

naturally and how strategies emerge over time, and with experimentation. This is important in a system that is fluid and less rigid, such as a well-functioning family business.

The strategy practices framework for family ownership is suggested in Figure 1.1. To the left of the figure are the ownership strategies we found. These practices were present in all the family cases across different cultures and types of businesses. The emotional and social resources, praxes and leadership used by the families, are shown to the right. We have divided the book into two sections according to this macro- and micro-level. Part I describes the macro-ownership strategies we found made families successful in their ownership. Important micro-activities or praxes, or leadership strategies are in Part II. This is how the families used social and emotional resources in leading the family group, and business, when implementing their ownership strategies. Important leadership strategies, or praxes, included negotiating autonomy when creating roles, being able to mourn loss of safety and creating authority.

Overlap of two systems: creative tension or destruction

Studies on why a family business fails are useful. These are plentiful, covering lack of planning the life cycles, conflict in succession or a failed succession and an inability to effect renewal (e.g., Gersick, 1997; Lansberg, 1999; Kets de Vries, 2001). Another risk with family ownership, and within the business, is a preoccupation with an overwhelming legacy (Gilmore and Ronchi, 1995), which can be an overhanging shadow for successive generations. Rivalry between or within generations (e.g., Kets de Vries, 2001) can lead to passivity, faulty decision-making or strategizing. Most of our families had confronted some of these problems. The research focus arose from exploring how the families strategized these threats, used leadership abilities to counteract them, and created resilient and thriving enterprises.

There is an intrinsic tension between the family system and the business system. As pointed out, this can lead to conflict and threaten to create destructive dynamics. But we also found creative tension and ingenuity resulting from the

Figure 1.2 Strategy practice: creative tension or destruction

overlap. In some cases, it triggered strategizing and thinking around the contradictory needs and paradoxes. The family has a primary task to create attachment and a sense of safety. The business seeks to be adaptable in the external reality, to be a transitional object. The paradox between the family as an attachment object can create conflict or creativity when the business, to be competitive and profitable, is a transitional object.The strategy practices we found successful enabled to avoid conflicts affecting the business and tension became the origin for creativity and innovation.

The succession theme

Less surprising is that succession, regarded as a critical stumbling block, was a prominent issue in the cross section between ownership and leadership strategies. We will therefore treat succession in both sections. A succession outcome is part of a process within the family as described in Chapter 5, Part I. The different options, and strategic elements, in a succession are described in Chapter 18, Part II. Succession forms a part of the other strategies and cases we describe. Stewardship overlaps with succession, and this is described in a subsection in Chapter 8. The same is the case with building social capital, as it can be transferred to the next generation (see Chapter 4). Succession and governance form part of a process of how to strategize authority, or can be approached as such (see Chapter 14). In Chapter 17 a non-family chair of the board describes how he makes role transitions for a new generation of family members and trains them. In the index there will be a complete list of where succession strategies and dynamics are described.

What is a family?

Applying a strategy-as-practice framework to the family unit challenges a romanticized image of the family. In western-based culture there is a social narrative of the family as a reproductive unit where the couple earns an income from employment. The family is the seat for romantic love; stereotypically with the wife's main task being to care for their children and remain relatively dependent on her husband for financial prosperity. There is a strong notion that income and financial resources are generated from somewhere other than within the family.

A surprising research finding, maybe based on our naivety, was that in every one of our cases it was a founder-couple that started the business. This was the case in an Arab-Israeli company, and in the German business and in the Chinese, American, French, Tanzanian and Swedish businesses. The business would often start, literally, in the kitchen. The wife would work, own and partake in the business often with equal if not more financial control than the husband. Women were instrumental in the strategy development and risk assessment that made the business successful. In this sense, the family should not be thought as being limited to romantic and emotional tasks. It can also be a business partnership and a space for risk assessment and strategy making. This is explored, together with a growing trend of powerful sisters, in a separate chapter. We discern a trend of 'sisters in ascent' that challenges a more patriarchal notion of the family unit and family ownership.

Educational approach

This book is for leaders, family members, owners and advisors involved with family businesses. For the reader not involved in any family business it may act as a window into a type of company that is an important value creator in our economy. Many management programs will have students, or executives, who are family owners or who at some point work for a family business. It is also for entrepreneurs considering how to grow and develop a business with her/his family. The book and framework should be of use to educators as a supplement to leadership thinking and ownership strategies for publicly listed companies or governmental agencies. It complements family business literature that focuses on failure and is a source for understanding what family owners do to become successful owners of family businesses. The chapters can be read in any sequence, shifting between chapters in Parts I and II.

In part I the chapters described a single case, the educational aim is to inspire the imagination of the reader. We found their stories inspiring and think this is a major educational aim. Each case illustrates an excellence in a particular ownership strategy and referring to the main theoretical perspectives on this strategy practice. The reader is shown, from the inside, how a family carved out a strategy, developed it and faced challenges. We will introduce the main perspectives within family business studies such as stewardship, entrepreneurship, technological innovation and succession. The best practice cases we chose to explore in depth, in separate chapters, are from the USA, Sweden, China, Israel (Arab-Israeli), Tanzania, England and Colombia.

In part II we discuss theoretical themes that shows enabling or challenging cap-acities, or praxes, that upholds ownership stategies. We use several cases from our study to explore each particular emotional or social capacity. They center on two leadership capacities that we found critical in family ownership: distributed leadership and the leadership of paradox. We also describe the social and emotional resources enabling such leadership capacities such as mourning of loss, developing autonomy, and negotiating authority. At the end of some of the chapters we list some guidelines. Some chapters follow an individual and their role. Chapters 13 and 17, respectively, feature an owner and a non-family chair of the board, both chapters illustrating recovery after selling a business and balancing the attachment and socio-emotional wealth with business needs in two family businesses. Again, the main aim is to enable the reader to develop new ways of thinking and unique solutions for the business they are involved with.

Research method and analytic approach

Family owners from geographically distinct locations were selected. We gained access to these families, interviewed owners, family members in leadership roles and non-family leaders in the business. The research cases were all of different sizes and in different types of industries. Some were very typical small businesses (10–200 employees). The UK, the US and the German (139 employees) companies were in this category and typical of small businesses, one still important as an employer in a local community. The other cases were mid-sized companies with 300–2,000 employees. The Chinese firm would be considered a mid-sized company in China, but in Europe, given its interlinked cluster of family and non-family-owned companies, would be considered very large. It was hard, if not impossible, to estimate how many people actually worked for this cluster of companies. The Arab-Israeli company employed, through different companies, people in Turkey, Italy and Greece in addition to Israel. This and the Tanzanian case involved big groups of seasonal or part-time workers and different types of businesses that had different roles in creating a complete tourist experience: transport, hotels, touring companies and so on.

In establishing the group of 'case-researchers', also advisors/consultants to businesses, one criterion was that they had to come from the country the case would be drawn from. This process took two to three years and was led by the editor of the book. The researcher's local connection made it possible to pick out companies that had a good reputation, that were known to be successful both financially and through other activities. Researchers could speak the language that everyone in the family used and knew the socio-political situation and context of the business. This would prove to be crucial when we analyzed the data and explored similarities and differences between the cases; local knowledge gave us the socio-political understanding of the business context, a matter of considerable significance.

Family members and non-family leaders were interviewed in depth, sometimes several times. A research protocol, ethical guidelines and semi-structured interview guide were developed. Interviewees would describe their roles, the story of the business and how the family and business system interacted, milestones, big challenges, and critical moments in the past. Cultural differences between the cases and between researchers lead, in the analysis of the material, to very fruitful discussions and if we needed to we contacted interviewees with follow-up questions. We eventually established a process of identifying similarities, or common denominators, between the cases. We used a bottom-up approach, exploring what actions and thoughts the families and other employees described. This, and the cultural spread, led to identifying what we think are some general features of successful ownership and leadership.

We have supplemented some cases that were not originally part of the research project. One family case involving legacy assets is described and written about by the controlling owner herself, who is from Colombia. Another is an in-depth interview and role analysis of an owner who sold his business. A third is an in-depth interview of a non-family chair of several family business boards, who provided his own perspective on governance. We will use a client case and an American case to discuss, in depth, the destructive potential when power and authority dynamics become unbalanced in the family and the business.

References

Chandler, A.D. (1990). *Scale and Scope*. Cambridge, MA, US: Harvard University Press.

Gersick, K.E. (1997). *Generation to Generation: Life cycles of the family business*. Boston, MA, US: Harvard Business Press.

Gilmore, T. and Ronchi, D. (1995). Managing predecessors' shadows in executive transitions. *Human Resource Management 34*(1), 11–26.

Gronn, P. (2002). Distributed leadership as a unit of analysis. *The Leadership Quarterly*, *13*(4), 423–451.

Heck, R.K. and Stafford, K. (2001). The vital institution of family business: Economic benefits hidden in plain sight. *Destroying Myths and Creating Value in Family Business*, pp. 9–17.

Ingram, A., Lewis, M.W., Barton, S., and Gartner, W.B. (2016), Paradoxes and innovation in family firms: The role of paradoxical thinking, *Entrepreneurship Theory and Practice*, *40*(1), 161–176.

Jones, G. and Rose, B.R. (1993). *Family Capitalism*. London: Cass.

Kachaner, N., Stalk, G. and Bloch, A. (2012). *What You Can Learn From Family Business*. *Harvard Business Review*, *90*(11), 102–106.

Kets de Vries, M.F. (2001). *The Leadership Mystique: An Owner's Manual*. London: Financial Times Prentice Hall.

Lansberg, I., (1999). *Succeeding Generations: Realizing the dream of families in business*. Boston, MA, US: Harvard Business Press.

Ruef, M. (2011). *The Entrepreneurial Group*. Princeton, NJ, US: Princeton University Press.

Tsabari, N., Labaki, R. and Zachary, R.K. (2014). Toward the cluster model: The family firm's entrepreneurial behavior over generations. *Family Business Review, 27*(2), 161–185.

Whittington, R. and Vaara, E. (2012). Strategy-as-practice: taking social practices seriously. *Academy of Management Annals 6*(1), 285–336.

Part I
Visionary ownership

2 Overview

Visionary ownership

Gry Osnes

Leading with ownership can be, as in our cases, the most forceful type of leadership. As we will show; developing new businesses and cluster ownership, long-term social capital building and taking on social tasks within a region are all connected with willingness and management of risk. It is often based on a vision, linked to strong individual or organizational goals pointing beyond what can be achieved with the established system. Ownership, and leading from this position, is in this way long-term strategizing for the next ten to twenty years. It can also be directed to fast adaptation to events that demand radical change. At its best it will oscillate between, and balance and align, this extreme long-term perspective and a short-term strategy of adaptation and grasping new opportunities.

Tasks and capacities in innovating a vision

Families and owners, as they grow their business, innovate and maintain a vision for their ownership. We will shortly describe the tasks in this process. For example, they *seek new opportunities* and start moving towards realizing them. They focus on *entrepreneurship,* and *consolidate* it into a business. These capacities and tasks create cycles of renewal and growth. When the business has developed, the family *accumulates the advantages* that business success creates. For example, sending their children to better schools and gaining new networks will eventually be used to increased advantage for the business. In some cases, the accumulated advantage extends to creating synergies and win–win arrangements between the local community, the family and their businesses. Managing these capacities concurrently are complex and challenging. We found that within a family, different members would be preoccupied with focus and argue for the importance of these different tasks. The family discussions would be concerned with the intrinsic tensions in trying to accommodate all of them and bringing them forward in a strategic manner.

Each family would have different capacities but also different starting points. Chapter 3 describes a US family that started out very poor and with no higher education. By the time the third generation was involved they were well-off and the children had achieved moderate but safe new ownership. They had succeeded way beyond their wildest dreams and consolidated their business, achieving a position they were happy with. Their entrepreneurship and consolidation had happened in shorter and longer cycles, the latter as the second and third generation children grew up. A new venture started by the third generation would initially be peripheral to the business but develop to become central or replace the original business. For some families their achievements could be experienced as a modest achievement, for others the fulfilment of a dream. In the last case in Part I an owner describes how she grew up in a family with substantial resources but, while developing in the role of owner, renewed and made a business out of the assets that had been in the family for several hundred years. She challenged the sense of entitlement that the wider family had of accumulated advantage in access to networks, prestige and education. The single focus on this accumulated advantage had slowly deteriorated the value of the assets over 20–30 years. By challenging this, and seeking new entrepreneurial opportunities fitting the different assets, a new cycle of entrepreneurship started, as it had at the founding of the assets over a hundred years earlier.

Successful ownership strategy practices

In the process of solving tensions, and balancing priorities, between the above tasks the family would develop specific strategy practices. The following strategy practices were executed by all the families: *entrepreneurship*, building *social capital*, and *strategizing successions*. Most of them owned several companies in *cluster ownership*. They *innovated* on the business model or technology, and displayed *stewardship* in different ways. They all, to different degrees, focused on and exercised these strategy practices successfully.

Each chapter in Part I is focused on one case and one of these strategy practices. Each family's approach to the practice in is idiosyncratic to them, but inspirational. No family managed succession, stewardship, entrepreneurship or built social capital in the same way. A unique strategy would depend on many factors: the context of the family, the history, the individual family members and random events. Stewardship would be important for all, but was developed to a particularly sophisticated level by the Arab-Israeli family. All the families, in different ways, innovated on leadership models, as described in the Swedish case regarding technological development. We chose to illustrate each of these strategies with the family that we found had executed it to the most sophisticated level. This was often triggered by socio-political challenges such as: political conflict and stewardship (Israel); emigration and social capital (Tanzania); entrepreneurship and social mobility (USA).

Chapter 3

The case from the USA demonstrates *ladder entrepreneurship,* a type of serial entrepreneurship that has enabled the family to build their strategic capacity and affluence. It is a touching example showing how a family extracted itself from poverty and achieved autonomy and a respected social position in its community. This family chose not develop and grow the business further. This was due to having reached a desired work capacity and a lack of further financial aspiration. Three generations are involved in a series of several businesses.

Chapter 4

The Tanzanian case is a bigger business with several safari camps and resorts, a farm and an airline business. The family was also a founder of, and active in, several charities. Due to the political risk they are exposed to, they mainly operate with a focus on entrepreneurship and consolidation. They are strongly seeking further accumulation for the family. A major objective was to establish a business so that their children could be residents in the country. Emigration and entrepreneurship often goes together and building internal and external social capital, used by most family owners, are accentuated by this emigration case.

Chapter 5

The French case covers a business that focuses on entrepreneurship and consolidation, opportunity and risk. The business has been transferred from the founders to the second generation, and the third generation is involved and being trained for future leadership roles. An ingenious succession is explored in depth, as it contributed to renewal of commitment and entrepreneurship.

Chapter 6 and Chapter 7

These cases are typical of successful, big family firms with local production and a global reach in sales. They seek opportunity, entrepreneurship and consolidation, to accumulate more opportunities for the family. In the Swedish case there was a deep commitment to employees' and customers' well-being. Such a commitment is in the Chinese case extended to the local community.

Chapter 8

An Arab-Israeli tourism business is described in this chapter. It originated in Jerusalem but later opened offices in Istanbul, Amman, Athens and Rome. It has, due to the political risks, expanded, with the help of the younger generations, so as to reduce financial risk. They have striven for accumulating advantages for the family but, as with the emigration issue in the Tanzanian case, political forces make this difficult.

Chapter 9

This chapter discusses the case of a business owner from Colombia who came from a family that, 100 years ago, were big land owners. These assets had been accumulated from the profits of a big family business from the early nineteenth century to the early twentieth century. Now, 100 years later, the still substantial assets have been divided between a wider group of distant and closer family members. One of these owners describes the history and legacy, the current political situation, and how she carves out autonomy and leadership so as to enable passive assets to become active businesses. Major socio-political changes have created new business opportunities for the assets. She tells the story of how she personally transformed through early exposure to ownership responsibilities and how this has developed over her adult life.

3 Ladder entrepreneurship

A social mobility case in the USA

James Grady and Victoria Grady

> When we opened our second restaurant in the new location, Betty and I realized we never really wanted but one restaurant to run. We had already realized early that the more restaurants you own, the more they owned you...
>
> Charlie (founder)

Introduction

The way a family structures its different business interests can be described as an ownership-company pattern. The immediate association one usually has with family businesses is a *one-business-one family* pattern. A typical family venture is united by either personal and/or shared goals that are similar to the passions evoked by their children or spouses. The venture gives the family member(s) meaning and provides for them a sense of purpose that guides their decisions and choices (Lansberg, 1999). Existing literature suggests that at least half, if not considerably more, of the family businesses fall into this category (Ucbasaran et al., 2008). However, the study of family businesses is connected to a growing interest in entrepreneurship that is involved in more than one venture.

Recent theory has observed an increasing trend for multi-company ownership, as families use the legal system to exercise more strategic possibilities than were previously available or apparent. Another related model of ownership is described by Michael-Tsabari, Labaki, and Zachary (2014). In this case the family, over generations, ends up with a cluster of companies—a *cluster model of ownership*. This type of family business originates around a core business founded by the first generation, and which serves as the primary interest of the family firm. Other firms may be added by succeeding generations and are considered peripheral businesses.

Opportunity and entrepreneurship

Some of the cooperative and shared spirit found in family businesses is revealed by observations of La Pira and Gillin (2006) who suggested that the energy that drives entrepreneurs "...comes not from deliberate intention or program but straight from the heart"... (p.19). A unifying factor for the family featured in this chapter emerged out of a strong relationship between family members based on a shared passion for their business, and was further strengthened by the depth of their faith. Opportunity is seen by La Pira and Gillin, (2006, p.33), in reference to Shane and Venkataraman (2000), as "the possession of information necessary to identify opportunity and the cognitive style necessary to exploit it". These are two attributes that define serial entrepreneurs. He further stated that a significant characteristic of serial entrepreneurs was the desire to make a difference. This characteristic may be unique among that group, but still, "they realize that their uniqueness does not entitle them to follow a self-serving path."

Serial entrepreneurship

Serial entrepreneurship is defined when an entrepreneur sells his or her original business, but at a later date inherits, establishes, and/or purchases another business (Westhead and Wright, 1998). Stokes (Stokes and Blackburn, 2002), in his review on small business closures, concluded that any person who has closed a business is a very likely candidate to become involved in a new venture. These owners, therefore, can be regarded as leaving a business through a 'revolving door', rather than a 'one-way exit' (p. 14). The re-created business is usually in the same sector as the original business. It often occurs in a series of three stages beginning with the sale of the present business, a latent or interim stage, and then a re-creation stage. The interim period is typically very long and may extend beyond five years, and "...the new business is often created around the needs of the next generation" (Kenyon-Rouvinez, 2001, p.180).

The USA case presented here does not fit this type of sequential pattern, nor does it fit any of the others mentioned above. We refer to this family's venture as *ladder entrepreneurship*. It does not exhibit qualities of serial entrepreneurship since there was no latent phase. For a short period of time there was a cluster around one central restaurant and two peripheral ones, but unlike the pattern typical of cluster entrepreneurship, later efforts were re-focused on ownership of one of the peripheral businesses. This approach demonstrates a type of entrepreneurship strategy, or sequencing, which had the particular function of allowing the family to improve the location and size of their facility without the risks of large loans.

In addition to solving succession issues and increasing financial safety, the family's entrepreneurship enabled a change in social status. Steier (2009) suggests the advantages of membership in certain social groups can often be leveraged. Charlie and Betty, the main founders in this case, did not have any of the advantages often attributed to social capital. They came from families that lived a marginal existence, and began in a new community with no connections. Beginning conservatively, they were gradually able to increase the size of their business and their role in the community. Even without the initial social connections giving access to good banking contacts, or further education, and the sense of confidence that is more often found in those with a middle class background, they were ultimately able to achieve and surpass their initial goals.

The *best practice* in this case is the acknowledgement of both their initial limitations and the growth of their abilities over time. They carefully adapted their family's growing financial needs to their capacity to manage a larger restaurant. This 'steps up the ladder' type of entrepreneurship allowed them to proceed with a sense of caution, slowly moving up one step at a time while increasing knowledge and managing the increased risk. This process is demonstrated in Figure 3.1 for the case being considered in this chapter. This is a process that is discussed in Chapter 16 as an increase in strategic capacity.

Box 3.1 Ladder entrepreneurship and strategic capacity

The transition from one business to another became a careful and deliberate strategy for taking up a new challenge in a business with more potential, without over-reaching or taking on too much risk. In each ladder, with each new venture, the possibilities inherent in the new business allowed financial growth beyond what was possible in the previous one. It also increased the capacity for managing complexity in the businesses.

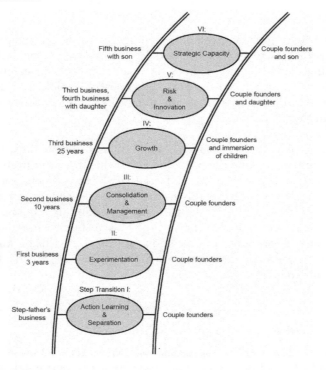

Figure 3.1 Ladder entrepreneurship

Strategic capacity and entrepreneurship

This USA case study follows the founder couple and their family through a series of related business ventures. They moved from a partnership with Charlie's mother out to a very simple and conservative first venture on their own. They learned enough over time to begin a series of steps up the ladder of success, and with each of these steps their capacity to manage larger ventures gradually developed, matured, and strengthened. Over the next 40 years they were able to relocate to four facilities, each one larger than the one before, with more opportunities.

> I think that if you go into business, especially with family, first of all it is very important that you communicate and not sweep things under the rug. You need to talk about anything that is bothering you, any conflict that you are having, and just talk through it. That is a good thing and that's where momma's strength comes in because daddy would sweep things under the rug. It is always better to communicate sincerely whether with a member of the family, an employee, or somebody else.
>
> Sam (son)

Background

Charlie and Betty both survived a very meager existence growing up. They met and married at a young age and worked shifts and second jobs. Charlie also used to hang around his step-father's restaurant, on occasion helping out by tending the fire as it roasted the pork. His step-father must have seen some potential in Charlie because when the restaurant manager suddenly quit, he offered him the job as site manager.

> When I took over the restaurant, I was not completely in the dark because I liked to hang around the barbeque place when I was off from work just talking with my step-father and stuff like that. I knew some of his techniques. When he lost his manager... he asked me if I would be interested in taking it over and naturally I was. So, my training, believe it or not, was very little. He showed me how to build a fire and turn the meat until it was done. I don't know; it just seems I had a knack for it because I always knew when the product was at its best. So, that was pretty much my training.
>
> Charlie (founder)

Box 3.2 Barbeque in the American mid-west

Many cultures have some type of traditional outdoor cooking, or barbecue (BBQ). Preparing really good BBQ is an art unto itself: it must be cooked daily and very slowly over low heat for several hours. The basics can be taught, but the nuances cannot. BBQ is a culture that exists throughout the south (southern USA), but may vary considerably in form and taste from one location to another. Separated in some cases by only a few miles, and in other cases by hundreds of miles, the differences are determined by the wood used for creating the smoky flavor, the cut of the meat, the side dishes, and the energy and philosophy that has gone into the development of the 'sauce'.

The one thing that remains constant is true BBQ is cooked over open coals at low heat for at least 5–6 hours. In the Deep South BBQ means pork shoulders, sometimes pork ribs and a lot of secrecy in the cooking methods and sauce preparation. If a restaurant is going to serve fresh BBQ, and no self-respecting establishment would consider otherwise, this means the person responsible for cooking must have the heat from the wood fire ready to start cooking before 6am if they plan to be ready to serve the first customers at around 11am. It is extremely labor-intensive.

Step-transition I: action learning and separation

As described by Stokes and Blackburn (2002) entrepreneurial learning often occurs through a process called action learning. It was in this manner, without a lot of training or foreknowledge, that Charlie took over the management of a small but growing barbecue business. He would prove to have a talent in handling people and preparing the food, while Betty had a head for figures and handled the accounts.

Charlie's step-father had designed a system that was easy to learn, easy to manage, and easy to supervise. It could be managed with a very limited staff which kept employee problems to a minimum. There was no table service. Orders were taken, paid for, and received at the main counter; the chairs were sturdy and the tables topped with a shiny, heat resistant, wipe clean laminate surface. It was an uncomplicated approach and Charlie and Betty adapted and learned quickly. When his step-father died less than two years after Charlie became restaurant manager, Charlie's mother inherited the restaurant. Charlie and Betty were able to take over the operation and the restaurant continued to flourish. Eventually the needs of Charlie's and his mother's still growing family began to outgrow the small restaurant's ability to keep up. Charlie and Betty decided to move out and start their own business.

> The separation was hard, but it was best for all concerned. We shared ideas in the beginning. At least we did back then, we don't much anymore. My mother is, well she's not a hands on operator any longer. She pretty much lets the people she has hired run it. But she still has a presence there— through today's technology she supervises the business using a TV camera over the register, a little TV monitor at home, and she calls them any time that she's not satisfied with something. But as far as us sharing ideas, that probably hasn't taken place for a few years now, but we, at one time or

another, would share ideas with each other, what would work for one and what was working for the other to enhance her business or mine. Our businesses are different now.

Charlie (founder)

Step-transition II: experimentation

They approached plans for their first business venture very conservatively. Considering their background, the uncertainties, and their conservative nature, what might be considered a modest financial commitment to many businessmen seemed massive to them. After having worked in this restaurant for three years, they knew the restaurant and the community were just too small to provide their family with the comfortable level of income they sought. They located a small parcel of land outside a much larger community 20 miles away. As they built this new and somewhat larger barbecue restaurant they had a decision to make—do we sell this first restaurant, or do we keep it and try to run both? After much discussion, they decided to focus all of their efforts and energy on one business.

Step-transition III: from consolidating into managing complexity

The transition to this, their second restaurant, was swift, and immediately successful. Charlie possessed good people skills that quickly endeared him to his new employees and his customers. He also displayed good judgment in his ability to gauge the size and the timing of the new venture.

I saw, you know, how good daddy was to his employees. He was never just a boss and I don't say that because I was his daughter. He is that way with all of his employees. He cares about them and wants to be a part of their lives and to influence them and to point them in the right direction. I think the employees had a deep respect for him and a very deep appreciation for him as a business owner and a boss.

Gail (daughter)

Complementarities and roles

Betty is quite different from Charlie and her abilities complement his. She is very practical, and accomplished at gathering and analyzing detail. She insists on clarity and hard information before any major decisions are finalized. Although she always maintained a lower profile, the complexity of their mother's role was observed by their children.

My mom is a bit of a perfectionist, a lot of people already know that. She had a reputation saying about any decision: "We are going to 'fight until it is right' for all concerned". My dad attributes most of our success to that.

He says, "If it wasn't for your mom, we would probably be cooking barbeque in a shack on the side of the road."

Sam (son)

This second restaurant location served them well for nearly 10 years, but eventually their success outgrew this facility. The confidence gained from this experience, and the skills and procedures that had been perfected in the process, would prepare them for a significant step forward.

Step-transition IV: growth

It was with a new level of self-reliance, and with consideration for the future of their two children, that after ten years Charlie and Betty opened a third restaurant, in a busy downtown region, and doubled the size of their facility. Again, they coordinated the sale of a restaurant, their second, to help finance the new venture.

This new restaurant became a great success in its own right, and also led to some unexpected benefits that would extend their influence into the community. The family began to notice subtle changes in how they were treated by the community at large. A new sense of community pride emerged in them; as Sam, the son, said: "I was proud of my parents being the owners of their own business. I was always proud of my family's business, even when I wanted to go out and do something else on my own."

In addition to their business successes and enhanced standing in their community, the family experienced a profound spiritual awakening and became active members in a Christian church. They still look today for ways in which they can be a positive example for others. Fifteen years after beginning their business, they had a recognized place in the community, a strong faith and a sense of purpose and meaning that extended beyond themselves. They began to look more seriously toward the future of their children and grandchildren.

From the day we became Christians, I ran my business as a lighthouse. We don't need to judge anyone, but our faith and our God are real and so we acknowledge it in our businesses and we do that in hopes that the message will somehow reach others.

Charlie (founder)

Step-transition V: risk and innovation

Building on tradition

As is the case in many family businesses, the business became a second home for the children, where they could learn the value of hard work, gain work experience and earn pocket money. When Gail finished high school she wanted to work for someone else in another aspect of the restaurant business.

She sought and obtained a job at a fast food restaurant. Having been brought up in the benevolent and caring ethos of her parents, she was appalled at how badly the employees were treated. A couple of years later, as she was preparing to start a family of her own, she approached her parents with an idea about opening a fast food type of restaurant serving fried chicken strips. This restaurant was to be maintained and operated by Gail with the assistance and support of her parents, especially her mother's bookkeeping skills. As had become characteristic of their ventures, it was an instant success.

> Working in this new restaurant was so different from what I experienced working for my dad. They were only concerned about themselves and making money and using their employees—draining them dry. After that experience I had a very deep appreciation for Dad as a business owner and a boss.
>
> Gail (daughter)

> It was actually Gail who came up with the new idea for a restaurant, and she sold us on it. But ... we all had to work together to get the ball rolling. I remember how we learned how to cook chicken. We got a deep fat fryer and put it out on the back porch. We already had our bank loan approved and everything. When the first big batch of it came out green and greasy, I thought to myself, "Oh, my goodness, what have we gotten ourselves into, we don't know how to do this!" And so, I said, "I'm glad the bankers are not in our back yard watching this or they would take back the loan they promised us." But anyway we did test cooking almost every day, it seems like for weeks, but eventually we came up with a product we all really liked.
>
> Charlie (founder)

Step-transition VI: strategic capacity

Family cycles and needs in succession

About ten years after the opening of their daughter's restaurant the parents began to consider a deal that would bring their son (Sam) into partnership with them. After nearly three years of discussions and planning, the family worked out the details of the concept, a venture that would provide security for Sam and his family and allow for an eventual exit strategy for Charlie and Betty. They had always said that the key to their success was their willingness, when necessary, to fight until it is right—and now 'it was right!'

Interval with cluster ownership

The innovation in developing Gail's restaurant was important, and gave the family confidence to launch another enterprise that was even more ambitious.

Charlie had the concept for a multi-service restaurant, building on the success of Gail's outlet. It would be much larger, but still an informal, family-oriented restaurant. It was also designed to be flexible and to gradually allow the addition of a more varied menu. Soon after it opened this new restaurant was exceeding their expectations, but there was an increasing strain that came from operating three businesses. In spite of their overwhelming success, or perhaps because of it, Charlie began having a recurrent thought: "…it was always our goal to own just one restaurant."

Separation and new identity

It was during this time that Gail was also beginning to feel the stress of too many commitments. During her fifteen years in the restaurant business she had started writing children's Christian literature, successfully, and she wanted to pursue this career. This meant she was no longer available to manage the restaurant. The success of the business opened up new opportunities for family members, enabling successive transitions.

> I knew the right thing to do was to sell my restaurant. Actually my parents and my friends and my husband really wanted me to let it go long before I did, but I just couldn't. It held too many memories. I really had a hard time letting go of it.
>
> Gail (daughter)

At the founder level this alleviated some of the pressures on the family and they wanted to return to a focus on only one, bigger restaurant. There was also an emerging 'generation gap' between father and son in the business the parents had developed with Sam. Sam was embracing the internet to develop his new business, an area where Charlie lacked knowledge and skills. This led to the next major transition on the entrepreneurial ladder: Charlie and Betty sold the older BBQ restaurant and took on the challenge of yet another bigger restaurant with Sam using new technology and new types of service.

Afterthoughts and reflections

Emotions and trust

The success of this family business depended on the natural development of qualities of leadership and mutual trust. These qualities were particularly remarkable in this case of sequential ventures. Trust is a form of glue that works to hold people together in collaborative relationships. The Foster family had trust enough in each other and the acknowledgement of their limitations was the foundation for how they would take up a challenge that was just big enough when their various new ventures were built. They saw their faith as enabling this implicit trust, the ability to work together as a family for a common cause, and the business was seen as call to be a 'lighthouse' for their faith.

Based on the convention of the world in which we live and work, trust may occur more naturally in healthy family businesses. This is the advantage often evident in a family business—the opportunity to build a more enduring trust that will outlast the many difficulties encountered over a number of years. When present its evidence may be contagious and can spread to non-family members and result in a willingness to become engaged. This was an important factor in the success most of our family businesses. In the case of the Fosters, trust enabled the capacity to move from one business to another while adjusting to various changes in leadership roles. In this way trust enables the growth of strategic capacity as it serves as a bridge that allows us to move from our old models or habits into the new one that is emerging (Parkes, 2001).

There is clear evidence of an ability to build strong social capital in the caring way in which the family treated their staff (see also the Tanzanian case, Chapter 4). The family also possessed a strong sense of wider purpose to their community and through their faith. Their approach also illustrates the merits of patient business-building, common to the more resilient family-owned businesses and in contrast to an approach of high debt and rapid expansion. The family was fortunate in that the respective strengths of the founder couple, Charlie and Betty, complemented one another perfectly: Charlie's strengths were culinary skills, entrepreneurial flair, and an easy manner with staff and employees, while Betty was strong on bookkeeping, detail, and communication and meeting skills. She ensured that important issues were discussed openly and honestly, minimizing rumors and misunderstanding, and fostering trust throughout the business and between the generations. The importance of trust has been recognized as part of an essential goal of family businesses, which is to build emotional capital as well as financial capital, the concept of 'warm hearts, deep pockets' (Kenyon-Rouvinez, Koeberle-Schmid and Poza, 2014).

Socio-emotional wealth and drive

As we explored the development of this family enterprise it was evident that an evolution had taken place. In the beginning, financial independence was an important consideration in their drive to achieve success—this was certainly accomplished, even in the first 10–12 years. Later, commercial success provided them with an identity and an improved social position. Gomez-Mejia et al. (2011) point out that the socio-emotional component is a strong incentive for many family businesses. This aspect is shown implicitly in many of the following cases and is further discussed in Chapter 18 on drive in family capitalism. While the Fosters may appreciate this aspect of their success, they do not exploit it, and they have always given back much more than they receive. Other scholars have detected a diverse range of motivations cited by habitual entrepreneurs: a desire for independence, autonomy, and wealth creation (Stokes and Blackburn,

2002, p. 374). All of these factors may have been important outcomes for the Fosters, but there was, also, an element of uniqueness that was all their own.

References

Gomez-Mejia, L.R., Cruz, C., Berrone, P. and De Castro, J. (2011). Socioemotional wealth preservation in family firms. *Academy of Management Annals,* Vol. 5, No. 1: 653–707.

Kenyon-Rouvinez, D. (2001). Patterns in serial business families: Theory building through global case study research. *Family Business Review,* Vol. XIV, No 3, September.

Kenyon-Rouvinez, D., Koeberle-Schmid, A. and Poza, E. (2014). *Governance in Family Enterprises: Maximizing economic and emotional success.* Basingstoke, UK and New York: Palgrave-Macmillan.

Lansberg, I. (1999). *Succeeding Generations: Realizing the Dream of Families in Business.* Boston, MA, US: Harvard Business School Press.

La Pira, F. and Gillin, M. (2006). Non-local intuition and the performance of serial entrepreneurs, *Int. J. Entrepreneurship and Small Business,* Vol. 3, No. 1: 17–35.

Michael-Tsabari, N., Labaki, R. and Zachary, R. (2014). Toward the cluster model: The family firm's entrepreneurial behavior over generations. *Family Business Review,* Vol. 27, No. 2: 161–185.

Parkes, C. (2001). *Bereavement: Studies of Grief in Adult Life,* 3rd edition. Philadelphia, PA, US, Taylor and Francis Inc.

Shane, S. and Venkataraman, S. (2000). The promise of entrepreneurship as a field of research. *Academy of Management Review,* Vol. 25, No. 1: 217–226.

Steier, L. (2009). Where do new firms come from? Households, family capital, ethnicity, and welfare mix. *Family Business Review,* Vol. 22, No. 3, September: 273–278.

Stokes, D. and Blackburn, R. (2002). Learning the hard way: The lessons of owner-managers who have closed their business. *Journal of Small Business and Enterprise Development,* Spring Vol. 9, No. 1: 17–27.

Ucbasaran, E., Alsos, G., Westhead, P. and Wright, M. (2008). Habitual entrepreneurs. *Foundations and Trends in Entrepreneurship,* Vol. 4, No. 4: 309–450.

Westhead, Paul and Wright, Mike (1998). Novice, portfolio, and serial founders: Are they different? *Journal of Business Venturing,* Vol. 13: 173–204. Abstract.

4   Building social capital

An emigration case from UK to Tanzania

Gry Osnes

[It] is not just another job. It is a dream. I have been lucky, we love Tanzania, we love the people, we love the country here. We have had a dream .... And the people who we employ are coming to join this dream. It is an exciting environment. And I think that makes for better management because they are happy and excited to be in this environment.

You have got to feel that you are not living your own life here. You have to merge and be part of the community.

(Jeff Fox, founder and former owner Fox safari)

Introduction

Social capital can sound rather abstract, but feels quite tangible, especially in a successful firm that collaborates closely with the wider community. In this immigration case we will show the creation and use of multiple supportive networks. Social capital is built up of ties, while harbouring tension is the building block for loyalty and trust. It creates multiple benefits: a strategy of building internal social capital nurtures a stable, loyal and hard-working workforce. External social capital constitutes the social network within the local region and business sector, and at the political level. A business-owning family can create political influence and use this to secure access to other types of resources. While such opportunities are open to all businesses, family owners have greater freedom than corporations to invest in social capital that benefits new ventures, in addition to the current businesses they are operating. A significant ambition for many business owners is to pass on social connections to the next generation. Moreover, their sons and daughters, through education and their own networking, expand the social capital further.

Social capital as competitive advantage

Family social capital can become an inimitable source of competitive advantage. A longitudinal study by Salvato and Melin (2008) identified that the competitive advantage of successful family firms depends to a significant extent upon the strengths of their social capital. They concluded that the ability to reshape and attend to building social capital constantly is a significant source of competitive advantage. It can be consolidated by the next generation and their school friends and university attendance; by their securing jobs with competitors or suppliers. The family can build both breadth and depth of social capital within the business sector and community in which they operate. Local networks become constituencies of support, which can be more lasting and beneficial than securing high-level political access. These are not mutually exclusive strategies. We will use an emigration case to illustrate a more general strategy of how all our family owners use social capital as a strategy to succeed. Emigration is, from a social capital point of view, quite an extreme position a family puts themselves in as they leave a local network. Emigration and entrepreneurship accentuate and illustrate how important social capital is, and the link between social capital and emigrant entrepreneurs is important. Research shows that lack of employment opportunities is an important reason for immigrants starting new ventures (Zolin and Schlosser, 2011).

Salvato and Melin (2008) define 'network centrality' as the extent to which central individuals have ties and strong influence throughout the network. 'Network closure', or intensity, is the extent to which everyone knows everyone within the network. In addition, the degree of trustworthiness was found to be a significant factor. Networks created for one purpose may be used for another, with high levels of trust being transferable from the family sphere to the business arena. Trust within the internal and external network aids the ability to withstand economic downturns, political instability or hostile regulatory regimes. In general, social capital helps any business, and in particular the family owner, to reduce resource dependence (see Box 4.1).

The importance of strong external networks tends to increase over time, and through the generations. Strong external networks also assist in attracting the best externally recruited talent, preventing excessive reliance on the skills base within the family. Access to elite technical education helps with the generational transfer of capital. It is also suggested as one of the crucial resources for entrepreneurship (Gedajlovic, et al, 2013), as this case will show.

Locally, internal social capital within the family and business can build on trust within communities, as recruiting in the community creates a committed workforce and local development of a skills base. Understanding and nurturing family social capital therefore helps the prospects for future generations of the family, as was demonstrated in most of our cases. In the chapter on technological innovation, Chapter 7, the internal social capital is used to facilitate a practice of continuous innovation. The Arab-Israeli family featured in Chapter 8 exercises stewardship of past and future generations. They use the employment strategy, and internal social capital within the business, to challenge political issues in their region. As such, internal social capital is linked to strategies on stewardship.

Emigration and entrepreneurship is also strongly linked (Peroni, Riillo, and Sarracino, 2016). Family businesses have been important for immigrants in many different countries, especially for highly educated and ambitious individuals who may find it difficult to enter professions in the host country. This can be due to regulatory barriers, discrimination, and lack of contacts (Waters, 2005). Creating a strong future for the succeeding generations is a major motivation, and entrepreneurial activity has often held more promise than a salaried post, especially for individuals overqualified for the available positions. The link between emigration/immigration and entrepreneurship adds another social dimension to the exploration of family entrepreneurship. We will here focus on social capital as a family and business strategy and not explore this in a wider social context. But it is an important added value, in addition to family ownership and economic value creation, that should not be underscored. Another aspect not explores here is the as social connection between families in different countries and what this contributes with of competitive advantage.

The following case study of the Fox family is a best practice case. The founding couple built a business from scratch, and created and nurtured strong internal and external social capital (Wiklund, et al., 2013) to support the business and the family. It is also interesting as it is a case of a family emigrating from the UK to Tanzania. Among their ambitions is to ensure that their children have the option of a career in Tanzania; and a 'green card' clearance to work in the country. The building of a family business in connection with emigration reveals how important a social capital strategy is. In this case it was built up over 30–40 years. This involved external social capital, enabling the firm to grasp opportunities and gain resources they needed for starting and developing the business. They built internal social capital safeguarding loyalty within the family, between the family and employees and with strong links to their local community. Through these strategies the founder couple could safeguard a green card and right of residency for their sons. A business of seven safari camps, a small-plane airline, a farm and a beach resort would develop during changing political circumstances. These political circumstances influenced their dependency on resources and a social capital strategy was used to manage this.

Box 4.1 Resource dependency

A key insight by the founders of resource dependence theory, Jeffrey Pfeffer and Gerald Salancik (2003) is that organizations are not autonomous; instead they are limited and constrained by a web of interdependencies with other organizations. Strategies to reduce resource dependence include social capital. The concept of resource dependence is a helpful dimension of strategic analysis to improve the autonomy of the owner-family (see Chapter 11).

This perspective implies an understanding of the company as a network of relationships of interdependence, not just a tactical set of economic transactions. Family-owned firms are among the most accomplished at building strong social capital, as a policy of enlightened self-interest. Some produce statements of values and principles that help sustain collective trust and a collective sense of purpose.

Salvato and Melin's research (2008), uses the case of the Frescobaldi family and their wine firm in Tuscany. Political connections helped Vittorio Frescobaldi, of the second generation, access EU help to improve agricultural yields. He set up a cooperative in order to be eligible for the scheme, enlisting help for his application through contacts at the Ministry of Agriculture. The case in this chapter deploys similar strategies; for example, where the owner intervened politically to ensure that the farmland was sold at a fair price, that the purchaser was the government and that the land was converted into a nature reserve. This would assist tourism, and do so in keeping with the domestic political preference for local control over land resources, rather than foreign ownership. The social capital developed gave the family credibility and political influence with donor countries, aid agencies and the government, which they later used to lobby for anti-poaching laws and protect nature reserves.

Creating a place in a new world

Many successful immigrant family businesses feature individuals from a low-income country establishing themselves in an advanced economy. The Fox family represent an interesting exception, but some perennial issues of aspiration, regulatory and cultural challenges and the value of social capital are evident. The case emphasizes the importance of the extent of the economy's development and the significance of internal and external capital in developing economies (Wright, et al., 2014). Vicky and Jeff, the founder couple, are British but feel more at home in Tanzania, having lived in the country for well over half their lives. They set up their safari business in the 1980s in a region of southern Tanzania. The Ruaha National Park is in central southern Tanzania and is home to a vivid array of wildlife.

The business comprises five different lodges, a seaside resort and a farm, run by Vicky. She also trains the chefs for the resort. There is a small airline run by one of their four sons, which serves the lodges but also other resort locations, including the beach resort. One of the four sons runs a tented lodge in the region, organizationally separate but closely linked to the main family business. Another son, who was paralysed by a spinal injury, runs the marketing operation with his wife from their base in the UK. Linked to the company, now run by Jeff, is an orphanage and nursery school in the region. They are both still involved in the business, Jeff being in charge of its related philanthropic work and Vicky running the farm and training employees. They have handed over much of the company management to their grown-up children – they have four grown-up sons, two of whom have wives who are also involved with the family firm.

External social capital

The couple had worked in Tanzania for 20 years and through this work they had built social ties to both business in the region and local communities. After Jeff gained early retirement from Unilever, they ran a cattle ranch where they devoted a lot of time to overcoming disease within the cattle, and made the ranch into one of the top cattle breeders and beef producers in Tanzania. When the owner had to sell the farm, an unwelcome development, Jeff started to seek other solutions and established social links to international NGOs and to politicians. Through brokering a deal making the farmland into a national reserve he built strong political links with the donor community and within the business community. In the 1980s tourism was not a priority industry for the government. Jeff recalled:

> It was believed that Tanzania's economy had to be built up from within. Which was right in a way, but tourism has a role and indeed to this day, tourism and the mining industry are interchanging as the number one foreign exchange earner in the country.

The Ruaha Lodge, built up by the family in an area often visited by them on bushwalks, would be the first business they had. From the beginning of the enterprise, the family were building their external social capital. They negotiated for permits and leases for having camps in national reserves. They recruited local people and secured the right to farm by land leases. The business has been extended by developing philanthropic organizations. An orphanage, some medical services and a nursery acknowledge the gratitude the family felt to the local community and how their social connections and wellbeing were linked. Such social capital has multiple benefits. Jeff said:

> We could not live here, and be given land and say 'Now this is my farm, thank you very much'. You have to give something back. I think it is just common sense really. I think any normal person should live like that. If you have received generosity and kindness from a community, from a community that has nothing, you strive to give something back that will be of advantage or benefit to them.

Internal social capital within the family

Roles were developed between family members so that they could be relatively self-reliant regarding some crucial resources such as high-quality food for customers, airline transport and logistical services between camps. In this way they created a buffer against the impacts of an underdeveloped economy, with the family forming the main internal social capital. A tragic accident on the farm led to one son having a spinal injury and being paralysed. He and his wife moved to England and from there they built up a marketing and sales unit that gave the business professional global marketing. This has turned out to be a key part of the enterprise, as they initially underestimated the importance of marketing in the first years of running the lodges. Another son, with the family's financial support, became a small airplane pilot and they developed a small airline. The airline business has six aircraft and five pilots and also sells their services to customers other than their own clients. Jeff observed:

> Safari Air Link, is the one that Peter, who was in Ruaha, my second son, started. And he is in Dar doing that. And that is successful in that most passengers are our own clients. They fly in our own aircraft. There would not be the guarantee that we would get the passengers there reliably and the system is travel between camps when making a package for clients is done in England in coordination with the airline.

Internal social capital and skilled employees

The centre of the family's operations family was a farm in Mufindi, located in the mountains with fertile ground. They also had a lodge for Tanzanians who wanted to escape the heat and dust of Dar es Salaam. Much of the food served at the safaris was produced at their mountain lodge and farm. Vicky explained:

> I decided that to upgrade, in all the hotels, the food was very important because the one thing you need when you go on holiday is to have good food really. I mean, apart from seeing all the game and enjoying yourself.

The family only recruited employees from this region and they were trained at the farm and lodge. This recruitment policy increased the internal social capital within the business and fostered a sense of community. Some MPs from other parts of Tanzania questioned this policy, threatening the political connections the family needed for conservation policies and lobbying. In addition to top quality food, they needed chefs, waiters and top English-speaking guides and they needed to try to keep these employees. Vicky said they have been able to find and develop the talent locally, as they are committed to training:

> We take on people from the local village and community who we like and who are bright and who are hard-working, and then we put them into a job and train them. We never take on someone else's cook. It is always someone we are training. The farm and lodge here is where we train the chef. We often have three trainees at the same time. When they are trained they go off to one of the other camps.

Samwel is our chief cook. He helps and is in charge of training all our cooks. I have been very lucky to get him. He started off as a trout hatchery chap working on a part of the farm lodge we are developing. He went to hatching out the chickens and overseeing that. Then he went to the butchers, so he knows all of that, the different pieces of meat, which is very useful. And then he moved to the kitchen when he was 19, he was only 19. I have had two who were only 19 to start with .... And they were just naturals, both natural cooks. You know how sometimes when there is a natural at doing something, really training is very easy.

Such internal social capital builds strong ties of loyalty and helps reduce theft from a company. An offender being dismissed for such a reason would create a sense of shame in the local community.

Sustainability and social capital

Strong external and internal social capital combine to create a powerful asset for a business-owning family, and are especially important for an immigrant family. There can be conflicts of interest, however, as this family have discovered. Poaching, and the closely allied problem of corruption, poses a potentially existential threat to wildlife and tourism in the country. One of the problems is that hunting is often defended as part of the national way of life, so a blanket ban is politically difficult. But without this, international gangs that trade in ivory and pay corrupt officials remain a menace. The Foxes lobbied the Tanzanian government for rigorous enforcement of anti-poaching measures, pointing to the obviously disastrous consequences of disappearance of significant species, both for the eco-system and for tourism. In this case, however, building tight contacts with the local people did not create leverage outside of the local clans. This influenced the position the Foxes had when they lobbied for national laws that would reduce poaching on wildlife.

A related issue is the question of sustainability and environmental responsibility. Their business depends absolutely upon responsible nurturing of the natural environment for its continued existence. An element of self-sufficiency is environmentally friendly – but also reduces resource dependence. Even with the family and the firm so deeply embedded in the community and the country, the shadow of colonialism still hangs over the Fox family in a nation that used to be part of the British Empire. This results in an uneven, at times suspicious, attitude towards foreign business investment. There are marked cultural and legislative differences with regard to land ownership between Europe and many parts of Africa. The family cannot 'own' the land, in a European or North American understanding of the term. While the concept of ownership, and associated contractual rights supported by the legal system, can help business and economic development, there is understandable resistance to this concept in the context of nations affected by colonialism in the past, where previously communal resources were appropriated by European settlers.

Political risk

In Tanzania, all land belongs to the government. There is no freehold, it is all leasehold. However, this arrangement can be made to work in a way that supports businesses. A Tanzanian citizen can have a lease of 99 years. Vicky is Tanzanian, so all the land is in her name. She had to give up her British citizenship as Tanzania does not allow dual citizenship. Jeff retains his, including the right to draw a British state pension income. He says:

> A lot of our ownership is very relaxed, we haven't even bothered to get secure title at all of the land lease. It is, a lot of it is at the stage, just an understanding of the villages concerned. We have been given this land, and we are developing it. We are protected by the culture of the country that ownership of what you have put on the land is always, cannot be taken away from you. So if you plant a fruit tree and then the land is taken away and belongs to someone else, that fruit tree is yours and you have to be compensated for your tree. So we have been planting forest. For the last 5 years I have been planting 1000 acres of pine forest every year.

There are also regulatory challenges. The family requires a renewal of its licence to trade every two years. Political risk is the biggest threat to the business. Aid from wealthy European countries comprises a significant part of public spending, but this has been cut from 50 per cent to 40 per cent, with the expectation that Tanzania builds up a domestic tax base. The problem that has followed, however, is a tougher tax regime for the private sector. Jeff comments:

> It is causing a lot of stress at the moment right now. But I have told the boys, 'Stick it out'…. All the time we have been here we have had our ups and downs, we haven't been too sure how long we are going to be here, we had a two-year work permit and were told this would be the last, and then they renew it.
>
> My dream as it were, is fading. In that I thought we could build up a viable business. Giving them a good life, pay for school fees, give them wages, that it could be passed down to our grandchildren. But all the parents, that is my sons, are not encouraging their kids to remain here in the business at this stage. Because of the rather gradually hostile climate towards firm investment. But that might change.

Afterthoughts and reflections

This case study demonstrates many of the key issues for immigrant entrepreneurial families, and the necessity of building social capital, including at the political level. The family displays a considerable ability to build and nurture strong networks, both locally, in creating employment and philanthropic initiatives. and at a national and international level, by networking with big funding donors, and regional and national governments. Over time they have discovered that creating a successful business and employing local villagers does not bring sufficient leverage on its own, to give them legitimacy and long-term security. The philanthropic initiatives locally, and the political lobbying nationally, have been essential.

There are examples of family businesses surviving populist non-business-friendly regimes, and continuing to do so over the generations. Becoming cornerstones of their local or regional economy is a strategy where multiple key players have an interest in maintaining the business. Strong social capital does not guarantee survival but can provide a buffer against political uncertainty. Strong family values need to be upheld in all business and private dealings. In the case of this family these strong values had their roots in their Quaker background, a tradition that has emphasized tolerance, peace and equality. There is increasing understanding around the importance of values in building a family's sense of social identity, creating social ties and preserving the socio-emotional wealth of the family (Berrone, Cruz, and Gomez-Mejia, 2012). Socio-emotional wealth will be implicitly described in many of the case chapters in Part II. It is also explicitly discussed in Chapter 17, with reference to a non-family chair of the board, and in Chapter 18, 'Drive in Family Capitalism'.

References

Berrone, P., Cruz, C. and Gomez-Mejia, L.R. (2012). Socioemotional wealth in family firms theoretical dimensions, assessment approaches, and agenda for future research. *Family Business Review*, 25(3), pp.258–279.

Gedajlovic, E., Honig, B., Moore, C.B., Payne, G.T. and Wright, M. (2013). Social capital and entrepreneurship: A schema and research agenda. *Entrepreneurship Theory and Practice*, 37(3), pp.455–478.

Peroni, C., Riillo, C.A. and Sarracino, F. (2016). Entrepreneurship and immigration: Evidence from GEM Luxembourg. *Small Business Economics*, 46(4), pp.1–18.

Pfeffer, J. and Salancik, G. (2003). *The External Control of Organizations: A Resource Dependence Perspective*, Stanford, CA, US: Stanford University Press, New Edition 2003, first published 1978.

Salvato, C. and Melin, L. (2008). Creating value across generations in family-controlled businesses: The role of family social capital. *Family Business Review*, 21(3), pp. 259–276.

Waters, Johanna L. (2005). Transnational family strategies and education in the contemporary Chinese diaspora, *Global Networks* 5(4), pp.359–377.

Wiklund, J., Nordqvist, M., Hellerstedt, K. and Bird, M. (2013). Internal versus external ownership transition in family firms: an embeddedness perspective. *Entrepreneurship Theory and Practice*, 37(6), pp.1319–1340.

Wright, M., Chrisman, J.J., Chua, J.H. and Steier, L.P. (2014). Family enterprise and context. *Entrepreneurship Theory and Practice, 38*(6), pp.1247–1260.

Zolin, Roxanne and Schlosser, Francine (2011). The role of immigrant entrepreneurs in international new ventures. In Maritz, Alex (Ed.) *Proceedings of the 8th AGSE International Entrepreneurship Research Exchange*, Swinburne University of Technology, Melbourne, Vic, Australia, pp.1187–1198.

5 Strategizing successions
Sibling loyalty in a French case

Gry Osnes

I don't want my daughters to think they have to go into this business; I want them to be able to have an education and be free in their choices, as I did not have that chance. Also, I have a small flower shop; if they want to get work experience and to earn money, they can work there.

Owner on his wishes for his daughters

Introduction

A succession provides a chance to review past strategy and performance, or lack thereof, and to explore new possibilities. Management of the emotions in the process enables an opportunity to change, or to sharpen a strategic course. As such, the succession dynamics are important for the long-term survival of the business and family ownership. It is frequently discussed as a process of conflict, rivalry and family tension; and succession can trigger several different disruptive or destructive dynamics. One difficulty for the leader or owner who is leaving is to manage the emotions that are triggered given that their identity is invested in the company. Over-involvement and over-identification of the founder or current owner/leader must be managed (i.e., Handler, 1990; Osnes, 2011).

Additional challenges can be faced by the successor. He or she might have to deal with an oppressive legacy or shadow from the predecessor (Gilmore and Ronchi, 1995), but not necessarily imposed by the predecessor. The family or the organization, even public opinion, can use the past to 'guide' or question trust in the new leader. The successor might internalize these expectations and mistrust, which would result in limitations in how the leadership role is exercised. Sibling rivalry is another threat. It can be triggered when a prestigious position or a controlling stake, depending on how the company ownership is constructed, is going to be passed from the old generation to the new. In such cases the family dynamic can be at its most destructive and reach Shakespearian dimensions.

The first succession in family ownership is typically from the founder to the second generation. The symbolic value of the company's product type, a process of production or a geographical area, building, etc. can be important for the founder's identity. This can be driven by a compensatory need (Kets de Vries, 1996) where the founding of the business and the social ascent are linked to other parts of the founder's background. The founder's ambition derives from an experience of having been humiliated or a grievance in the past and the task, or business idea, provides the needed compensations for such experiences. In this way founders, according to Kets de Vries, repair the past but also create a strong bond and identity with the business. Such identification with the business can make the boundary between the individual and business blurred. This bond and identification between the founder and the company often needs to be challenged when the next generation takes over. Distrust and conflict may arise and the incumbent can consciously or unconsciously obstruct the successor's entry or leadership (e.g., Handler, 1994; Kets de Vries, 1996). Another important aspect of founder to first generation successions is that the family does not yet have any experience in managing succession processes. Succession processes are also learning processes and a family may not have stories to tell about past successions, how they worked or did not. Resistance to letting go is a classic challenge in these founder to first generation successions. In the case that we will describe it was skilfully thought through in order to deal with these classic challenges.

A best practice case

The siblings of the second generation, in their early fifties at the time of the succession, were acutely aware of the emotional problems facing the first succession from their founder parents to themselves. Both had been involved in the founding of the company as teenagers and young adults. The siblings returned to work for the family business in their forties (sister) and fifties (brother). They chose to recruit a non-family CEO to ease the transition of ownership from the founders, the mother being the sole owner, to themselves. The siblings further strategized their own future leadership roles and a third generation immersion into the business. Three succession processes were in this way concurrently strategized. Being honest about their own limitations and facing difficult discussions and dialogues made this possible. A flexible mind-set that did not idealize a particular type of succession made them able to innovate and to be flexible.

Box 5.1 Perspective: roadmap for transitions in successions

Role histories and role biographies are important units of analysis in succession. A succession involves individual transitions of leader(s) leaving and entering a role, and an organizational event. That means one has to explore what is happening for the organization and, in addition, one needs to explore the situation for the person exiting the role(s) and the person entering the role(s). The interlocked levels of the individual transition and organizational needs are particularly complicated in a family business. An analysis would need to include a focus on transitions for the individuals and the organization. Figure 5.1 shows an overview and is a roadmap for the different transitions that are active in a succession.

To slow down the thinking and process, in order to digest emotions and build reflective capacity, there is often a need to review the understanding of events and facts. Then one can explore the stakes involved for both the individual and the organization in the actual succession transition. The individual stakes can be explored through a detailed account and analysis of key participants' role biographies. This would be both for the incumbent(s) and successor(s). The organizational aspect is explored through the history of the role; the events, leaders and strategies that have shaped the role over time. Focusing on these dimensions, we will illustrate a bottom-up approach to gathering information that can capture the unique aspects of a succession case. Terms used are 'leadership tenures' and 'role history', the 'role biography of top leaders' and/or 'active ownership roles'. Discussions explored different historical factors and future scenarios for the succession, with a focus on the actual strategy needed for a particular succession. Figure 5.1 is a roadmap setting out which dimensions need to be explored. The important thing to notice is that the succession is not only an individual event (see also Chapter 16). The strategizing of the next leadership tenure is influenced by the past and future ambitions of both the incumbent and the successor. It is also influenced by the organizational need and how the role has been strategized in earlier successions.

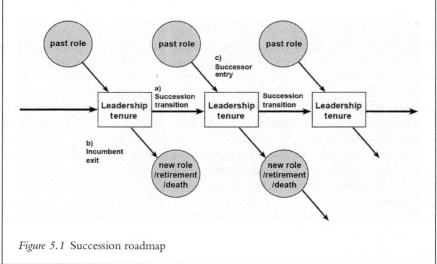

Figure 5.1 Succession roadmap

Transaction atmosphere

The family business under study was founded in France in the early 1970s and was in the fashion industry. They had one flagship store, three boutiques and, later, also a sales website. The fashions and lifestyle products were at the very high end of the market. The success of the business was seen as directly linked to the leadership of the buyer, the role held by the mother and founder. Her talent was the start of the business and gave the competitive edge that had kept them at the top of the game in Europe for 40 years. Other buyers from Europe, often competitors, would visit their shops to learn and be inspired by the 'editing' they observed there. In a chance conversation a CEO of an up-and-coming fashion brand made this comment: 'We would give them clothes for free just so they would be seen in their shops... if only we were given an opportunity!'

Overview generations and businesses

In most successions there are at least two, if not three, generations to take into consideration. Three generations were taken into account in this succession. The founder–couple as leadership team and mother as sole owner were handing over their control of the company. Their two children carved out their roles as future leaders and co-owners. A grandchild in the third generation had started in the business and they planned for her to become a future leader and/or active owner.

A focus on the family and its ownership is important when developing ownership and leadership roles. An added complication, but an important one, is that there might often be several businesses involved. This can influence succession dynamics. We found in most of our cases that several businesses were involved and this will be explored further in Chapter 16 where we discuss succession strategies. In this case there were several businesses through marriages. These companies were part of social networks with loosely or strongly connected businesses. Different roles in such networks enable family members to develop skill and authority. A diagram of the family networks and their businesses accordingly shows three different family businesses (Figure 5.2). The first business

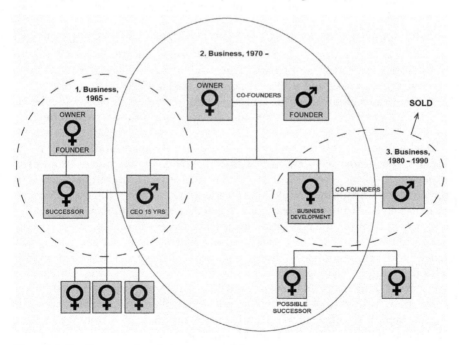

Figure 5.2 Family network and cluster ownership

(unbroken circle) is the main business under study here. The second business was a big business owned by the second generation son's wife and mother-in-law. He started working there before marrying the daughter of the founder. He later became the CEO and successfully grew and globalized this business. He had planned for an early retirement and for more involvement in his parents' business. During this process he and his wife divorced. His sister, Elisabeth, had established a business (the third business) with her husband and when their marriage failed they sold it. She had worked successfully in the business for twenty years and developed new businesses and stores.

Role histories and their imprint on succession dynamics

The founders and over-involvement

One main challenge in this succession was an over-involvement of the founders in their roles, which led to the founder hesitating or only reluctantly handing over the leadership role(s) to their children. The founder of the business, Mrs Cohen, started the boutique and was sole owner. She became renowned for an excellence in selecting clothes from fashion collections, introducing new designers and future stars and recognizing fashion trends. This unusual talent was connected to her own upbringing and childhood experience, as is often seen with entrepreneurs and founders (Kets de Vries, 1996). Her daughter, Elisabeth, offered an explanation and link between her mother's childhood, emotional involvement, talent and embodied identification with the business:

> My mother was doted on as a child. The youngest of much older siblings, she was brought up during the war in England. The family escaped there before the occupation of Paris. Her mother was a tailor, her aunt was a court dressmaker and a second aunt was a glamorous actress. She was a very beautiful child and in a time of very scarce resources they enjoyed dressing her for this glamorous and selective world they provided for.

The childhood of the founder, the socio-political situation and the type of business she created were in this way linked. The family were Jewish and their experiences during World War II brought a historical imprint, and drive, to the business. The business could be seen as compensating for this past. Dressing or being dressed in the most carefully selected, beautiful and expensive clothes compensated for the discrimination experienced after the war. A compensatory need had been fulfilled. This created a strong attachment to the business, which would come to symbolize a triumph and proof that being Jewish is beautiful. This drive might have been instrumental for the founding and was crucial for the success. However, this link is often not directly experienced by the next generation, as in this case. They had not shared the same war and post-war climate and had other motives and wishes for their involvement. Strong emotional ties between the founder and the business can in this way be challenged in a succession. It can lead to a sense of loss for the founder and be channelled as criticism and conflicts among family members. Lack of mourning for a loss, often unconscious or a taboo, can have profound consequences, and be the origin of destructive dynamics.

The former leadership tenure

Analysing the succession as a phase between two leadership tenures enables one to look at what is happening at the system level. This can be independent of the individual emotions and trajectories involved. This case illustrates how a founder business often has a lack of clarity in roles between the founders as leaders and as owners and the roles of other family members and employees. This problem had yet to affect this business in an irreversible way. The founder's leadership had been to focus on what she saw as the crucial skills and authority. The editing of fashion, the role of scout and the embracer of innovation, would be voiced by the mother as always 'editing, editing, editing' the fashion collections, 'having an eye' and 'empathy for and deep understanding of the client'. Such idiosyncratic but often deep-seated assumptions of what gives authority, either for ownership or leadership, is a part of what is explored and reviewed in a succession. The mother came across as a typical founder with a loving but slightly dismissive approach to her children, who in turn expressed resentment about her lack of appreciation. As the daughter, Elizabeth, said:

> After the first shopping trip I made with my mother, I can remember feeling useless and not up to standard and she was very critical. I was very hurt by it... I later thought it was unreasonable as it was my first buying trip ever.

A non-family CEO as a 'golden strategic event'

The founders had an unclear idea about what the succession process would be and the specific leadership criteria. Within the founders' mind-set, no mandate for a new tenure could be developed. The blurred and informal arrangements between being the owner but active in the business as leader, with no differentiation between when they were acting as either, made a succession very difficult. The mother would exercise her right as the owner not to discuss inheritance and future leadership succession. Elisabeth, for her part, would make the point that 'It is James and I who own the future.' This statement reflected their legal position of inheritance, which could only be thwarted by disinheriting them. Both James and Elisabeth said outright that they would have found it emotionally difficult, if not impossible, to take on the CEO role. They rightfully anticipated fights with their parents in implementing necessary new ideas and systems.

The crucial strategic event in this succession, initiated by the brother, was to employ a professional leader for an interim period. Most of the father's functions, and some of the mother's, were taken over by this non-family CEO. The parents and their children, and the siblings among themselves, would use the CEO as a buffer when they carved out a new strategic course for the company. This contained conflicts, tensions and different generational experiences. Strategizing the succession helped to mature the authority structure within the business so that ownership roles and leadership roles were clearer. A professional human resource policy and a new approach to PR and marketing followed. The siblings, both openly and secretly, supported the CEO in professionalization and new initiatives. The use of a CEO with a time limited contract also created some time and space for them to resolve tension and discuss their ambitions regarding ownership and leadership roles. It also provided the opportunity to further review this in the context of the long-term challenges for the business.

Maturing the authority structure

Analysis of role histories can bring to the surface issues involved in how authority has been constructed and re-constructed in the succession; a succession can reset assumptions about authority. An active process of strategizing the next leadership tenures can lead to constructing new types of authority. As described above, the mandate for the CEO was both to modernize and to be an emotional buffer. This was different from the mother's focus on her role as scout and 'editor'. A differentiation of the top leadership and the active ownership was also clarified which would influence the way decisions were made. A new set of authority arrangements and a new top leadership role were carved out. This created clarity for the family, the CEO and the employees on decision-making between the active owners and the CEO. This succession process led to the differentiation of an ownership group and a management team. Importantly, this authority development did not change the idiosyncratic aspect and vision of the business; it remained an embracer of high end fashion and innovators. The challenges of building governance and clarifying leadership authority are, of course, also a feature in non-family entrepreneurship.

Role biographies and achievements

The politics of storytelling

Stories about the founding of the company are a source of identity and a value system for the family and also for the employees. The story will often change over time as it interweaves new aspects of the past, new challenges the business faces and new choices. An interesting discrepancy was hidden in this family's initial story about the founding of the business. The founders, employees and siblings would tell the story of how the business was started by the parents. When 'digging into' their role biographies it appeared that both siblings were highly involved as co-founders, working with the parents when they were very young. It was James, as a teenager, who spotted the possibility of buying what was a small shop. This had been expanded over several houses into the flagship store. The work over those years had a high price as he did not go to university, something he regretted. A storytelling including and acknowledging the children's work as adolescents, and the sister's later involvement, was triggered by the succession. It would challenge the assumption that the parents were the sole founders. A boundary between the generations, in order to conform to a conventional family structure, had been upheld by this story. Although this sense of normalcy had been upheld, it undermined the siblings' entitlement.

A sense of achievement

In this family it was difficult to build a sense of achievement, a classic feature for offspring in successful family owners. The perception of nepotism from others and oneself can lead to a fragile sense of accomplishment. However, the siblings in this case had, crucially, experience from working outside the family business. This is necessary to build authority for oneself and within the family business. An analysis of the role biographies in this case showed several businesses influenced the way in which knowledge, skills and authority had been developed by the siblings. The son had been the CEO in his wife's business and built global experience and authority that influenced what he brought with him to his mother's business. The sister, with her husband, had founded and sold a luxury scents and cosmetics business. This was important for her capacity as innovator and in developing new businesses. She complemented her brother's administrative and marketing competence with innovative and product development skills.

After the succession Elisabeth's role developed and was formalized as creative director; her main task was to conceptualize and build up new business ventures. She would then, for the first time, have an office of her own. James planned a return and had been taking over some of his aging father's responsibilities on a part-time basis. However, as he was still CEO of his mother-in-law's fashion house the workload became too onerous. After the interim CEO had been in the role for six years he retired from this job and became CEO of the mother's business.

Legacy and shift between generations

This family had to manage a succession with inter-generational tensions and conflicts, which, as is common, often came across as resentful criticism. Such negative focus can often become too important in how the family, and others, perceive the dynamics. Importantly, a strong sense, and numerous acts, of altruistic nurturing was also a feature. The mother, while criticizing her children, was proud of them. She had nurtured them by offering roles and opportunities, allowing for risk-taking, making mistakes and development of knowledge and skills. The siblings, while experiencing hurtful events, gained experience and knowledge very early in life. While there was pressure on them not to continue into higher education, to which the son gave in, the financial autonomy the business gave to them was important. Discussion around autonomy was triggered by the succession. Dialogue between the siblings, over some years, evolved the reasoning and justifications for keeping the business. Thus the past was dealt with and they became able to challenge the legacy of their mother, rather than continuing, reverently, with the existing state of affairs. Frankness about their talents and financial needs was a part of this. It allowed for exploration and construction of meaning, and for a drive independent of the founder.

> We talk freely about the future, the business, how one of the shops has to be redone and put in shape. We also discuss if, in the future, we would like to sell and then develop another type of business, not necessarily fashion, but lifestyle, what type, other products and so on.
>
> Elizabeth

Nurturing and entitlement

A genuine affection and altruistic nurturing formed the basis for enabling and encouraging the third generation to develop careers outside the business. If they insisted, they were given the opportunity to work for the family. The second generation siblings did not want to force their children to join the business, and in fact discouraged it. They wanted to hand over the business, if any of the third generation was interested, differently from how it was handed over to them. At the time James' children were still in their teens, and unclear as to which career paths they would choose. He had a small stationery shop he thought of as a place for them to have work experience and earn pocket-money. Elisabeth's daughter, on the other hand, was employed in the business. She was in her early twenties and expressed satisfaction with her work. She planned a career in fashion but was not blindly committed to the family business. With her good degree of detachment, it was easy to engage her in talk about competing fashion businesses and their 'edge and newness'. She admired her grandmother's talent and business acumen, but maintained some distance and detachment. She negotiated her involvement with the family by not participating in the grandmother's Friday Sabbath. This caused some friction in the family, and criticism from her grandmother, but she also strongly supported the grand-daughter's immersion into the business. In this sense boundaries and autonomy were developed and maintained.

Intra-generational relationships and trust

Trust is intrinsic to all successions, and this case is no different. Issues of trust and the need for trust repair is often essential in any succession. Most families have skeletons in the closet that influence trust within the family. Trust is essential to make any organization, including a family business, work. Incidents of family members forced out of the business and marriage complications are events that can suddenly become relevant. Even when the events are long in the past, the way they were managed may have led to mistrust, complicating relationships in a way that affects a succession. Elisabeth initiated and managed some discussion with her brother around painful secrets within the family. For several years she had felt excluded from her brother's deliberations and strategizing processes for the business. She worried that he might intend to buy her out and become sole owner. She attributed a tension between them to conflict between their parents. The parents had a complicated marriage and in different ways they created conflicts between the siblings. They would confide secrets and display favouritism between them which, for a while, made the relationship between the siblings very difficult. . James had felt betrayal at several levels and his sense of family belonging, loyalty and entitlement had been disturbed and made difficult.

In the discussion and exchange between them, Elisabeth had to repair a sense of distrust and the exclusion of her brother. There was a sense of rejection of James by the father. James had worked in the business from his late teens and left it in his mid-twenties. His lack of success in achieving a profit in men's clothing had been the surface issue causing anger and criticism between him and his father. Elisabeth had not supported him, and this led to a breach in sibling loyalty. A part of the repair was an apology from the sister and this contributed to the management of the succession. Some history rewriting was necessary around the troubled relationship between the father and James. The process changed the siblings' relationship radically, and established them as equal and active co-owners. They would develop this over three to four years, and this became the basis for how they developed their roles and supported each other.

Afterthoughts and reflections

Sibling 'we-loyalty' and succession

A 'we-feeling' between siblings is a crucial emotional factor in the establishment of trust and strategic capacity. This factor has been overshadowed in psychological or psychodynamic thinking by the attention to parent–child relationships (Coles, 2003). While there is often a focus on sibling rivalry, this can be counteracted by, or co-exist with, loyalty. A succession should, therefore, not only be seen as a dynamic between a parent and successor but also as about the sibling relationship. A successful succession offers siblings an opportunity for life-long closeness. The emotional benefit from this, in a sense of meaning and safety, can be more important than the financial aspects of the business. Coles focuses on siblinghood and the development of a sibling 'we-sense' as being important for a sense of self and the capacity to trust. This is crucial for the support and dialogues that are important in a family business (Sorenson and Bierman, 2009).

Hybrid governance structures and leadership

A founder or second generation business will often have a need for maturing its authority structure. If this is accomplished, the later generation can build on, and further develop, these. Adjustments and changes will also happen during the course of a leadership or ownership tenure. Review of governance structures is a continual responsibility, and should be a main strategic task for any business or organization, including a family business. The family as a governing body is often informal, fluid and a source of innovative thinking and fast decision-making. A succession triggers so many emotions that instituting some structure, at its simplest form planned family council meetings with an agenda, is a big improvement. A hybrid structure can be developed according to the family's needs, not necessarily complying with corporate governance structures. The fluid interaction and dialogue intrinsic to a family unit's informality is not replaced by such 'home-grown' structures. Rather, it can give a safer space and more systematic discussion where painful, often avoided, topics can be discussed. This is recommended, in different forms and shapes, by the main advisors and practice oriented academics in the field. Further discussion can be found in books about family councils: Eckrich and McClure (2012) and Carlock and Ward's (2010) cover management of business, family and individual cycles when planning for the ownership of the business.

Even if one designates a member of the family as the successor early on, the support that such structures provide is crucial for the establishment and maintenance of trust. Such hybrid structures also achieve other things, for example, review and assessment of the business performance. Trust is built between family members and other stakeholders such as employees (e.g., Sundaramurthy, 2008). Important human and group dynamics that can be destructive are counteracted with such safe spaces for face-to-face discussions. The family might choose to have a trusted outsider to facilitate the discussion. Powerfully destructive group and individual dynamics, such as scapegoating or idealization of individuals, can undermine cooperation, trust and ultimately successions. When important conversations are held away from open forums, taking place mainly in private conversations, processes of fantasy and suspicion easily develop. Unfounded claims can take hold without being refuted or confirmed, and can easily spiral out of control. This can create self-fulfilling prophesies and downward spirals in cooperation and strategic thinking, which can very rapidly lead to a complete collapse of trust and the entry of lawyers and often-irreversible dynamics.

In the case discussed in this chapter, the development of an ownership group as different from the CEO role enabled an emotional and personal process building the necessary trust between the siblings to overcome grievances, ask for forgiveness and take emotional risk. Trust became the platform for dialogues about their own commitment and strategies, addressing the needs and possibilities for the business. Complementary talents and knowledge possessed by the siblings could then be explored without triggering unnecessary competition. Such analysis and strategizing is important in designing leadership and ownership teams. It defines and clarifies authority. Some basic trust, or willingness to commit to explore trust, is crucial for the process to start. It can become a virtuous circle where trust increases over time. Such co-ownership makes it possible for the owner and leaders' team to manage increased complexity.

References

Carlock, R. and Ward, J.L. (2010). *When Family Businesses are Best: The parallel planning process for family harmony and business success*. Basingstoke, UK: Palgrave Macmillan.

Coles, P. (2003). *The Importance of Sibling Relationships in Psychoanalysis*. London: Karnac.

Eckrich, C.J. and McClure, S.L. (2012). *The Family Council Handbook: How to create, run, and maintain a successful family business council* (A Family Business Publication). New York: Palgrave, Macmillan.

Gilmore, T. and Ronchi, D. (1995). Managing predecessors' shadows in executive transitions. *Human Resource Management, 34*, 11–26.

Handler, W.C. (1990). Succession in family firms: A mutual role adjustment between entrepreneur and next generation family members. *Entrepreneurship Theory and Practice, 15*, 37–51.

Handler, W.C. (1994). Succession in family business: A review of the research. *Family Business Review, 7*, 133–157.

Kets de Vries, M.F.R. (1996). *Family Business: Human dilemmas in the family firm*. London: Thomson.

Osnes, G. (2011). Succession and authority: A case study of an African family business and a clan chief. *International Journal of Cross-Cultural Management, 11*(2), 185–201.

Sorenson, R.L. and Bierman, L. (2009). Family capital, family business, and free enterprise. *Family Business Review, 22*, 193–195.

Sundaramurthy, C. (2008). Sustaining trust within family businesses. *Family Business Review, 1*, 89–102.

6 Cluster ownership

A multi-generation, entrepreneurial family in China

Olive Yanli Hou

My father shared many common characteristics of his generation in the 1970s – he cared about how to develop this factory and how to help the people survive and live decently. Last year (2011) some local businessmen and I donated our money to renovate a temple, where everyone could have a nice view of Yunhe County. I think it would be beneficial for us to unite together as one and think about the whole industrial picture.

He Shangqing

Introduction

Traditionally we think about the family business and its relationship to the family in terms of the family's ownership of a single business. This frame of mind can oversimplify the way the family strategizes and thinks about their business or businesses.

There is oversimplification at two levels. First, the family might own, or family members might co-own, several businesses in different constellations. In the cases featured in this book, just one out of all the families, the Swedish family, owned only one company. Second, the family and its ownership might be a part of a wider social fabric of businesses that are within the same field, or providing related products, often known as a *cluster region* (or *regional cluster*) as proposed by Porter (1998). We will explore a best practice case that will illustrate how a founder business developed into a cluster of companies, owned by different family members. The development of these businesses was instrumental in, and happened concurrently with, the development of a cluster region for the production of a particular type of product.

Within the family business field the family and its engagement with the family business has often been explored through the three-circle model. This rests on the assumption of one family-one business. The original bivalent two-circle model well describes a family that owns a firm and three overlapping circles: (1) the family, (2) the business and (3) the ownership (Gersick, Davis, McCollom Hampton and Lansberg, 1997; Tagiuri and Davis, 1996). This model is also presented in Chapter 8. It focuses on the roles of owners, family members and employees and how they interact, and can be used to understand authority and the internal dynamic where there is one business and one family. However, only one family in our case material had a single company ownership structure and the three-circle model cannot capture the strategizing done with multiple businesses, shifting ownership between family members and how this complex pattern influences successions.

A model that Michael-Tsabari, Labaki and Zachary (2014) suggested can offer a more comprehensive picture for more complex ownership structures and how they develop over time. The cluster model is useful for analyzing complex family business structures and changeable multiple ownership. We will call this *cluster ownership* so that it is not confused with a cluster of businesses in a region – that is, how a region develops as a cluster of similar types of businesses that are not necessarily family owned. Well-planned cluster ownership can prevent destructive competition and rivalry (Michael-Tsabari et al., 2014) and gives family members the opportunity of new ventures and opportunities for entrepreneurship. Creating a new company may help to buffer the risk of tunnel thinking and enable the business to better prepare for potential changes in the market. Cluster ownership also allows the family owners/managers more flexibility and choice over strategy, including choice of location. For example, in this case the two units with the task of innovation and R&D were located close to the best arts educational institutions, to assist recruitment of new talent. The units would not be stifled by being a part of a bigger hierarchy with complicated and slower decision-making processes geared toward mass production.

Succession and new entrepreneurship

The process of ownership transition and succession in private firms is influenced by several factors, such as the family structure, the personal goals of the owner-manager, the ability and ambitions of potential successors, and legal and financial issues (Le Breton-Miller, Miller and Steier, 2004). Among these elements, "very little attention has been paid to how family dynamics affect fundamental entrepreneurial processes" (Aldrich and Cliff, 2003: 573–574). The traditional notion of strategizing life stages and succession in family ownership falls apart if one takes into account cluster ownership. Some researchers try to identify different ownership structures, stages of business growth and family experiences in the business based on life cycle (Gersick et al., 1997). It is still a useful norm yet it lacks accuracy and vividness as cluster ownership often is not a linear process; it is, rather, interactive with many interwoven constituencies.

Within economic thinking a cluster is used to indicate a geographic concentration of interconnected companies (Porter, 1998). As a combination of cooperation and rivalry (Reve and Sasson, 2012), a regional cluster is a gradually developed space where common resources, knowledge and experience are shared, and where increased specialization and comparative advantage are accumulated. Raising capital through alliances in a cluster is more likely to happen and easier to achieve. Still, it can be argued that extensive overlaps on knowledge and between partners in a cluster may constrain the potential for innovation, especially in small and homogeneous regions (Fitjar and Rodríguez-Pose, 2011).

In the case featured in this chapter, the cluster ownership of a family was instrumental in developing such a cluster of specialist companies in the region. We will combine the two phenomena: the development of cluster ownership and the cluster region, and try to find out how the family structure and dynamics, and the context in which they operated, encouraged certain types of entrepreneur behaviors. The cluster region at a macro level outside of the family business, and cluster ownership at micro level within the family business can both be examined. One business may act as an "anchor" firm in a cluster region that induces spin-offs and attracts firms from related industries (Greenstone, Hornbeck and Moretti, 2008). In this case, the He family is an extended family, not a nuclear one, and owned several different types of firms including production and innovative companies in cluster ownership. The latter corresponds to the model suggested by Michael-Tsabari, et al. (2014). Through the cluster model, the ownership evolution and entrepreneurial process can be well recorded and analyzed.

A best practice case

In our Chinese case these two clusters, the family business and the region, are closely connected. The interaction between the two also actively influences the entrepreneurial process and business outlook. There are four separate businesses owned by the He Shouzhen family. The family started with a founder business that was handed over to the elder son as new director within a commune ownership structure. Five years later, the retired founder started the region's first local private family business, with his younger son, after the Chinese government relaxed the rules and permitted private ownership. Six years later, the elder son in the second generation started the second private family business on his own. His daughter went on to start a third business, later sold to her brother who took over their father's business. Further, two cousins in the third generation started two other businesses. All these businesses would produce the same type of product, be suppliers for parts or services or linked in other ways. Former employees from the commune enterprise also started their own smaller spin-off businesses. These companies would sometimes cooperate on bigger contracts, but they would also compete. In addition, the family had invested and started a business that would be a small incubator for new design ideas and for product development. The ownership transfer among siblings within the family indicates the family business is not a linear development process but a complex development of cluster ownership. E-commerce and self-brand innovative firms launched by the third-generation grandson proved his capacity to take over as manager of a second family business set up by his father.

In this Chinese cluster region, the He family collaborates as different firms in cluster ownership. They also collaborate with external firms so as to advance the industry and attract more established overseas clients, which none of them is able to achieve independently. Replicating the proven successful models, the village has become a cluster region for one unique product. One in three local citizens work in this industry; and the village accommodates some 800 manufacturing enterprises that employ more than 30,000 people and produce 19 categories of wooden toy products, resulting in several hundred thousand items. The products are exported to 74 countries and regions, representing 30 and 60 percent, respectively, of the global and Chinese domestic market shares.

A case of cluster ownership

The He family from southern China has run a wooden toy business for over three generations dating back to 1973, when China was about to undergo dramatic social, political and economic change. The whole country was transforming from a planned economy to a market economy, which requires a radically different mindset. The wooden toy business opportunity was spotted and exploited by the first-generation founder while he was working on the task given to him of leading people out of poverty. The driver, or motivation, behind the enterprises is similar to our Swedish case discussed in Chapter 7, where the entrepreneurs' purpose was about collective survival and improvement of the living conditions among the local community.

The ownership of this extended He family relates to four different businesses. The central business is the Hexin Group, which has now become a diversified conglomerate with seven firms ranging from exports and imports to trading businesses, R&D, artistic design, animation production, franchise businesses, e-commerce and education to a micro-loans finance firm. These were all developed from a sole OEM (original equipment manufacturer). The succession between the second-generation elder son and third-generation grandson has been accompanied by innovative breakthroughs at different stages.

The business and its context

The business originated from a founder operating within the collective political system (communism) that governed China in the late 1960s and early 1970s. The founder, He Shouzhen, was the director of a commune enterprise appointed by local government in Chishi County, Zhejiang Province. Due to national industrial policy, all the craftsmen in the cities had to be reallocated to rural areas. He Shouzhen managed to develop a wooden toy production business from what had previously been a simple wood-processing factory, as he realized that wooden toys would create more added value, and therefore bring more benefit to his community.

Entrepreneurial bricolage: spot, grab and develop

Lévi-Strauss' (1967) concept of *bricolage* explained many of the entrepreneurial behaviors we observed in this case. The founder, He Shouzhen, was able to create something new when faced with resource constraints. Bricolage is "making do by applying combinations of the resources at hand to new problems and opportunities" (Baker and Nelson 2005: 333) and in this case it enabled the business to grow and flourish.

High-quality trees constituted one of the few available natural resources in the local area. Initially, He Shouzhen and his fellows only did basic treatment of timber, but later he added more value through more advanced processing. With more revenue coming in, He began exploring new opportunities, particularly an import/export business in close-by Shanghai city, which was the economic center then and still is today.

> At that time, we could not go to Shanghai directly. You had to get an introduction letter with several stamps from the commune and handicraft bureau in the county and then the authority of the province. In the early morning, we arrived at Shanghai and then lined up for the accommodation. It would take two hours queuing outside the travel agency. The travel agency would give you a list, indicating which road or which bathhouse you should go to. Because the craftsmen were not qualified, we had to stay at bathhouse (with basic accommodation condition).
>
> He Shangqing, recalling early days working with his father

He Shouzhen discovered that one Shanghai company was exporting hammers, pick-hoes and hoes. He went there and pitched directly. The Shanghai company requested samples to be submitted within one week. He Shouzhen's farming tool factory had never previously made these articles, moreover the transportation was poor, so it was impossible to deliver the prototype in such a short period of time. So he bought a handle from the local market in Shanghai, scraped off the production serial number, polished it and handed it over to the contact. By showing this modified prototype and with the help of sincere persuasion, he finally secured an order to provide hoe handles.

Sensitivity to contextual change can create *bricolage* opportunities for entrepreneurs with a well-prepared mindset. A state policy required Shanghai city to support the surrounding area including Zhejiang Province where the Chishi commune factory was located. Shanghai companies recommended He Shouzhen, whose factory supplied wooden tools for them. He Shouzhen was able to bring back some gadgets from Shanghai, including castanets, skill balls, and peg-tops. After a trial production for more than a year, the first batch of wooden toys was produced. In 1973, the Chishi Toy Factory was officially established. Other smaller factories soon followed suit, and the wooden toy business started to boom.

The first succession: a public vote

Under the Chinese regime of the day, the pattern that was common in private businesses and in most other countries, in which the founder could almost freely select his/her children as the successor, was not possible. What occurred was that the father-first son succession in the commune enterprise was based upon public consensus. But the son did win over the employees' support.

> The factory belongs to [the] commune yet the commune had no share and didn't invest a penny. As for who would take over the factory, it was not my father's business really. Rather, the commune and local government had the final say. Eventually the factory held an open election for a new manager when my father was about to retire. Almost 100 employees voted for the new management team. My wife and I ranked the highest.
>
> He Shangqing

The first-generation founder He Shouzhen retired from the Chishi Toy Factory in 1980, but with his entrepreneurial spirit undiminished, he established the first private enterprise with his second son, He Shangqing's younger brother, He Yulin, in 1985 in Yunhe County. This company was named the Zhenpeng Arts & Crafts Factory, and from there the He's private family business began. Zhenpeng Arts & Crafts Factory has now been run for 31 years since its inception.

Loss and reconstruction of the first business

After He Shangqing took over the Chishi Toy Factory, it quickly became the top exporter in Zhejiang Province. Unfortunately a severe flood in Chishi County destroyed the original factory. He Shangqing commented, "The flood took away almost everything. We were back to Yunhe County with nothing but knowledge, concept and technology. No revenue, no product, nothing. But I had resources, acquaintances and networking."

He Shangqing applied to return to Yunhe County. He initially joined the local Foreign Trade Department and worked as an official. In 1990, He Shangqing initiated a company, the Foreign Trade Arts & Crafts Factory, under the umbrella of the Foreign Trade Department. The next year, all the other nine shareholders withdrew from public-private business, as they lost interest in the enterprise. So in 1991, He Shangqing set up the Hexin factory, a second private business within the He family. By then, the family business set up by He Shouzhen (the father) and He Yunlin (the second son) had been running for six years. The catastrophic events of the flood, and the subsequent rebuild and relocation of the new business, created several spin-off businesses were set up by former employees in Yunhe County. He Shangqing's cousin, who used to work with him, started his own business with a Hong Kong partner and become successful in his 30s. Another cousin in the third generation from his wife's side did the same.

Expanding the cluster with new entrepreneurship

Like his father, He Shangqing was highly attuned to policy changes and their potential impact on private business. As policy-making in China gradually opened up opportunities for exports, He Shangqing made a bold decision in 1994 and moved the Hexin factory from Yunhe County to Shenzhen City, hoping to deal directly with overseas customers, as Shenzhen was close to Hong Kong, the stepping-stone for international trade. This proved difficult in practice, owing to the distance between Shenzhen and Yunhe County, the lack of timber and facilities. In addition, the financial crisis in Southeast Asia in 1997 hit the company hard. As a result, it sank deep into debt. He Shangqing had to borrow money from his mother to sustain the business, before finally closing down the factory in Shenzhen and returning to Yunhe County. He absorbed the financial loss but while the enterprise seemingly failed, the family had gained valuable knowledge and skills in the process: their management ability, control of processes and understanding of western etiquette had improved due to the frequent and in-depth communication with overseas customers. By the end of 2000, Hexin Group had managed to clear its debts and earned profits of 1.2 million Yuan.

E-commerce transformation and the next generation

There were four shareholders in He Shangqing's family business. As the second-generation founder, He Shangqing improved production skills, enhanced process management, and expanded the business to overseas markets. The third-generation siblings (a son and a daughter) contributed to the company's transformation by developing e-commerce.

The third-generation son, He Bin, spotted the new internet platforms and also built an online business but this was closed down shortly afterwards, owing to a high degree of uncertainty for online Chinese businesses, including fears for the security of online transactions. In 2005, the daughter, He Xuefei, was encouraged by her mother to sell some wooden toys in her e-shop on Taobao. com (the Chinese equivalent of ebay) and proved to be more successful in developing a Chinese domestic distribution and credit rating within Taobao. After five years, He Xuefei's online store received the top rating of the "Imperial Crown" level as a trusted seller and in 2010 she sold her online business to her brother, finalizing the ownership/credit transfer and only keeping about 10 percent as a minor shareholder.

Renewed authority and the second succession

When He Bin returned to Yunhe County from Shengzhen City with greater exporting and online experience, he realized the importance of further business education. Supported by his father, he resumed his studies. After college graduation, he was prepared to put theory into practice and make some changes to the family business. A conversation with his father made him more determined to make a difference: his father asked him if he just wanted to be a shareholder or if he wanted to complete the preparation for becoming a CEO as well. He Bin was innovative in creating new brands and reconstructing the value chain, while most other businesses in the cluster were content to stay as an OEM and take outsourcing orders. His grandfather and uncle's family business continued to use the conventional business model and debated with him over his risk-taking strategy. Like his grandfather who created added value by moving from wood processing to toy production, and like his father who expanded the export business by relocating to Shenzhen City, he also raised the family business to a new level. Many people in the company were suspicious about He Bin's plan, as building a self-made product brand takes a long time and the prospects are uncertain. His father, He Shangqing, expressed his support however, "Eventually he will do this business by himself, he needs to take the responsibilities and bear the consequences even if he fails. After all, he is the one who will manage the company in the future."

The He family business had transformed itself from a mere toy manufacturer to a conglomerate with seven firms, whose businesses included R&D, production manufacturing, online business, franchises, design, animation and education. The design center and animation studio is located in Hangzhou city, where the company can recruit creative talent from well-established art institutions. The franchise headquarter is located in Yiwu, the biggest wholesale market center in China, and the direct sales center is in Shanghai which has a mature retail ecology. Although diversified, the multiple firms are all centered round the core business of wooden toys. There is one exception though: the family business did invest in a local micro-loan company firm as the alternative finance market was rapidly growing in China with considerable potential for returns on investment.

When He Bin, of the third generation, reached the age of 25 he had already built his authority through strategies like e-commerce and independent brand building. He Shangqing, of the second generation, handed over the business to him at this young age. He believes that the succession should be done sooner than later.

> If the succession was late, you cannot rectify if he is [heading in] the wrong direction. I will challenge him if I think the decision was incorrect. I will let him do new things if I have doubts. When you are capable of controlling the company, you should hand it over. When you are old, you have to rely on your son to look after you; sometimes you will even become a burden.
>
> He Shangqing

Legacy, stewardship and creative flow

He Bin was exposed to an entrepreneurial environment within the family when he was a child. His grandfather, He Shouzhen, had helped local fellows out of poverty through leadership of the commune enterprise and is seen as a legendary figure. His father, He Shangqing, continued and expanded the business overseas. His uncle launched the first private family business with his grandfather, and his cousin (son of his aunt) set up a joint venture with a Hong Kong partner after working for several years with his father, He Shangqing. Another cousin, also from the aunt's family, started up his own business as well.

> My cousin did a great job; he is my role model. I often boasted in front of my peers that he was very powerful and capable. Actually my father, uncle and cousin were all my role models, so I set my benchmark and target in my mind from very early on.
>
> He Bin

For members of the extended family, there were opportunities to express their creative ideas, and to encourage learning and development. He Bin's uncle stepped in when he noticed overseas orders shrinking after the financial crisis. He came to He Bin, asking him to be the mentor of his son, He Wei, who had just graduated from college. He Bin invited He Wei to attend a toy exhibition in Nuremberg, Germany so that the latter could get some hands-on experience. He Wei realized that branding was crucial for a sustainable business when he saw the LEGO stall. He then discussed with his father about investing in computer facilities to keep pace with developments in e-commerce.

Cluster ownership and knowledge transfer makes it possible for the family business to take considerable risk or "disruption" without worrying too much about short-term financial results. The trading firm in Shenzhen was shut down due to an unfavorable economic environment and misjudgment of its prospects. But the second-generation owner saw it effectively as a necessary tuition fee, concluding that they had gained rich management experience, which would have been impossible otherwise.

Box 6.1 Serial entrepreneurship and cluster ownership

The cluster ownership of this family business means that the family can combine flexibility and adaptability with closeness and bonds of trust. They can add new businesses in response to the market changes, while maintaining a platform and meeting point for collaboration, and help lower the risk by learning from each other's business practices. Inevitably, there has been internal conflict between family businesses, especially when they were bidding for the same overseas clients. The second-generation owner He Shangqing would often step in and chair the discussions when there was a dispute. On the other hand, closeness can also encourage referrals and other types of collaboration. For example, the third-generation son He Bin moved away from the OEM business, so that the company could move up to the high-end value chain. As a result, he sometimes declined the OEM orders and handed them over to other family members' companies or non-family member factories in the region.

The synergy between the He family business and the cluster region can be seen in the Zhen Peng Arts & Crafts company, the grandfather/second son family business, which opened an industrial park including ten other local firms so as to improve the productivity and better serve overseas clients. The education subsidary of the Hexin Group is a new venture co-invested by ten leading firms in the same industry. The second-generation owner/manager still plays a facilitating role among the local business community as the key opinion leader.

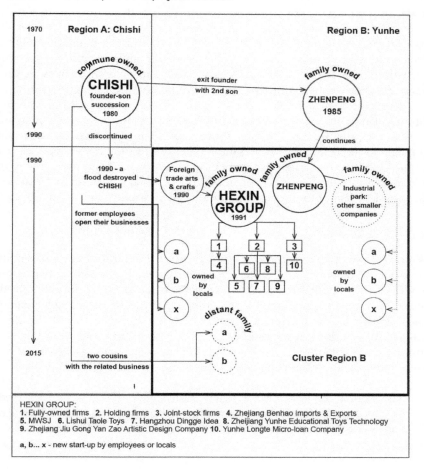

Figure 6.1 The He family and its cluster ownership in a cluster region

How a family business defines its success

Financial results are often not the only goal of a family business. The sense of stewardship and responsibility discussed in Chapter 8 can be a significant part of the motivation. For family businesses, there are times when owners/ managers have to make non-business-driven decisions, or ones that are responsive to both business and family needs. With the He family, there have been some events where family needs were the major drivers of the decisions, or at least contributed to the business direction, so that "the wider entrepreneurial reality of capital utilization and accumulation process" (Michael-Tsabari, et al., 2014) could be captured. In our Chinese case, the third-generation daughter decided to sell her online business to her brother, mainly because she was not keen on commerce and wanted to focus on family and children. Such ownership transfer was driven by family needs instead of purely financial considerations.

There have been different levels of emotional ties to the business with the different family members, yet the family legacy was always seen as a precious asset. Some firms are based in different locations, but all the generations retain nostalgia for their hometown in Yunhe County and the original wooden toy business. Profitability aside, family members may see success as the capacity to live and operate the enterprise according to a personal value system, or to pass the founder's legacy to the next generation (Denison, Lief and Ward, 2004)

A note on gender

Women have, previously, been very much behind the scenes in family businesses, as described in Chapter 15, and the image is of a soft yet persuasive power within a family business. We saw that in this case they were as involved, and as co-founders were important as the family carved out complementary roles, skillsets and leadership styles. Both the son and daughter in the third generation described their mother as "straightforward" and "outspoken," compared to their father's "mild" and "gentle" characteristics, and spoke of her irreplaceable role in the family and the business.

> My mother did not receive much formal education but she has great influence on me. She is very responsible and dares to face up to any challenge. She does not accept any excuse and will fight for what she wants.
>
> He Bin, third-generation son

> I think my mother should be seen as the pillar or backbone of our family business. Hexin Group can't survive so long without her. My dad always thinks positively and focuses on the advantages of doing something while my mom is usually a "what if" person. What would be the risk of doing this and how you could handle the bad situation, etc. She is very capable and I think you could call her "Lady Boss".
>
> He Xuefei, third-generation daughter

Afterthoughts and reflections

As a family business grows, it is natural to build a portfolio of related businesses with the extended family filling key positions (Cruz, Justo and Gomez-Mejia, 2011). Changing the core business or adjusting the business model and strategy is a major step. The He family transformed itself from its core OEM operations to a diversified array of businesses, enhancing family autonomy. Each generation utilized their skill sets and led the business from different perspectives. The first-generation founder-grandfather explored a promising product, the second-generation owner, the elder son, advanced the engineering technology and expanded the business overseas, and the third-generation owner/manager upgraded the business to a higher level covering various value points on the industrial chain. The animation and IP development, still linked to the original wooden toy products, is a good case in point.

Regional cluster

In China, there have been several cases of family businesses directly converted from commune enterprises through an MBO, (management buyout), which often requires delicate negotiation with the local government. It did not happen like this in this case, as the commune enterprise collapsed due to several catastrophic events. However, the skillset, know-how and leadership that the family founder and key members had developed from the commune enterprise were revived in their new ventures.

Cluster ownership enables flexibility and adaptability in a family business as such a structure can respond to the needs of both family members and the business itself where appropriate. Most families described in this book, except the Swedish one, chose to have more than one firm so as to strengthen their competitiveness in one way or another, hoping to seize the new opportunities by adding entities, or reduce the risk by selling the business as seen in Chapter 13.

References

Aldrich, H.E. and Cliff, J.E. (2003). The pervasive effects of family on entrepreneurship: Toward a family embeddedness perspective. *Journal of Business Venturing*, *18*(5), 573–596.

Baker, T. and Nelson, R.E. (2005). Creating something from nothing: Resource construction through entrepreneurial bricolage. *Administrative Science Quarterly 50*(3), 329–366.

Cruz, C., Justo, R. and Gomez-Mejia, L.R. (2011). Solving the paradox: A multifaced approach to corporate entrepreneurship in family firms. Unpublished manuscript.

Denison, D., Lief, C., and Ward, J.L. (2004). Culture in family-owned enterprises: Recognizing and leveraging unique strengths. *Family Business Review*, *17*, 61–70.

Fitjar, R.D. and Rodríguez-Pose, A. (2011). When local interaction does not suffice: Sources of firm innovation in urban Norway. *Environment and Planning* A *43*(6), 1248–1267.

Gersick, K.E., Davis, J., McCollom Hampton, M. and Lansberg, I. (1997). *Generation to Generation: Lifecycles of the Family Business*. Boston, MA, US: Harvard Business School Press.

Greenstone, M., Hornbeck, R. and Moretti, E. (2008). *Identifying Agglomeration Spillovers: Evidence from million dollar plants*. Cambridge, MA, US: NBER Working Paper No. 13833.

Le Breton-Miller, I.L., Miller, D. and Steier, L.P. (2004). Toward an integrative model of effective FOB succession. *Entrepreneurship Theory and Practice*, 28(4), 305–328.

Lévi-Strauss, C. (1967). *The Savage Mind*, Chicago, IL, US: University of Chicago Press.

Michael-Tsabari, N., Labaki, R., and Zachary, R.K. (2014). Toward the cluster model : The family firm's entrepreneurial behaviour over generations. *Family Business Review*, 27(2), 161–185.

Porter, M.E. (1998). Clusters and the new economics of competition, *Harvard Business Review*, Nov/Dec98, 76(6), 77.

Reve, T. and Sasson, A. (2012). *Et Kunnskapsbasert Norge*. Oslo: Universitetsforlaget.

Tagiuri, R. and Davis, J.A. (1996). Bivalent attributes on the family businesses. *Family Business Review*, 9(2), 199–208.

7 Technological innovation

Family commitment in a case from Sweden

Liv Hök

We are the third generation; it was our grandfather who started it all. He was a mining engineer; he saw how the workers in the mine would be at risk from the hazardous working environment. It started with protective gloves, respirators and safety goggles. In the very beginning, everything was made by hand. He and his wife would sit up nights and make this protective equipment. The thing is that this was during the Great Depression. He became unemployed, so he thought he could dedicate more time to this. And it just became bigger and bigger.

Sister, third generation

Introduction

In his classic work, Joseph Schumpeter described technological innovation as 'creative destruction' (1942) for the economy. The creation of new technology would be the basis of growth for emerging companies and would lead to the destruction of other companies if they failed to adapt to these advances. The development of information technology over the last 30–40 years has led to many examples of such creative destruction. Another aspect of studying technological innovation is to observe how big companies innovate. It is often assumed that the greater the amount of money a mature company uses on research and development (R&D), the more likely they are to be technologically innovative. It is often assumed that family owners are less likely to invest in technological innovation as they are risk averse and conservative. Contrary to this assumption, De Massis, Frattini, and Lichtenthaler (2012) found that family involvement as owners and leaders directly influenced the use of, and investment in, R&D. This innovation has had a positive impact on leadership in product development and an increase in the number of innovations. It is often suggested that the family will identify with the past and its products and traditions, and be driven to protect this, the owners' aspiration being to protect their socio-emotional wealth (Gómez-Mejía et al., 2007) resulting in reduced drive for technological innovation. In this case, we will explore a family whose tradition is to constantly improve and be technological innovators as a part of enhancing their socio-emotional wealth.

Capacity for strategizing innovation

Most innovations, not only technological ones, are the result of a diffuse, elusive and fluid creative process. The ability to capitalize on an established technology, production system and administration is linked to a mind-set of stability and safety in maintaining and growing a market share. Technological innovation, by contrast, is inherently uncertain. Sometimes a breakthrough is unexpected as it can happen where there is general intent for innovation but results in thinking outside the box. It needs a focus on customers, but also a more explorative mind-set and experimentation. For employees and leaders, the capacity to maintain different types of mind-sets can depend on intellectual capacity, training, personality, drive and identity. While some people and therefore companies can switch between these two modes – operational and innovative – in a strategic way, many cannot. An inability, both in family and non-family businesses, to develop or adapt to new technology is often seen as technological inertia (Ghemawat, 1991).

Innovation in family businesses

Research on family businesses' ability to be technologically innovative is disputed. Some infer that they are less innovative, others suggest family-owned businesses can be more innovative. Many family businesses start with an innovation. It can be in the form of a new business model and/or taking advantage of a gap in the market with a new type of product. When it comes to technological innovation, the disputed question is whether the company or family are able to have or maintain an innovative capacity compared to non-family businesses. Results of research investigating the amount of R&D investment indicate that family businesses invest less than non-family businesses, but these findings are not always consistent. One complicating factor in these types of studies is that families often own several companies. The development of new products or technologies might take place in new, independent companies. Different patterns of ownership structures such as serial entrepreneurship or cluster-ownership allow the family to manage innovations differently. In the Chinese case described in Chapter 6, the family have a cluster of companies where product innovation (the design of wooden toys) is allocated to a separate company located close to the best industrial design schools in the country. This structure reduces bureaucratic complexity and hierarchical levels within each of the businesses. Reducing the risk of introducing a new type of technology can also be managed better by isolating the activity into an independent company.

Obstacles and advantages in strategizing innovation

A family business can be more flexible. It has a high degree of informality that contributes to fast and flexible decision-making. In family businesses there is often an overlap of the owner and leadership roles that can facilitate fast and risky decisions when or if the family manages to deal with the inherent uncertainty that an innovative drive entails. The owners' and employees' social network is the social capital of a company and serves as an advantage when it comes to the capacity to innovate. The network outside the company provides room for dialogues that can create new ideas and serve as 'listening-posts' for new development, for finding resources and for recruiting the right people. Sometimes such loose ties in external networks (Granovetter, 1981) enable one to gain information and inspiration from fields that are on the periphery of one's core tasks.

At the same time, family ownership can be a disadvantage. Any informality can lead to a spill-over of conflicts between family members into the company, making it less flexible and more risk averse than other companies (Chrisman and Patel, 2012). In the end, money invested in research or costly new technology development programs affects revenue given to shareholders. There may be a positive short-term effect for family members who work in the business, less so for family members who are only owners. As such, lack of trust and negotiation of autonomy between family members can become crucial. When the company does well, or the family are able to manage these tensions and conflicts, informal decision-making can be a huge advantage.

A best practice case

In this chapter, the best practice case that we will describe is a family firm with a simple ownership structure: one company and all activities, as within a corporation, maintained within the business boundaries. They have streamlined the production of high technology products and have an elaborate innovation review and decision-making procedure integrated with the informal dialogues and discussions between employees, leaders and owners. They have managed to maintain this structural ease and dexterity in fast decision-making for innovation. Beyond providing respiratory protection, the family invest in their social identity in a constant quest for improvement. This is seen as their 'future-proofness' (De Massis et al., 2012): the only thing that makes the owners confident they will survive beyond the next 10 years.

Eighty years of commitment

This case study is about a three-generation family business of medium size in Sweden that manufactures respiratory protection products such as masks, filters, escape hoods, fan assisted respirators, filters and air-fed respirators. The products are first and foremost used by industrial workers, but also by other professionals and by hobbyists. The production presents a complete system of masks, filters and accessories for all market areas. In 2014 the company had a turnover of approx. 193 MSEK and approximately 95 employees, 8 of whom were working at the headquarters in Stockholm. Their factory is located in the south of Sweden with a subsidiary in Hamburg (GER), one in Hull (UK), one in East

Providence (USA) and one in Moscow (RUS). Protective masks and filters produced by the company are sold to more than 35 countries through representatives. The commitment to technological excellence is voiced by the Managing Director (MD):

> An important value that both our grandfather and father advocated was that we would stay true to our core products – protective goggles and respiratory protection. We need to do what we do very, very well. This is vital.

The founder couple started making masks in their kitchen during the Great Depression. The first modern respiratory protective mask made of natural rubber with an anatomical design appeared in 1972. The design of this approved half-mask took place in close collaboration with the Swedish Defence Research Institute. A company representative was unofficially told at the time that they had constructed the best half-mask in the world. Their respirator with adaptable facial component parts was touted as offering the highest degree of protection of any mask on the market. When the company launched their first silicone mask in 1989, its ease of use was tested and evaluated in the Stockholm Marathon. The artistry of the second-generation son, who also acted as MD, still characterizes the products today. In the past 40 years, the business has invested heavily in product development. Since 1993, the company has been ISO 90011 certified, an international recognition of its quality management system. They have two main goals: to have an on-going creation of an extensive and flexible product range and to benchmark it with the highest quality standards.

As is often noted in family business literature, it can be a challenge to manage family relationships and conflicts. A typical issue is whether a family member is thought to be capable in his/her role of running the business. Choosing between siblings or dismissing a certain family member from a role, or from the whole operation entirely, is an extremely difficult process that usually evokes strong emotions. In this particular family business, there was a series of difficulties. After these matters were resolved, the owners carved out different executive roles between them. Three out of four siblings are working in the firm today. As the only owners, they are involved in every stage of business operations.

They have a distributed leadership model where the sister is the Chair of the Board, one brother is the CEO, and another brother is the Head of Technological Innovation and in charge of the major production unit. The main bulk of the employees are trained in engineering, as is the eldest grandson of the founder, the head of the production unit. This, described below, constitutes a distributed leadership model where they all complement each other's competences. Today's MD, the youngest brother, lacks an engineering background. He sees this as an advantage as he contributes with outside-the-box thinking and comments:

> Not having a technical education is often an advantage. I can ask silly questions.

Innovation and cycles of decision-making

The family have generated widespread involvement from all levels of employees. Any decision on new products and developments includes production employees and board owners. There is a list of on-going projects kept by the sales team who have a large stock of ideas born of their contact with customers. The sales team includes some of 'the old boys' who have worked in the firm for over 20 years. Their experience represents an extensive knowledge base about the company and its products.

Pre-studies, projects to be implemented and promising project ideas are continuously reviewed. Everything goes through decision-making processes between the owners and different employees (e.g. engineers and salespeople meet periodically throughout the year to analyse all promising ideas and pre-studies so as to decide what to develop further). This is the basis for determining which projects will be carried out in the current year, the following year or the year after that. The MD describes the process:

> We have to prioritize together how we are going to manage these things. There can be of course a lot of back and forth, but when we leave the room, we have decided on something together. It's a process. There are three executive management meetings, one after another.
>
> We have a long list, and we mark up A, B, C. It's important not to forget the projects that have fallen lower on the list. We do lose sight of some things along the way – but the fact that we document this whole process means that after a year or so we can say, 'have we not talked about this before; has something changed?'

Managing the tension of innovation

Informality and initiative play a part in the process, and these elements of the company's culture are developed and fostered. These are a part of the internal social capital. They encourage creative thought, but also lead to differences of opinions and thereby tension. The tension caused by the fierce competition of ideas is fuel to the innovation cycle. The owners have fostered an atmosphere within the company so that people dare to come forward with new ideas, and employees can then lobby for those ideas. The owners are positive and listen without taking any decision, instead putting good ideas on 'the list'. The ideas then become part of the innovation cycle. In addition to these intensive project work periods, there are other periods when the leaders and employees go into more administrative phases. Any enthusiasm that emerges during the administrative phases is balanced by putting the idea on the list where it awaits the more formal structure and cycle of meetings.

Ideas can come from several sources and there is, but not exclusively, a focus on customer contact because of the knowledge they expect the salespeople to have. As the MD commented:

The business aspect is to consider our salespeople more as consultants who advise customers on how to solve problems. They can focus on technical factors and customer needs…

In addition to ideas stemming from the sales force, there are ideas from employees in production emerging from the availability of new materials or new technical solutions. A tension between different types of knowledge and levels in the hierarchy is therefore also allowed and managed by the process. This brings other sources and types of ideas into the innovation cycle. The people in charge in the factory and their co-workers are also continuously talking and monitoring technological challenges and ideas for improvements. This idea of aiming for continuous product improvement is intrinsic to the job and is taken for granted as part of the employees' role in the bigger picture. If someone wants to push something through that might be a little outside the box, it is the custom to check with others first.

Social capital

In the same way, family members and employees are acutely aware of the tension within a competitive market. Everyone understands what each product is used for, and they are convinced that the day they become sloppy is the day that their competitors eat them alive. A priority in recruitment is to identify those people who understand this aspect of the business culture and can sustain it, but it is not always easy to get a healthy dose of staff turnover and new blood. Maintaining trust is a priority, as are ethics:

> That's what it's about – treating your staff, suppliers, and customers with respect and having a stable income, bringing in new brooms now and then. [There is a Swedish expression: new brooms sweep the best.] It's a simple philosophy. Maybe we lose a deal here and there, but we sleep well.
> MD

This family business places a high value on cultural sensitivity. A potential employee who displays such sensitivity has authority and is a huge advantage to the company. A main goal is always being at the top of quality standards set by governments. The MD noted:

> The sales staff are responsible for much of the knowledge business and call themselves missionaries.

A culture of trust means that the management can rely on the employees and concentrate on other things. The development department keeps a sharp eye on the industry sector. This enables strategic cooperation with suppliers, and ensures that relevant market intelligence is always on the agenda when representatives meet. There is also an international association for breathing protection. The American and Swedish Departments of Defence arrange meetings where competitors present their latest research to each other.

'Future-proofness'

As is typical of a family business, one finds a strong identity and a long-term focus on survival in this company. This has also been described as 'future-proofness' by De Massis et al. (2012). It can backfire by making families very conservative in embracing new trends and challenges, but it can also be an advantage. The link between a long-term perspective and the identification of the family with the business can be complex. In this case, the family and the company, their name and their reputation, are a part of building and fostering external social capital. This is both social and emotional, building on a legacy of quality and family reputation as well as family integrity and ownership. It has been built up and transformed over 70 years. Both for the business and for the family itself, this identity and emotional value have been crucial for long-term thinking. At the same time, there is a high degree of informality and involvement of active owners who can take very fast and often risky decisions that build on this legacy but do not increase profit at all. When telling the story of their business, most of the families in this book have mentioned moments that were important for confirming and consolidating the interdependence or interchange between the family, the business and the surrounding context.

When the terrible 9/11 disaster occurred, the company immediately donated masks for the clean-up effort. Instantly the family's gut instinct was to help. They perceived the world through the lens of protection from dust, sometimes quite obsessively, and immediately saw the need for this protection amid the disaster. This answer to an unimaginable catastrophe illustrates their powerful drive and deep involvement in the business. It also shows a type of decision-making that few, if any, other types of organization could make. In this case, they confirmed the family's and employees' commitment to a sense of meaning, but also created goodwill. Both prior to 9/11 and after, the company has donated products like this – for example, for the tsunami victims in 2004 – but without the company name made visible.

This decision renewed the basic premise of the founder: to help others breathe. This began with a focus on miners who became sick from the dust of northern Swedish mines. He had been a mining engineer and was made redundant during the Great Depression. He and his wife started developing masks at home, literally on the kitchen table, and this was the start of the business. One year after the 9/11 donation, a large New York business became a client. Making a profit from a disaster donation raised some ethical issues within the company, and with their focus on innovation, they used the new profits to develop a new mask.

Owners' role history

Family businesses can, if they want their leaders to be family members, become very vulnerable to members lacking strategic capacity and business skills. When innovation is a core part of the business, the capacity to innovate is added to the necessary qualifications for the coming generation. It is not a must that the innovator is the top-leader. It might be an advantage, however, that one of the family members, maybe as an active owner, has a good grasp of the technology involved. In this family, there has been an inventor in each of the three generations. As described above, the founder couple were innovators together. In all the family business cases in this book, a couple started the business together.

The second generation in the Swedish family business described in this chapter, the founders' son, had initially not seen a future for himself in the company. His main interest was art, not the technical aspects of vents, filters and material used in masks. After standard military service, he studied art and industrial design and later applied this education to the production of masks in his family's company through the organic development of his personal ideas about nature and shapes. His focus was on industrial design and a well-thought-out idea of how a mask should look and feel. As part of his art studies, he analysed human anatomy and facial features, which added a new aspect to innovation and improvement of the product and became the basis for his involvement when he took over as MD. His artistic talent and understanding of facial structures led him to place high demands on the protective properties of the family's masks. Good respirators must be easy and convenient to use, and he is said to never have been totally satisfied, always improving his masks, with emphasis on comfort and a firm fit.

The third generation developed a new leadership structure distributing the responsibility between them. As active owners and leaders, they partake in the innovation cycle described above. In this way they can decide which risks and investments they want to take on. This mandate is neither allocated to the board, nor solely to the technical unit. The oldest brother, engineer and head of the production unit, holds the important hands-on ownership role. Being in a role as an active owner in the innovation cycle, or in the leadership roles aligned in the hierarchy, they are able to build on the flexibility of family co-ownership and manage the involvement of different layers or perspectives of the organization. There are several tensions that could create conflicts, but these are linked to the mantra and founding idea of the business, to always innovate and improve on their products.

As active owners with an equal number of shares divided between the siblings, they each have an equally strong ownership vote on the board. The oldest brother had long been employed by the company and was head of the technical unit. Neither he nor his sister was interested in taking on the MD role. In the end, their youngest brother took it on. The sister is the sole family member who has worked outside the company. Her experience of being a pre-school teacher in 'the real world' has benefited her. She has since studied business communication, and in addition to being the Chair of the Board, she holds brand responsibility.

> This means communicating what sits within these four walls. The company culture is really found amongst the staff. I am able to communicate this

feeling quite well to new employees, actually. Ivan is really good when we hire new employees too. Telling the whole story, I think they may get a little 'hallelujah' feeling from how proud we are of our company. This pride gets carried over to your new employees. I think that I have made use of my pre-school teacher experience, especially when it comes to managing people without them being aware of me doing it. Some of the old foxes here figured it out eventually, but it's gone well.

Chair of the Board

A new wave in thinking began to take shape when the youngest brother, today the MD, arrived in 1989. He had graduated from upper secondary school, been in military service, and started at the company. He soon ended up in the Marketing Department working in sales. He called customers and helped the salespeople send out brochures, samples and such. He was then 'thrown into the deep end' having to do customer service and sales representation – anything from visiting a paint shop to going to major companies with complicated security issues and needs.

> That was a really big difference. So I busted my chops on the shop floor as people say and built upon everything that I learned along the way.
>
> (MD)

Intergenerational transmission

The tradition was that the wives of the first as well as the second generation were drawn into production and product development. The children had their working roles to play, helping the parents in different ways. They were brought up in this family company from early childhood without ever reflecting on it themselves and without it being a subject of discussion. The sister of the third generation tells the story about how the founder's children would help him with small tasks and later would advance to 'fastening screws and that sort of thing'. Many times, a mask would be pushed onto a child's face and the father would command: 'Breathe!', and after a while he would ask, 'How does it feel?'

There were two children in the founder family, a son born in 1920 and a daughter in 1919. According to the granddaughter and today's Chair, their father always showed an intense loyalty to his sister, who had also worked in the company in the early days: 'He helped her with everything she asked for, after she left the company, as some sort of compensation. What he took over did not amount to much to be frank, what he took over was an idea actually.'

Only one member of the fourth generation is currently involved. This family have the philosophy that, of course, their members can come in, but not directly, rather they have to gain experience somewhere else first. In this way they can better contribute with skills and knowledge that have been tested in a larger arena.

It's one thing to work here and another to be an owner. The bigger we become, the more important it is to have the right person in the right position. I mean, it could happen that things even get too difficult for me sometime in the future, in which case I need to be prepared to step down. The day we sell is the day we lose our identity. If the next generation doesn't fill new roles, ownership is what matters…

Skill as well as being hard-working and experienced must come with humility as one can be very skilled without giving a damn. However, you can also be eager and willing to learn. That is what being skilled means to me.

MD

Afterthoughts and reflections

This family had identified and constructed a history about the past that acknowledged and cherished their ability to be transformative. The business idea and family drive have been the same since the 1930s. They go on providing solutions while innovating those solutions at every turn. They have moved from masks produced for coal and cotton processing to a completely new system where the user can easily customize the product based on site requirements. The sister summarizes:

As an inventive family, we want to find solutions to things. This is in all of us, that we are not satisfied. It's in our genes. You don't leave things alone. It sits right here [points to her heart]. My father was phenomenal at it. It was because he was this type of person that set the wheels in motion.

The founder started the business in 1926 when he, a geological engineer, became unemployed due to the Great Depression. As an engineer, he had seen workers in the mines becoming ill and dying from the damage caused by the dust in their working environment. His primary task then, as it is to this day, was to protect human life from inhaling harmful substances. When he first started to pursue this idea, it was by producing respiratory protective devices made out of leather with a cotton filter. In those early days, production was mainly carried out by hand. What drew the founder couple to the workers' situation was not only the desire to protect human health and life, but also creating an income for the family. The founder story, in the business described here and in many family businesses, is instructive and important. An active process of reconstructing it with stories about important moments confirming or indicating a change will often be found. This is a story about the social identity of the business and the family members' own identities invested in the business. These stories are often a framework for the decisions made at strategic and tactical levels. For the current family owners and leaders, there was an acknowledgement that the choice of being active in the business had called for personal sacrifice and that it was not possible to realize some dreams.

Note

1 ISO (International Organization for Standardization) is an independent, non-governmental membership organization, made up of 163 member countries with a central secretariat based in Geneva, Switzerland. ISO 9001 refers to quality control standards.

References

Chrisman, J. J. and Patel, P. C. (2012). Variations in R&D investments of family and nonfamily firms: Behavioral agency and myopic loss aversion perspectives. *Academy of Management Journal, 55*(4), 976–997.

De Massis, A., Frattini, F. and Lichtenthaler, U. (2012). Research on technological innovation in family firms: Present debates and future directions. *Family Business Review,* DOI: 10.1177/0894486512466258.

Ghemawat, P. (1991). Market incumbency and technological inertia. *Marketing Science, 10*(2), 161–171.

Gibb, A. (2002). In pursuit of a new 'enterprise' and 'entrepreneurship' paradigm for learning: Creative destruction, new values, new ways of doing things and new combinations of knowledge. *International Journal of Management Reviews, 4*(3), 233–269.

Gómez-Mejía, L. R., Haynes, K. T., Núñez-Nickel, M., Jacobson, K. J. and Moyano-Fuentes, J. (2007). Socioemotional wealth and business risks in family-controlled firms: Evidence from Spanish olive oil mills. *Administrative Science Quarterly, 52*(1), 106–137.

Granovetter, M. (1981). *The Strength of Weak Ties: A Network Theory Revisited.* New York: State University of New York, Department of Sociology.

8 Stewardship and integrity

A Lutheran Arab family in Jerusalem

Gry Osnes

So this is our reputation and everyone knows it. I might say to a visitor, 'Look, here you see my Christian guide and my Jewish guide'. I show the Israelis, 'my driver is a Muslim'. And it is not exactly what you read about in the newspaper. We live together and we are enjoying each other's company. And it works. And nobody can tell me it doesn't work. We have practiced it. The guy who just came in here now is my general manager. He is an Israeli and Jewish. I don't have a problem working with Israelis. We are being threatened by this side, threatened by the other side.... That side doesn't like what we are doing, this side doesn't like what we are thinking!! It never stopped us.

Second generation older brother

Introduction

Stewardship is a theory that explores how interests other than financial interests motivate leaders or employees (Davis, Schoorman and Donaldson, 1997). This is an applicable theory for family businesses (Miller and Le Breton–Miller, 2005) as family ownership, when both financially and emotionally healthy, strategizes the interest of several generations of owners. The most classic way of thinking of stewardship within family businesses is when a family takes into consideration a future generation in decision making (Ward and Aronoff, 2010). The long-term benefit for the next generation is balanced against seeking short-term profit or taking out revenue, and influences how they invest in assets. This generation can be young children or as yet-unborn generations. The owners of a family business have the power to make these types of decisions without justifying them to a disparate group of shareholders. The freedom to reduce profit in order to fulfil such goals is unique for family owners and their businesses.

Stewardship is often also done for its intrinsic value for the family and can include ethical considerations (Phillips, 2003), as shown in this case. The interests of stakeholders other than the owners, such as employees, can be important. There are conflicting views as to whether the family will take care of only their own financial interests or also that of other stakeholders, such as employees. Research on decision making shows that families who are involved in the business as executives and/or employees will respond to, and take into account, non-financial interests (Miller, Le Breton-Miller and Lester 2011). Our case shows that families can combine the two interests. External stakeholders in the local environment can be crucial as a pool for recruitment; their engagement creates local commitment and goodwill for the business. Such types of stewardship that expanded outside the family were seen, to different degrees, in most of our cases. This would differ depending on the need in the local community and how embedded the family was in this community.

Business development and family life cycles

The established thinking about stewardship often has a focus on the stewardship of future generations. In several of the cases we found this focus to be too narrow. The Arab-Israeli case illustrated this well. They were taking into account the life cycles and needs of both past and future generations and sought to find creative solutions. They had an extraordinary focus on strategizing different needs in the family and this was also expanded to a strategy for how the family ownership would act in the socio-political situation in Jerusalem. Carlock and Ward (2001) have written extensively about life cycles and how they have to be managed, or be thought about, when the family review, discuss and take decisions about the family members' involvement and the future of the business. This perspective is very useful in understanding how stewardship would evolve from the founding of the business, to the second and third generations and their involvement.

A best practice case

Stewardship in this family took into account four generations' current needs and achieved this while maintaining a strong focus on profit. They strategized a complexity of needs within the family and the local community together with short and long-term profit. The complexity of strategizing different family members' and generations' needs was exacerbated by a complexity in strategizing a commitment to social issues. The social issues were connected to the conflict between different religions and ethnic groups, creating a continuously difficult and entrenched political situation that was a political risk to the business. This activism would pose personal and business risks for the family. Strategizing such multi-layered stewardship was not achieved by choosing between priorities. Seeking to establish personal meaning triggered the development of a complex strategic capacity by working toward several goals at the same time and resulted in an ambitious scope. Tensions, and striving to resolve them, led to innovation and unconventional solutions. All the generations were involved in understanding and maintaining this strategic complexity as a source of innovation and as an identity for the family and the business.

Complex strategizing of stewardship

The business has its main office in Jerusalem and is one of the biggest tour operators for pilgrimage tourism in Israel. It has been organized into a cluster of family-owned companies with several hotels, a tourism agency and a bus company. The first business was a tourism agency in Jerusalem, which now also has offices in Rome, Istanbul, Amman and Athens. The customer base has traditionally been from the USA, but, increasingly, also from Europe. This family operates in what must be regarded as an extremely difficult and polarized socio-political context. It is dominated by protracted religious fundamentalist groups in conflict, often supported or fuelled by global geopolitical forces and interests. One second generation owner describes the historical context for the stewardship vision they have for the business below:

> Take a look at history! There is a street in the middle of old Jerusalem. Everyone exchanges services across it, across the main street. But each one has a unique identity. And that makes it function quite creatively with the other groups. So I don't think you can exclude the Jewish identity as not belonging to the Middle East. They are part of the Middle East. You cannot remove me as a Christian from it, from the mosaic. And nobody can tell me that I don't belong. And you cannot take the Islamic out either; it is part of the mosaic.

This second generation owner added and developed a political position and a value system, based on co-existence and with the business as a non-violent protest against polarization between religious and ethnic groups. They thereby took on political risk at the personal level and for the business. The ideas and values built into the particular type of stewardship were expanding on how the business was founded by their parents. It was derived out of how the business had developed before them and what it symbolized at the political level. This transition from the founders to the second generation expanded the strategic scope for stewardship dramatically.

Founders: from survival to stewardship of the next generation

The family are Arabs from Beit Jala in what is now in the Palestinian West Bank. The current owners' grandfather was converted from Catholicism to Lutheran by German missionaries in the late nineteenth century and established the first Arab Lutheran Church in The Holy Land. He was also a tribal leader. His youngest son, together with his wife, founded this business before the establishment of Israel. He did not like school and through friends and family he started to work as a driver/guide for academics visiting the area. His role as driver developed into guiding in the 1930s with an influx of American academics and other groups of visitors. His wife would work from home administrating the business. Eventually it developed into an office outside the home, with employees, for the growing business. This shift was triggered by regional geo-politics. Jerusalem was under administration by Jordan and regulations dictated that if one employed people for one's business one had to have an office outside the home. With growing demand and the complexity of requirements for archaeological excavations they needed plenty of employees. Increasingly the guiding would include groups from both Christian and Jewish communities. The wife-founder and mother of the current owners described the start-up as follows:

> It was in 1932 we heard academics needed drivers. They wanted to be picked up from the port in Haifa or from Beirut. They wanted to go to Damascus and here, to many other different places. At that time there were no hotels. Wherever they went we had to arrange for their lodging and food. It wasn't easy. But, I mean, this is how the business started. My husband was in his 20s when he started working with his brother as a driver. This is how he learned about all these attractions and places....
>
> In 1948, during the war, there was no business. No tours, of course. But in 1951 American scholars started coming again. All these professors of archaeology came here to dig. And my husband, he knew some of these professors and worked with them. Took them to the digs, stayed with them. He learned lot of things. These professors recommended him to their friends, and their friends would tell others, and this is how we started. It started to become groups, I should say 1958 to 67, most of them very educated people.

Next generation

At this point the concern of the couple was to have an income and to provide for their children. The children would in a natural way start doing some mundane work, then as teens take on more serious roles in addition to school. When their two sons had finished upper secondary school, the couple were able to provide them with sufficient resources to travel to the USA and study there, one starting his PhD in petro-chemistry. This is the classic way that one often thinks about the stewardship that family owners create. A second generation is provided for with higher education, other social networks and futures. They were offering a life outside Israel, which was full of tension and conflict.

Former generation

The founder was, at the time of our contact with them, over 80 years old and still worked for the business. In all our cases the founders or senior generation continued to work past what would be seen as normal retirement age. A founder or former leader would be active and working in the business and this was not seen as problematic. They had given away ownership control but continued in less complex but important roles. It meant they did not retire and it was not seen as a disadvantage in the business. If tensions arose they would be solved. Innovation was used to tackle the possible tensions the different family units and generations would have, to ensure that financial security was not impaired. Issues and the implications of having three generations and a mix of genders in the business is described in Chapter 15 on Gender and Leadership.

Second generation: from family stewardship to a new meaning

The owners extended stewardship to the financial and emotional wellbeing of four generations: the founder, themselves, their children and grandchildren. We will show other less acknowledged stewardship considerations also taken into consideration. The current owners, two brothers, had been ambivalent about coming back to Jerusalem after living and studying abroad. They had been presented with other work opportunities and could create good lives in the USA or other places in the Middle East. One of them was married to an American. In Jerusalem there would be no work opportunity matching their level of education. Having created the opportunity for careers in the Gulf States or USA as well-paid professionals, the brothers made a stark choice in choosing to return to Israel. It was clear that their parents needed help to run the business. They had a strong sense of belonging to Jerusalem, a sense of obligation due to the difficulty of the political situation. A return to Israel triggered a deep ambivalence in establishing their own families in such a conflict-torn society.

Innovating a vision

They decided to run the business to reflect a microcosm of how Jerusalem could be if political forces had not caused the fragmentation between different religious groups. A policy to have employees from all the ethnic and religious groups became the main strategy practice. In this environment it was highly unusual and went against the political message and dogma of extremist political forces. A consensus between otherwise warring factions was that Jerusalem would need to be divided into a Palestinian part and a Jewish part. It rested on the assumption that peaceful co-existence was impossible. By running a business that employed Jewish, Palestinian and Christian people in all roles, and was financially profitable, proved the opposite. At the time we had contact with them this would be the only company in Israel that had Arab owners and a Jewish Managing Director (MD). Innovating and implementing this vision would show that conflict and fragmentation was a political construction and could be avoided.

Creating roles and complementarities

The founder husband and wife and the second generation of brothers had all carved out roles between themselves. Complementaries in talents and interests had been important in role development. Currently this was in progress with the third generation. Young adult family members were taking higher education and specializing in different kinds of management training. Others were acquiring language skills that would fit markets in Europe. A normal hierarchal structure does not fit into this way of developing roles. Eventually a family member had a domain where they had relative authority and, with consultation, a more fluid and flat structure for decision making is used. We found this in all the family businesses we studied and it is exemplified by the two owner-brothers of this business. In Part II this will be described as 'distributed leadership'. Stewardship is linked to distributed leadership as a notion of family justice, the vision and respect for other family members brings forward a more complex pattern of authority and execution of roles.

Complexity and strategic scope

Sami, one of the owners, was head of the hotels with their separate hierarchies and staffs. In addition, he was responsible for marketing and PR for clients in the USA and Europe for the whole group. He was seen as the main entrepreneur focusing on expansion, growth and increased margins. The second brother, Hani, was the president for the group of businesses. He was more politically active. In addition he was responsible for reviewing tailor-made itineraries of groups within the touring company. The latter could seem to be a trivial matter in the eyes of an outsider but was highly complex. Most of the tours they arranged would be pilgrimage tours for tourist groups from Europe and America. The role entailed matching the type of religious group visiting with their different needs, visits to different religious and ethnic neighbourhoods, and different sites with several religious functions for different groups on different days. This required respect for and knowledge of different religious and political realities on the ground and religious festive events. Hani explained his mind-set for, and complexity of, this role:

> I will tell you ... I'll explain, I studied both economics and chemistry, and I started my PhD but came back here before I finished. When you study chemical engineering it teaches you to focus. And in engineering you take your initial conditions, you take your boundary conditions and you can focus on the solution. This systematic way of thinking helps. There is no doubt in my mind, in business it helps a lot. Okay, because when you are dealing with businesses in Jerusalem the varieties are much more than in engineering. It is much more complicated but the training, the way of thinking, the focusing on the solution, it is good training.

The current owners have developed a set of values and priorities that have been integrated into the business and mind-sets of employees and family members. In this way the past is, either by breaking with it or expanding it, a part of creating meaning, commitment and strategy. The following shows how the owner, reflecting on the past, created a commitment to lead in an innovative and different way.

> Among Arab people, two or three generations ago, there is no homogeneous line defining that these are Palestinian, these Muslims, Jews and these Christians. No side is homogeneous. So the idea of putting a border in between [in Jerusalem] is stupid. And how do you do the jigsaw puzzle that is the Jewish area, Israeli area, you know, with the security cordon around it? Everything within a Palestinian State, or only Israeli... It doesn't work. There will always be this feeling of commitment to the rest; no one will give up a part. So how do I recognize my continuity there? And I have to recognize the continuity, I cannot just dispense with it.

The choice and capacity to take on such an expansive scope of thinking for stewardship was triggered by several factors; tensions created by balancing the needs of the past and future generations, the local political conflict and the few jobs in contrast to work opportunities abroad. These tensions were the source of ingenuity and innovation. We will later describe how it also led to new entrepreneurship.

A balancing act: stewardship and financial profit

The family was constantly focusing on profit in addition to stewardship. It had restructured the business into three main companies. The hotel business was owned by the family and managed as a part of the group but one of the brothers had a majority of the ownership. As part of the group it would provide synergies and add to the profit of the group. The following quote is from Sami describing his thinking as owner in the earlier days:

> It is a natural, for me it is a natural part of the process to go through this. In the beginning I was only doing tours. Bringing groups, exactly like my parents were doing, putting them in hotels, guides, you know, buses and all that. But I was only exchanging money from one pocket to other pockets. So at the end of the day you deal with big money but put a little in your pocket, you know. So I thought, well, I have been successful in the business, why should I not get into the infrastructure? That is where I started thinking about opportunities. And the first one I thought of was in transport, and we started the bus company. Then came the hotels, first small, not good ones, later I bought a more central and nice one.

Second to third generation: strategizing long-term survival

One of the owners and a member of the future third generation were involved in building new offices and businesses outside Israel, as a contingency for the political risk of operating any tourism business in Jerusalem. As they pointed out, the cost of a third Palestinian uprising, or intifada, could destroy their business. The relationship between Palestinian groups and Israel became increasingly hostile, triggering the First and Second Intifada (1988 and 2000, respectively). Growing the business was intended to mitigate the political risk to which they were exposed. Strategizing a more expansive and complex business model went in parallel with the involvement of the third generation.

The family first opened an office in Athens and in Amman, Jordan. A daughter started working in Amman and, while developing businesses there, also worked to open an office in Damascus, Syria. The latter attempt was complicated and would, after three years, end in closure of the office due to the Syrian war. The third generation then opened an office in Rome and established the business there. A second daughter is now working in an office and business in Istanbul, Turkey. While these businesses also faced risks, such as economic recession and other political risks, they could act as a buffer for the risk in Jerusalem. A synergy was that these offices could arrange for pilgrimage tours for groups that had already visited Israel. In this third generation, immersion, entrepreneurship and stewardship were all expanded with a strong focus on long-term survival.

Values and succession

The children of the owners were, as the owners themselves had been in the past, present in the business and participating in activities from an early age. They would have small tasks in the office, run errands and so on, and later work during their holidays while studying. Increasingly some decided to plan a career in the business, others did not. Since the local work opportunities were limited, the possibility of employment in the family business was important in itself. The expansion of the business made it possible to offer the next generations modest roles, and increased responsibility. The family's approach was to encourage the children to pursue higher education. If they chose to start working in the business, they had to start at the bottom of the organization. There was no entitlement to leadership jobs and they would reputedly be more strictly evaluated than other employees. Making a mistake was acceptable for all employees, making the same mistake over and over again was not acceptable. At times, several of the third generation were working and learning different languages in Europe, working in hotel management or running tourism offices.

Storytelling and family identity

Strategizing of stewardship increased in complexity as the fourth generation emerged. The overlap of so many generations in the workplace allowed for retelling stories that stretched over a time span far beyond what one would find in other types of businesses, and discussing the related issues. In this case the stories would span experiences and how they were understood, with changing contexts, from 1930 to 2014. The stories related to strategies and changing context, technological changes and how the needs of different generations were met. Stories about family ownership illustrate something striking in successful family owners. The family and employees love to talk about the business, often in a process where over time stories get repeated and retold with banter and amusement, arguments and tension. Storytelling seems to function as a reworking and reliving of past experiences at the collective level. Keeping the stories alive helps maintain a strong sense of meaning and social identity.

> I know about my children, what they think. Definitely they are aware of what we are doing. And also they are non-violent. I love for them to be in that position, and I give the credit for that also to my wife.
>
> Second generation younger brother

Application of stewardship through personal integrity

Stewardship as a policy was integrated into the business and further strengthened by a strong sense of personal commitment. This approach supported a sense of self and identity without compromising commercial success. The business was growing and financially profitable, always seen by the owners as a tool for their self-interest. One of their goals was to create a microcosm of a peaceful society within the company. If they had employed people who could not work within this framework they would have to leave, regardless of how much this would cost financially. The vision was to integrate internally a harmonious community, within a society that was polarized and fragmented by extreme political groups. It had implications for the daily running of the business, for example to accommodate an employee living in The West Bank who could not attend at short notice owing to closure of check points. Despite this they would employ people from The West Bank, dealing with any inconveniences and obstacles as they occurred. A replacement guide would be found, if someone were unable to attend for reasons beyond their control. The MD and owners maintained constant discussion and review of these internal processes. Their approach also provoked hostility from different political groups that the owners or MD would have to deal with.

Internalizing of stewardship had for this family become a part of their identity. It was, as described above, integrated into how the business was run, a part of family identity and personal integrity. Hani offers the following description:

> Being a Christian, in this country, or Muslim, or Jewish is an identity issue. You know, I am not a person you'd see hanging around in a church, I have not been in a church in so long, but I definitely identify myself as a Christian. ..... if you want my definition of who I am, I will tell you exactly how I define myself. My name is Hani, and the reason why I am, who I am is genetic. You are who you are because of your parents, but... I am a Palestinian. Of... Arab heritage. Or an Arab because I belong to

that bigger thing. Culturally I am Muslim but Christian by faith. So that is how I define myself. … Anybody who tells me one is more important to you than the other … well, you cannot say which is more important to me, they are all important. That mix makes me who I am. It makes you who you are and makes everybody who he is. You cannot, in my opinion, you cannot separate, and say that my Christianity is more important than me being a Palestinian. Or that… I don't believe in this.

Acknowledging the connection between the family and the local community, and the business as integrated in both, is the fundament for the stewardship that was developed. An observational viewpoint was created that went beyond boundaries related to religious strife, the 'ownership' of ancient sites and their historical and religious meaning and claims from different religious groups. This case illustrates stewardship as a strategized relatedness where the external context, the business and organization practice involves the construction of identity and a mind-state. Stakeholder management theory, often discussed as a perspective taking into account interests other than short-term financial results, does not take this into account.

Afterthoughts and reflections

We were surprised at how important stewardship was, in our cases. In all the cases featured in this book former owners had not retired when leaving a powerful position but continued to work in the business in a less crucial role. We found that all of the families would strategize at least two generations when making important decisions.

Stewardship and strategic complexity

Strategizing stewardship includes innovating in the face of complexity: shifting between the short term and the long term, between individual needs, family needs, business needs and the context. Figure 8.1 is used to illustrate the scope, or area of needs and concerns that a family can take into consideration. One dimension concerns the past and the future. The past could be taken into account and include the financial interest of older generations, a legacy and a tradition. On the other side, creating possible tension and conflict, would be a focus on the future of young or unborn family members. The other dimension, or axis, depicts the social context in contrast to the needs of the family group and the individual family members.

The family as owner operates in the centre of this and will make decisions and priorities that are connected but which can be in conflict. The family is in the position where they have to manage conflicting and paradoxical needs – that is, strategize a wide range of possibilities that would only meet some of the needs. The scope of their strategic capacity could be extended along the temporal dimension or, with the family in the centre, also from the individual

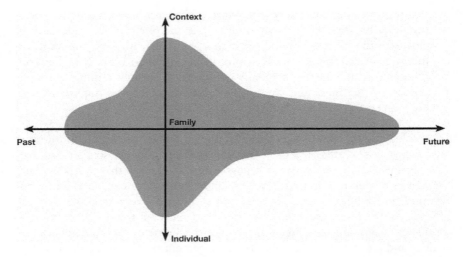

Figure 8.1 Strategic scope in stewardship

to the wider context. Through mapping different actions and strategies one can get a picture of how wide a horizon or how complex a strategy is exercised at different stages in the family ownership.

Family business in a social fabric

All the businesses have a commitment to the social fabric in which their business exists. Such commitment has been executed in different ways and to different degrees during the history of the business. The local community, skills and a particular socio-economic context were often the origin of the business idea. In the Arab-Israeli, US and Tanzanian businesses the founding of the business was connected to the financial survival of a couple or a small family unit. Wider stewardship was strategized when new generations got involved. The Swedish and the Chinese businesses were founded with a concern for the local community, in addition to family financial survival. In the Swedish case, described in Chapter 7, the start-up was based on what a mining engineer had seen of health hazards for the workers in the mines. In the Chinese case the business was initially a part of the commune. The founder was the elected representative who had to find some work for the village and so built on skills they had in using wood to create simple tools. From this, as described in Chapter 6, it developed into a village within which were many companies, with the family owning several of them.

   In contrast to a corporation listed on the stock market, family owner(s) and leaders have the opportunity to adopt such an extensive approach to stewardship. They can take into account any stakes they want, even if there is a negative impact on the financial results of the business. Mainstream strategic thinking would regard this as irrational. Within family business research it has come to be discussed as socio-emotional wealth (Gomez-Mejia et al., 2011). The social identity the family has with the business and how they, for this reason, will take decisions is not necessarily leading to optimizing financial interest. It could be, as in this case, that the family had a strong social identity linked to its stewardship of the business; this was the main idea that made running a business in such a difficult political climate worthwhile. The socio-emotional wealth perspective is described more in Chapter 18, 'Drive in Family Capitalism'.

References

Carlock, R. and Ward, J.L. (2001). *Strategic Planning for the Family Business: Parallel planning to unify the family and business.* Basingstoke, UK: Palgrave Macmillan.

Davis, J.H., Schoorman, F.D. and Donaldson, L. (1997). Toward a stewardship theory of management. Academy of Management Review, *22*(1), pp. 20–47.

Gomez-Mejia, L.R., Cruz, C., Berrone, P. and De Castro, J. (2011). The bind that ties: Socioemotional wealth preservation in family firms. The Academy of Management Annals, *5*(1), pp. 653–707.

Miller, D. and Le Breton-Miller, I. (2005). *Managing for the Long Run: Lessons in competitive advantage from great family businesses.* Boston, MA, US: Harvard Business School Press.

Miller, D., Le Breton-Miller, I. and Lester, R.H. (2011). Stewardship and agency? A social embeddedness reconciliation of conduct or performance in public family businesses. *Organization Science 22*(3), pp. 704–721.

Phillips, R. (2003). Stakeholder theory and organisational ethics. *Business Ethics Quarterly, 13*(4), pp. 479–502.

Ward, J.L. and Aronoff, C.E. (2010). *Family Business Values: How to assure a legacy of continuity and success.* Basingstoke, UK: Palgrave Macmillan.

9 "For 100 years, nothing needed to change"

A Colombian owner's account

Angélica Uribe

My dear, you will ruin everything.

Architect to Angélica

Introduction

My name is Angélica Uribe. I was born in Bogotá, Colombia to a well-established family. I studied law and practiced in senior positions for many years. This is the story of how I came to be in charge of a school my mother founded and owned, and my father's land and real estate assets. I will describe how I managed the transition from a successful legal career to a role as owner and business manager. It is a story about developing autonomy for myself, ensuring the survival of the businesses, and maintaining and enhancing the family's assets.

The quote by the architect that opens this chapter was said to me when I assumed responsibility for modernizing what had been an inherited country house for the whole Uribe-Vargas family. Due to division of land assets between brothers four generations ago, and between my grandmother and her brother and sisters, my sister and I ended up with a property called San Jose. Several of my relatives have cherished memories of staying with grandmothers at this farm, often over the weekend or longer holiday periods. The house itself was completely un-modernized, had lacked upkeep and even an electricity supply. I made it a priority to modernize it, so I would be able to use it for the family over weekends. I made a plan with an architect, hence the quote. Throughout the renovation project each bit of the house – doors, colors, pieces of furniture – would be reviewed and a decision would be made of what to keep or change. It was a constant process of deciding what to keep of original features and what to modernize. I had very little cash so necessity also dictated the end result and the blend of the old and new. During the process I received several opinions and emotional grievances and support from the wider family. When the renovation at last was finished we held one of our regular family parties. Family members would go through and comment, revisiting the memories triggered by features I had kept, surprised positively or negatively by what had been changed. I learned that changing such inherited assets alters how others can access their memories and their history. This experience, or critical event, influenced the process of renewal of the land assets and the school that I describe below.

My personal account builds on work that I have undertaken with advisers in analyzing my role. The role as owner has been established and developed over a period of 15 years and was influenced by earlier critical incidents which I discuss in some depth later in this chapter. All this happened in the context of a rapidly changing socio-political reality in Colombia. It offered both huge obstacles and opportunities. This asset modernization proceeds in step with that of the nation, as we move from quasi-feudal arrangements to a modern market economy. Colombia is thankfully moving away from many years of civil war, weakened security and economic underdevelopment, but with many social problems as a legacy. I assumed responsibility for putting an uncoordinated array of inherited assets into some order.

Box 9.1 History of the Uribe-Vargas family and independence for Colombia

The history of the Uribe-Vargas family as entrepreneurs, traders, retailers and owners of real estate goes back two centuries, to the early years of Colombian independence from the Spanish empire. The Vargas family firm established itself as a supplier of material for footwear and a variety of agricultural and household goods to the newly independent nation. They imported the products from Great Britain with traders located in both London and Colombia. They established a successful retail store in Bogotá, the country's capital, Francisco Vargas & Hermanos.

Bogotá is in the cooler, central mountainous region of Colombia. The country lies on the northern tip of the South American continent, possessing both a Caribbean and a Pacific coastline. The main ports are on the warm, tropical Caribbean coast so goods were conveyed on a long and slow journey to the retail outlet. They were transported from the port of London directly to a harbor on Colombia's Caribbean Coast, Barranquilla, and then by the Magdalena River to a river port from where everything was transported on mules through the Andean mountains to reach the capital, Bogotá, which is 2,800 meters above sea level.

The founder Inocencio Vargas began importing a variety of goods from Britain in the 1820s. He was married and had a family. One of his children, Francisco Vargas, my great, great, great, great grandfather, consolidated the success of the business and managed the store. The third generation also continued the enterprise successfully. The brothers in this third generation would alternate between London and Bogotá. One brother would spend time with his family in England buying and exporting goods. Other parts of the family would market them in Bogotá in the shop, which was located on the ground level of their home. After a period of time, the brothers would exchange these roles and the brother who was living in England would come to Colombia and vice versa.

The Uribe-Vargas family firm ceased trading as an import and retail establishment in the mid-twentieth century, owing to changes in the nation's policies. A move away from free global trade towards more protectionism with the intention of developing local industries made it more expensive to import finished goods, and so the business was no longer viable. However, much of the wealth was converted to tangible assets. The family had major but uncoordinated assets, principally in the form of land but also property. The land that remained was agricultural, typically farmed by tenant farmers under Colombia's quasi-feudal system. Some of the land owned had been agricultural, but in areas that have subsequently become urbanized owing to the growth of the Bogotá conurbation.

Developing the role as owner

Along with my sister I inherited an array of diverse assets, principally, my mother's school, a significant amount of agricultural land and some property. The land assets constitute the legacy of a family ownership that is now 200 years old. In the nineteenth and twentieth centuries it was a thriving import and retail business (see Box 9.1). In 2005 my mother passed away, and a few years later my father became ill. It has been an extremely difficult adjustment. He was a brilliant man: during his career he was a leading human rights lawyer, diplomat and politician, who helped draft Colombia's constitution. However, he had no interest in or aptitude for business, and did not actively manage the land and other assets that belonged to the family, but delegated the responsibility.

To enter and develop the role as owner constituted a profound shift in career, mind-set and life trajectory. It was related to my own development and a sense of autonomy, the relationship I had with the wider family, how I constructed and developed the business and how these were influenced by the socio-political context. There were several critical incidents in my life that have contributed to how I was, in an unplanned way, prepared for the role as owner. This was a complicated process as there would be several limitations I had to acknowledge, some of which I sought to change. It was influenced by a wish to manage the assets so that my children would enjoy a better organized inheritance than I did. It included managing the legacy of a feudal system in the context of a changing political reality in Colombia, and renewing the school to ensure it would be a thriving business.

My role and the complexity of autonomy

The individual level

As a young adult, I followed my father's example by reading law and beginning a successful career in the legal profession. I finished the undergraduate studies, completed a diploma in financial law and a masters of law in Georgetown University, USA. This qualified me for some challenging roles in the public and private sector in Colombia. I took part in diverse tasks, such as reviewing public credit agreements, giving legal advice to a pension fund and selling public banks after a financial crisis. I was on the Boards of Directors of different banking institutions. I married and had two children.

When I began to take over management of the assets, initially in my spare time, it became clear that they were losing money and we could not pay the taxes. Due to lack of attention we had not optimized the income while the taxes had increased as the properties had increased in value, as the political situation in the country had improved. Without a turnaround strategy we would have had to sell assets to pay taxes. I decided that it would not be responsible to let the assets fall into an unmanaged decline, but I also realized that I lacked the relevant training and experience to lead the turnaround. My sister had married and was living in Europe.

A cousin of mine told me: "there are two ways to approach this challenge: hit your head against the wall or learn." I enrolled on a three-year Harvard course for business owners, the Owner/President Management Program. The impact on my thinking was great and I began to think more in terms of professional asset management. I had to put to one side my career as a lawyer. There was a sense of loss. My priorities had been to have a salary, something stable and secure. Handling the family assets was a big challenge for me. It was difficult and I felt it as if I was putting on someone else's clothes. I somehow pretended it would be temporary, that I later could return to my life.

From the different strategies I experimented with, I learned that asset management required not just a new set of skills, but a different mind-set. Lawyers are trained to avoid risks, work for themselves and their clients and believe they are right. The training I got, informed among other things by my mistakes, was that as an owner you will have to have a very different mind-set: you have to take risks, hear other people's points of view and be as flexible as you can to adapt to the world. In the experimentation I learned how to make strategies so as to maintain asset value and financial autonomy in the long run.

The system at the level of business and assets

The school had been continuously in business, and actively managed, but had been in need of reform and modernization for some time. I have developed a good relationship with the head-mistress, the two directors and my mother's closest advisers. I had to get used to being not only my mother's daughter, but also the owner who would give directions for how the school was to develop and to start to renew and become more competitive. We increased our application volume and began to see higher enrolments. We constructed new buildings and created classes for younger kids. We have begun preparing a leadership succession. This does not necessarily mean an exit for previous leaders, but it does involve changed roles. We have built up a stronger administrative staff group in addition to the teacher hierarchy. The new challenges are to renew a progressive ideology for the school and to expand into other educational activities for the alumni. The land assets were not yet a part of a planned enterprise. They constitute a myriad of assets, many of which have been neglected for many years.

The system at the socio-political context: Colombia

Concurrently with my realization of the scope of the ownership responsibilities things changed in the political arena. There have been several decades of civil war but the security situation has been improving since the early 2000s, and the country has moved towards a market-based economy, increasingly open to international markets. Many people have moved to the cities, because of the war and to seek new opportunities. There is entrepreneurial and technological innovation, and many people have readily adopted an urban life. The peasant life is disappearing. While there is still economic inequality, more ordinary citizens have consumer goods and an improved standard of living. A middle class is growing. It has developed a more professional lease system with more

---

Box 9.2 Autonomy and the family business

Autonomy is often defined as the capacity to act with some degree of freedom from others and not be forced into a choice. This has to be negotiated and developed at several levels and as such an owner or family owner group will be in a situation where they will have to negotiate this at several levels. When an individual is autonomously motivated, they take actions they find genuinely interesting and/or important (Schröder & Schmitt-Rodermund, 2013). The source of the action is intrinsic to the individual as a person and their drives and ambitions. This is different from acts motivated or controlled by someone else, to avoid feelings of guilt or shame. Critical incidents, different events or processes can be used to explore what triggered or lead to a shift or development in how a family member developed a sense of autonomy. The shifts can be analyzed at different levels. Self-determination theory, with a focus on autonomy, was articulated by Deci and Ryan (1985). Choices and actions are classified respectively into autonomous (or self-determined) and controlled motivation.

Autonomy is created in two ways: by being in a role because one finds it genuinely interesting (i.e., intrinsic regulation) or important (i.e., identified regulation). Controlled motivation actions result from avoidance of feelings of guilt or shame (i.e., introjected regulation) or interpersonal controls like rewards or punishments (i.e., external regulation). When this is adapted into a family context, there are two more elements: relatedness and perceived competence. Relatedness is the support and encouragement within the family, and in this instance also within the business and society. Relatedness within the family refers to dimensions such as involvement, caring, helping, supporting, giving advice and encouraging (Deci and Ryan, 1985). Since the individual, the family and the business operate with overlapping systems this relatedness of the family owner goes beyond the family system and includes the business and its environment. Developing autonomy for oneself within the business is one dimension of relatedness, another is the actual business context, with regulations and socio-political factors and social change also influencing individual autonomy. A third dimension of autonomy is a sense of competence through the immersion or introduction to the business (Schröder & Schmitt-Rodermund, 2013). Building on this we will explore how the successful family owners have developed and negotiated autonomy, based to a large extent on intrinsic motivation, while at times acknowledging the influence of external factors.

transparent dealings with those renting the land. There is a "peace dividend" for the Government with the reduction in conflict releasing funds for social spending. For many years it had to devote considerable resources to the armed forces, but now it is able to invest more in education and social services.

In the 1980s and 1990s, the war between the leftist guerrillas FARC and the armed forces, and the uncontrolled power of many drugs cartels, meant that personal security was severely compromised outside Bogotá, Cartagena and other conurbations. Kidnappings were part of the tactics of the guerrilla movements. As the conflict reduced in intensity, the way in which people lived and used land began to change. One could contemplate travel around the country with the risk of being kidnapped having all but disappeared. Bogotá and other cities expanded and what had been dormant land assets could be deregulated to become industrial sites or used for residential and commercial areas. This increased their value and the tax burden. An owner would tactically wait for the asset to mature while managing the tax burden and generate income to cover it. Only strategizing the assets, income and governmental regulations would enable me to have the freedom to make decisions favorable to my family, including, in the future, my children. An early sale would bring losses and missed opportunities to create value. Other family members were inclined to sell to release cash, but a good price for the sale of the assets could have been difficult to attain. I observed this slow decline in assets, a downward spiral leading to a bad deal, and further loss in financial autonomy. Overall, I saw my tasks as entrepreneurial: to explore good options for realizing value from the assets. As far as the land was concerned, it was a case of creating a modern asset-management company. The school, on the other hand, was already a viable business, but did need some investment and modernization, while maintaining its liberal philosophy.

Critical incidents in my role development

The significance of these events in my life was not apparent at the time they occurred. They seemed minor at the time but would, in hindsight, give me information, skills and help to form some views about the world that later became very significant. I identified four different critical incidents that at some level have prepared me for the role as owner and the formation of my abilities. This would only have an impact on the family and its ownership after a prolonged period. I have had some major decisions to take; yet some of the formation of my role came about through the intervention of fate. In all these events my family system, the type of assets and the political assets were important. As a sequence of events they accumulated into an awareness of these levels. Only when they all were thought about and strategized could I develop some rules and freedom for how I wanted to be as the one managing the assets.

Lunches with grandma

My grandmother on my father's side, Elena Vargas, was a quite remarkable woman. She was born in the first decade of the twentieth century, at a time when women could not vote in elections. The Uribe-Vargas family had not followed the cultural norms, had been liberal for generations and practiced equal status for women and men. She became deaf at a young age following a measles infection, yet became an aware, active custodian of the family properties. She had a head for figures, allied to common sense. She lived into her 80s and died in 1990. She married Gustavo Uribe, who was an entrepreneur and did not come from a rich family. Her father had advised Gustavo after Elena's illness and disability that he was free to marry someone else, but he stayed true to Elena. He had good business skills, enlarged the real estate business and was very active in the management of Elena's business. He died in the 1960s leaving Elena as the sole manager of her assets, nominally, with the help of my father Diego Uribe-Vargas, an adult by this time.

I came to know my grandmother well because she lived close to my school. Neither my sister nor I went to our mother's school; the thinking being that the daughters of the Principal would be highly conspicuous. I attended a traditional French establishment, while my sister attended Marymount School, a private American Catholic school that our mother had attended. Every week on a school day I would have lunch with my grandmother and we became close. I was curious about her work, and she taught me some of the basic aspects of running a business. Although the knowledge imparted was not advanced, this exposed me to commercial realities. I developed some idea about what the family assets were, and how income and expenses moved in and out of the system, at a very young age. While these lunches would continue over several years, only when I returned from university, as young adult, would it trigger another shift in my involvement and further immersion into the role as owner.

Counting the cows

This incident marked a shift from how my father had managed the assets and how I was forced to take over some of this work. It involved me carving out a business model that would maintain the assets in a financially healthy way. It was related to the legacy of my father's arm's length approach to asset management. In particular, a cattle and dairy farm belonging to the family was in a neglected state. My initial exposure to the land estates was a culture shock – in fact comical. Day-to-day management was in the hands of a *campesino*, a manager, who was very elderly. I saw myself as an urban young woman and knew absolutely nothing about animals or the land when I paid a visit to the estate with a veterinary surgeon. I did not know about the cycle of impregnation of cows and subsequent milking! When the vet asked me how many cows were giving milk, I did not even know why some cows would not give milk!

Thus began the slow process of identifying and tagging each cow and building individual medical records. It transpired that we had around 80–100 cows but the milking was still being done by hand. To recommence the milking cycle, we had to arrange artificial insemination using modern dairy farming methods, and so on. That was how neglected the situation was.

When it became clear that the dairy and cattle business was losing money, I sold the cattle. But the arable land was also under-performing as a business. I assumed the role of investigating and managing this on behalf of my father. This meant becoming assertive with people who had taken advantage of my father. It meant refusing to believe in their version or follow the rules they had made up, and setting my rules.

"The cabbage king"

The quasi-feudal system under which the agricultural land was managed is known in Colombia as *Siembras en compañía*, literally translated as "sowing seeds in partnership." In principle, this is a shared-rewards system that arranges for a certain proportion of profits from the land to be retained by the landlord. It is, however, informal, non-written and vulnerable to abuse. My father's approach as a largely absentee landlord was to accept the word of the tenant farmers in a benevolent, paternalistic way and not to negotiate with any rigor, in line with his liberal politics. Over time, however, as I discovered, some had started to take advantage of the situation; while they were nominally peasant farmers, they had become prosperous and the traditional picture of the landlord exploiting those working the land had become inverted. With the confidence that my legal training had given me, and increasingly aware of the need to get on top of affairs, I began to negotiate with tenant farmers, rather than simply accept what I was told.

There are perverse incentives in the *siembras en compañía* system, and it lacks transparency. The owner theoretically receives 30 percent of the harvest, but that depends on what the farmers say – they go to the market; it is subjective and self-reporting. The system is totally informal and cash-based; they don't pay taxes. They will say: "There were too many cabbages," or "It was raining a lot." It is very difficult to monitor and often the owner loses money. There are also mafias. There were two types of thief stealing from my father and the business: those linked with the land, and those "hangers on" who worked with him. However, it used not to bother him, he would say: "I have money, I should share it."

A key confrontation came with one farmer when I refused to accept the price quoted. He insisted that I take up the matter with my father. I bluffed, saying that I had my father's support to negotiate and asked him to tell me the price he would receive for the crops before selling the vegetables. He arrived at my father's office with the usual payment for a cabbage crop, and once again reported that the prices were going down. I refused the offered price. I offered him a post-dated check for his 70 percent of the business. He was furious but left the office with the post-dated check. The farmer had a strong negotiating hand. No fewer than 25,000 cabbages were still in the ground and would rot if they were not harvested. I called my mother's school to ask if they would buy the cabbages but their need fell far short of that. Other farmers or buyers refused to become involved. Through a cousin I learned of a wholesaler called Omar Cosma also known as "the cabbage king." He represented a new, entrepreneurial generation of farmers. He was also the owner of a dealing slot in the main wholesale market, and offered me a price that enabled me to cover costs and gave me some cash for other expenses.

I decided I wanted to end being a part of this feudal system, based on cash and with no transparency. We are now switching to a system of market rents, written contracts, and stable prices, a macro, strategic approach. It does not matter to me if the tenants sow crops or not, just that they pay a market rent to use the land.

Integration into visionary ownership

Modernizing San Patricio, my mother's school

When the assets were divided between my sister and me, I was assigned the San Patricio school that my mother had founded in 1959 in Bogotá. My earlier experiences in active ownership came together in defining what I would be passionate about doing as owner of the school. Earlier it had been a progressive and liberal school. Pupils were encouraged to express themselves, form their own views, and take part in debates over public policy matters. This included questions of school administration such as uniform and discipline. A strong ethos of social responsibility included an outreach program to slum areas; pupils took part in this at a young age. My mother was completely immersed in the management and development of the school and an education authority in Colombia.

After her death in 2005 the school was in need of renewal and certain aspects needed modernization. Although much of its ethos and approaches were democratic and ahead of its time, it had invested insufficiently in information technology. Not all of the newest learning aids were used, and there was insufficient teaching of computer and internet skills to equip pupils for the twenty-first century. Although some teaching of English had been introduced in the 1970s, this had to be increased significantly. Nowadays a modern private school needs to be bilingual to prepare students for modern business careers and most professions. More generally, the infrastructure was in need of renovation.

The challenges facing me in taking over the reform of the school are considerable. I have arranged to take a lead on the school's modernization and reform. Fortunately the head teacher and the senior teaching staff are supportive of the reforms. I had complementary strengths to the employees but my own education had been more traditional, at the French school with its emphasis on discipline and thorough academic learning. I have had to learn ways of getting involved in the education field and work, to learn the nature of the institution in order to make changes but not erase its "essence." I have experienced, as with San Jose, changes that are necessary for a new century but which are also "treading on people's memories." I believe it is possible to retain the liberal and enlightened policies that my mother introduced while introducing elements necessary for the new century.

Afterthoughts and reflections

In family business literature, questions of legacy and succession are often discussed in terms of the implications for the second or third generation, where the business approximately resembles the original firm in terms of its structure, markets and way of operating. In the case of the Uribe-Vargas inheritance the business, the society and the wider economy are unrecognizable from the world of the founders, which featured the sail boats and mule trains of the recently departed Spanish colonists.

Moreover, Colombia itself has undergone rapid change in the past two decades, with a marked and welcome decline in the civil conflict between government forces and communist guerrillas: urbanization, development of the market economy, wider use of the English language and increased social and commercial interchange with the rest of the world through the internet.

While the Colombian economy was modernizing, much of the disparate and unplanned assortment of assets that my generation inherited had not. The land was still operating under a feudal system which had been manipulated to their advantage by tenant farmers. Without intervention and professional asset management, eventually the value of the assets would have withered away to nothing. The private school, though modern and avant-garde in the 1960s and 1970s, was in need of investment in infrastructure and a more up-to-date, outward-looking curriculum.

At the beginning of the process I had mixed feelings, of optimism and fear, as I began to deal with a new reality. I had the challenge of renewing, without changing the essential core, every business. The house had to retain its charm and become modern at the same time; the farm had to figure out the best way to develop the land and at the same time obtain a very much required cash flow. At the school the goal was to keep my mother's enlightened educational philosophy, while ensuring it remained a successful and sustainable business.

Sometimes, after I had introduced changes, the results were not visible, and I felt frustrated. At other times I was taken by surprise at the extent to which things moved forward. Even though I have always looked for a smooth transition, many times this is not possible. Moving smoothly creates a claustrophobic feeling, while moving quickly may be reckless. Family members and associates want to see a change achieved but I realized many years ago that there is a process which is as important as the result, because it is not possible to arrive at a different reality without understanding what it is.

The major choice I had to make on behalf of my generation was whether to permit these assets to continue in their slow decline, or to equip myself to manage them in a professional manner, turning them once again into profitable enterprises. In order to enable the family to retain its autonomy, I chose the latter. But to do so, I had to undergo a major career change. My role and mind-set was to have to change from that of a lawyer in public service to that of a modern businesswoman and tough negotiator. This has been a profound change in skillset and outlook, not just a case of acquiring extra knowledge. To the extent that I have achieved this will be tested over time, but I hope that my story is instructive and encouraging in terms of maintaining a family firm's autonomy, and understanding the importance of role within such a transformation.

References

Deci, E.L. and Ryan, R.M. (1985). The general causality orientations scale: Self-determination in personality. *Journal of Research in Personality, 19*(2), pp.109–134.
Schröder, E. and Schmitt-Rodermund, E. (2013). Antecedents and consequences of adolescents' motivations to join the family business. *Journal of Vocational Behavior, 83*(3), pp.476–485.

Part II
Leadership strategies

10 Overview

Leadership of paradox and distributed leadership

Gry Osnes

The family is faced with two important arenas for leadership. First it is the leadership of themselves as a family. Second it is the leadership of the business. They are linked, and both will be explored in the following chapters. We found issues and processes that were particularly significant to family ownership and businesses, though they might appear in a diluted form in other types of businesses.

Our findings challenge an approach to advocate 'best practice' used in non-family businesses and then 'preach' it to the family owners. These are often based on normative assumptions that imply that a family business can achieve optimal performance if only it stops being controlled by a family. Family business and non-family businesses struggle with different sets of intrinsic problems. To operate like a non-family business might simply lead to the business taking on challenges that non-family businesses struggle with. This could be lack of risk taking, stifling and rigid procedures, problems with developing long-term strategies and short-term commitment from professionals. Idealizing either system is not particularly useful. That being said, successful family businesses use management and leadership practices used in non-family businesses. They often assimilate these through training and education taken by the next generation. It is less clear if non-family businesses can assimilate and use unique family business strategies as the trust and risk willingness, explored in Part I, might be unique to the family owner.

Distributed leadership and *leadership of paradox* are family capacities that manage the tension within the family and between family and business needs. Overlap between family and business interests can lead to conflicting and destructive dynamics, and they need to be acknowledged. Interestingly, the structure within a family business can help the family with containing, sometimes resolve, family conflict. In Part II we will explore the emotional and social resources the family members use when they are leading the family and the business, to achieve both family and business goals. The strategy-practices described in Part I were enabled by the leadership described here. In the following chapters, we describe these types of leadership in depth. First, in the Chapters 11–14, we discuss and exemplify different aspects of leadership of paradox. In

Chapters 15–19 we explore how leadership of paradox develops into different types of distributed leadership within the family and with employees in the business.

Leadership of paradox

A paradox is seen as a situation of contradictory needs that co-exist simultaneously, persist over time, and have as their origin an underlying tension that can be strategized. In family ownership the needs and goals of the business and the family are often contradictory. Leadership of paradox is the capacity to manage complicated and contradictory needs and demands. This is put into practice via leadership that innovates in paradoxical situations with a high complexity of needs and challenges (Smith & Lewis, 2011).

Chapter 11

Family owners need a focus on *autonomy and roles* to meet several contradictory needs. A drive for autonomy is intrinsic in a healthy family system and in starting and maintaining a family business. It is drive for increasing both individual and family autonomy; as such there can be contradictory needs within the family. The contradictions and paradox increase when the family roles have to be negotiated with respect to the needs of the business. A best practice approach is to negotiate roles as an ongoing dynamic, ensuring the family remains flexible and adaptive to new needs. We use the cases from Sweden, China and Israel to illustrate how this is done within the family, in relationship to the business and a wider social or business community.

Chapter 12

We discuss the *role of mourning*; how the capacity to mourn loss is crucial for the strategic capacity of the family. An example is a product important for family identity not being viable anymore and removing it from the company's offering. The paradox of being attached, choosing to execute a strategy that will trigger a sense of loss and emotional pain, is explored. The need of the family to offer safety, and maintenance of sentimental objects that reminds family members of a cherished past, can be contradictory to keeping the business financially healthy. Breaking with the past can be painful but is sometimes necessary, as a feature of the leadership of paradox.

Chapter 13

This chapter, titled 'Selling the Business', describes an individual owner's *mourning and recovery*, with his family, in recovering from a very profitable sale of the family assets. We put this in the context of commitment escalation and successor intention, and crucially, to exemplify that not all types of businesses, within a particular competitive context, are fit for family ownership. The chapter follows up on the themes of Chapter 12, and explores the recovery process described there. The founder had several strategies to recover from the loss of a work role and the family cohesion the business had contributed to. Importantly it discusses the management of loss for employees and sensitivity to mutual loyalty built up over 40 years. While this type of business sale is often seen as a failure, we describe how selling a business can also be an example of best practice.

Chapter 14

Chapter 14 explores the ability to create *authority* for individual members, the family unit within the business. It is a complicated process of shifting from a power to an authority mind-set. Creating power, relinquishing it and negotiating it poses a paradox for the mind as we are born with an instinct for short-term survival and striving for dominance. At the system level power is seen as legal rights and other sources of sovereignty, as one basis for leadership. In contrast is authority. Authority derives from a process of negotiating or defining tasks for individual members within the family group and inside the organization. Authority strategizing safeguards the individual against being corrupted by power, and builds trust and a sense of achievement. There are dangers in overuse of power, and our successful families were able find a balance. We describe this balance with different cases, illustrating the use of the 'golden share' giving undiluted power to one owner.

Distributed leadership

All the businesses we studied had been started by a founder-couple. This might be a coincidence or linked with a capacity to strategize complexity. Wives had important owner and leadership roles together with their husbands. Often they had financial control and could act to bridge the financial needs of the family and the business. Likewise newer generations of siblings would create roles of active ownership and leadership between themselves. A new generation of highly educated and skilled daughters had, in our cases, changed patriarchal assumptions. This has led to a distribution of leadership and influenced choices on succession. With distributed leadership there is an emphasis on understanding the complex, ambiguous and interconnected dynamics that are often ignored (Bolden, 2011).

Chapter 15

In this chapter we discuss what we discern as an emerging trend in many family businesses in relationship to *gender and leadership*. The traditional image, which is also often the case, is of a family business as a male dominated arena where the men handed it over to their sons. We found that most of the businesses could not have been founded without the work of a founder-couple. The wives had important roles also strategically. Cultural and political systems, at least in the USA and Europe, have changed radically the last 40 years. This influences new generations where women have education and work experience outside the business.

Chapter 16

We describe three different *succession strategies* for family businesses. Further, we show how two of these are upheld by different praxes. The capacity to switch between these three options was applied by all our families. Some families use new entrepreneurship as a strategy – supporting and co-founding new businesses for some offspring or family members – to avoid or dilute the difficulty of succession choices. This is a succession strategy unique to the family business and can build a network of partly independent businesses with business ties and close cooperation.

Chapter 17

The role of a *non-family Chair of the Board* in Norway is explored in this chapter and how a board structure, and use of a non-family Chair, as one way of using governance so as to distribute leadership is illustrated. In this way the family will attract and use external competence and resources they need when the complexity of the business increases. A challenge in the governance of family businesses is to balance the family and business needs, maintain social identity and the strengths of family ownership. At the governance level, this presents a set of challenges: to ensure the closeness of the family, and commitment to its vision, while also ensuring sufficient transparency and accountability. We describe the challenges of ownership and governance, illustrated by the successful example of an experienced non-family Chair, who is Chair of the Board of two family owned businesses.

Chapter 18

This chapter describes some of the powerful *drives that shape ambitions and relationships*. It summarizes the book with a focus, and some added theory, on the different drives we found important; why and how the family engaged with their ownership and the businesses they owned. We use theory on preservation of socio-emotional wealth, some attachment theory and selected contributions from psychodynamic theory to illustrate the complexity. Further suggested reading is provided for the reader with a particular interest in this aspect of family ownership and family businesses. These issues are equally relevant in business-owning families as in any other, with the added complication that the stakes are high, as the family wealth is tied up in the enterprise.

References

Bolden, R. (2011). Distributed leadership in organizations: A review of theory and research. *International Journal of Management Reviews*, *13*(3), pp. 251–269.

Smith, W.K. and Lewis, M.W. (2011). Toward a theory of paradox: A dynamic equilibrium model of organizing. *Academy of Management Review*, *36*(2), pp. 381–403.

11 Autonomy and role

Liv Hök

Control leads to compliance; autonomy leads to engagement.

Daniel H. Pink

Introduction

Autonomy means being in control of one's own destiny and defines a person's or a group's ability to decide over her/his/their own decisions and actions. It is about to what extent one is able to think, feel and act independently. It can be seen as a healthy amount of self-respect and self-confidence in combination with other resources and financial independence. Autonomy is a crucial motivating factor for those families founding and maintaining ownership of their own business. It conceptualizes a main drive behind how founders seek to start ventures and how families maintain and grow their own business (e.g. Sharma, Chrisman and Chua, 1997). It is important to bear in mind that there are degrees of autonomy, not any ideal states, as our discussion will show later. Autonomy is often defined as the capacity to act with some degree of freedom from others and not be forced into a choice. When autonomously motivated individuals perform the actions they find genuinely interesting and/or important (Schröder and Schmitt-Rodermund, 2013). The source of the action is then intrinsic to the individual as a person and is a drive linked to cause and issue in the context. This is different from acts motivated or controlled by someone else in order to avoid feelings of guilt or shame. Then an external expectation is made into an introjected internal demand.

Another type of external control can be made through rewards or punishments, i.e. external regulation (Ibid.). While all families demostrate elements of these, we found that in our best cases, the children were not forced to take over. There would be a mix of genuine interests; the family member could start new businesses aligned with both the family interests and her/ his own interests. Autonomy would, in these instances, come with purpose and identity and capture an element of duty, a milder form of guilt making one take ones role in the family business.

Importantly, the founding of these businesses was driven by what the founders themselves found interesting and important. This was in combination with financial survival where the control of one's own effort was not in the hands of an employer or someone outside the family. A family would try to reduce the interpersonal control of other non-family individuals and organizations but would accept and negotiate, interpersonal dependency within its family members. In our cases, we saw how successful families had creatively and dynamically carved out their own roles with the unique sovereignty that a family ownership gives. While seeking to create and maintain autonomy, they could even take decisions risking their own assets. When these families were later considering decisions about how to develop their businesses, their own autonomy would often be given more weight than short-term financial returns.

Task and leadership

Motivated by a wish for survival and financial prosperity, the primary task of family ownership is to consistently manage family assets. In our research, we met strong conviction concerning the importance of consensus when it comes to task and values in a family business and its context. We found the leadership to be about enabling dynamic development and supporting a willingness to change when circumstances so demand. In family businesses, this happens in the tension between a) harbouring and working for business success and b) protecting family autonomy. This tension can sometimes be the root of a downfall, but also of innovation, long-term strategies and successful entrepreneurship. Creating financial success and business autonomy as well as negotiating with the family members in their different roles, both within the family and in the business, involves many contradictory needs and demands. This is the basis, negotiating these needs and external realities, for paradoxes that pose a complex leadership task of how to negotiate and create room for compromises, win–win situations and innovative solutions. The leader needs to be able to, on an on-going basis, both acknowledge and have agency within this realm. In defining this task, one usually encounters a system of interlinked roles within the family as well as in the business.

To be able to manage oneself as both a family member and leader in role, one needs to mobilize one's resources and contribute to the task (Obholtzer and Roberts, 1994). The willingness as the capacity to take on a certain role is linked to autonomy as well. Taking on a certain role can be an act of drive resonating with personal capacities and ambition, aligned with what the family as a group has to do and to what is seen as important for the survival of the business. The family venture or established family business is the overall strategy practice for autonomy through ownership. This is exercised through the other strategy practices described in Part I in this book.

Having to manage the complexity of being in different types of roles in the two systems, family and business, is one of the big differences from having a role in other types of businesses. It is generally seen that the family business has the competitive advantages of commitment, efficient decision-making, independence and long-term perspectives as well as a loyal and hard-working business team.

This is, of course, when the family dynamic does not become too toxic or disruptive. Davis and Stern (1988) also underscore that a strong cultural connection, good working relationships and cooperation among co-workers and family, as well as good developmental possibilities are crucial competitive advantages that family businesses have over other types of businesses.

Financial success

All entrepreneurial families have to face external realities to survive financially. At times, expectations and demands from the market and from partners outside the family can be perceived as threatening and limiting or as posing opportunities. We show how family businesses are able to resolve this. They can achieve increased autonomy through financial success, though differing in terms of what they consider to be enough financial saturation. Tensions might arise from being engaged in the local, social or economic context or derive from employee relations or markets. Financially, the autonomy of the family member is linked to the autonomy of the family unit, the business. By being dynamic (in the sense of negotiating one's needs, creating win-win situations and accepting compromises) about autonomy and financial return, the families we met were often able to succeed in all these aspects.

We explore our family cases with respect to how they have *dealt with different upcoming challenges* while striving for autonomy and managing *their roles* in constructive and creative ways. We found *seeking autonomy* to be a main drive, both psychologically and socio-politically, when creating and developing one's roles, thereby generating business. The theme of autonomy is also linked to other strategies that families may employ. This will be discussed in different chapters. It is illustrated in varying cases: a family building autonomy out of poverty and social mobility is discussed in in Chapter 3; and a family building autonomy after emigration is examined in Chapter 4. In addition, in Chapter 9, a family business owner from Colombia describes how she carved out autonomy at all these levels.

System analysis of autonomy

In Chapter 9, we studied in depth how an owner could be in a position where they have to negotiate their autonomy within the family, within the business and within a wider socio-political context. In this chapter we illustrate these levels again three additional cases from China, Sweden and Israel. When owners, or owner families, have to manage autonomy in multiple systems this is done through the development and change of roles and is linked to how they feel about the roles, the drives and the motivations for them. This is complicated within family ownership due to the overlap of different systems, sovereignty and the accompanying wide range of options, highly emotional stakes involved for the family and strong emotional ties within the family.

A role and system perspective

A role can be described in several different ways. Here, we use the word role in the sense of 'the link between the individual and his/her organization' (Borwick, 2006, p. 7). In an organization, a workgroup or the like, taking a role is about being able to formulate or discover 'a regulating principle inside oneself which enables one, as a person, to manage one's behaviour in relation to what needs to be done to further the purpose of the system within which the role is to be taken' (Reed and Bazalgette, 2006, p. 46). This is a complex integration of feelings, ideas and motivations evoked in working towards the aim and task of a certain system. Integration takes place both consciously and unconsciously and is expressed in purposeful behaviour.

A system view focuses on how the organizational factors such as structures and performance are linked with the individual experience. Each role has its own dynamic and developmental process, and when individual role-takers find meaning and experience good job satisfaction, it will affect the outcome. Exploring roles and how families and their businesses are working as systems, we will focus on how to optimize individual, family and business autonomy. The different needs at these levels are most often be in conflict with each other. In this sense, absolute autonomy does not exist but is negotiated between individual needs and individual role taking within the family and between the family and the business. This places the family members' roles in a larger context with an acceptance that a family member is part of both smaller and larger systems (von Bertalanffy, 1975). The larger system would be the business and its context, the smaller system, the family.

Emotions and roles

Taking up and being in a role is also linked to emotional experiences. In seeking to solve a task, roles are also about applying emotional competence, skills and general knowledge. With a system perspective on family business and seeing it as dynamic, we look at different emotional phenomena as parts of a whole system (Öquist, 2010). The glue holding families together is the emotional bonding and affectionate ties between and among the members, a sense of responsibility and loyalty to the family as a system (Kepner, 2004). The theme of attachment and different emotional affects or emotional capacities is discussed in Chapter 12. In addition to the emotional part of roles and autonomy, a role develops in relation to how other roles are taken up. Roles are taken up and exercised in relation to each other at any time. If, for example, a certain family member is pressing for a development or change, we may see how another tries to put on the brakes and stall the on-going process. An important task in the dynamic of the family is to be aware of and to take control of how such roles in the family and in the business take place. This is important so as to avoid tensions and conflict. It takes into consideration how the organization's/system's parts are connected. The acknowledgement of how roles are interlinked, how they are negotiated, and the emotions that sometimes drive them, affects the learning of the family and the organization. Learning to see the whole together (Senge, 2010) will enable families to continually expand their capacity to create the results they want to achieve, as well as develop new patterns of thinking.

Overlap of systems and roles

Owner families are in a particular situation with several combinations of tasks. They are often seen as not 'normal' when on one hand considering a romantic image of a family or on the other taking an economic business view where leadership is based on merit. With a family as owner, the form of business distinguishes itself from other business-performing organizations. Family members are often active in several formal and informal roles such as leader, employee, owner and family member all at the same time. A person can be in all the roles of employee, owner and family member, or just in one of them at any point in time. As an owner, one might have a role within the business as employee or leader. In our research we focused on the families that would have both strategic and/or operational roles within the business. At times, some would be working somewhere else and children in their younger years would be involved as the business would be a place where the family would work together. In the same way, the business is a part of family life and, as such, even family members not working in the business would develop informal roles related to the enterprise.

From the owner family perspective, the overlap between family and business means that the business holds essential parts of family life: its history, family roles, family relations, social identity and future wealth. From the perspective of the business, its future is in the hands of the family who owns the business, and the members' role taking has an impact on development. This is why we pay attention to the family members' mutual relationships and roles in relationship to the business tasks. Successful families have had to develop a high degree of perception and awareness of the roles they are in within the family and within the business system. They must carry their awareness with them when discussing business strategies and affairs among themselves and/or with non-family employees and leaders.

Negotiating roles and autonomy

Our first case illustration is from China, and it is about safeguarding financial income. Here the negotiation is between the local village community and the municipality, the founder and, later, his family. The second example is from Sweden where we found the negotiation was between individual and family needs. In the third case from Israel, individual and family autonomy were successfully negotiated. By the time the second generation was the right age to get involved, money was not their primary concern. Their autonomy was more connected to freedom in a political sense. Despite having much better paying jobs in the USA and the Gulf States, they relinquished these and moved back to Israel. This illustrates how a family may negotiate autonomy, or use it for change in the local community.

Collective systems and family autonomy in China

This case illustrates a tension between family autonomy and the context of the local community and business environment. Entrepreneurship and innovation grew out of managing the tension and contradictory needs. There is often an element revealed about autonomy in the founding story, often concerning financial hardship. In China in 1970, a family of craftsmen was relocated from an urban area to a rural one in line with the national policy of relocation of villages during the height of the Communist era. As the leader in the village, the founder decided to try wood processing work using the locally rich timber resources. This would provide for most of the families in the village. Through several successions and shifts in the political system, the business eventually became privately owned by the founder's successors. As such, individual and family autonomy beyond employment was created relatively late. There was a capacity to hold communal financial well-being and individual and family well-being in mind and, in this way, autonomy was built into all the spheres. In addition, several spin-offs, for example, former employees starting their own businesses, created a cluster of specialized businesses in what would become a town. The founder used what was available at that time and at that geographic location in his own creative, independent and long-term way. Family and individual autonomy could not have been achieved for anyone without improving the general well-being, competence and financial situation of the village.

The founding and development of what is now a cluster of family owned companies, where several family members own different companies or are in leadership roles, shows the complexity of negotiating different systems. After having received a lucrative contract to make wooden handles for shovels, he started the business in 1973 as a municipality-based wooden toy factory. He and his wife worked in the business which became a part of the village. He was subsequently elected to the governing body of the village. While negotiating and creating roles between these three systems, and the needs represented in each system, the external business context had to be taken into consideration. An initial contract involved exporting shovels and pickaxes to Japan, in itself controversial as relations between Japan and China had been tense politically for a long time. Counteracting this was a state policy that aimed at facilitating export.

The first succession pinpointed the overlap between two different systems: the family and the municipality with the business and its employees. When the founder retired, his oldest son had been working in the business most of his adult life. The municipality did not want the founder to appoint him successor himself, but rather wanted the employees to elect the new leader which was along policy lines of collectively-owned companies. The eldest son was duly elected to be leader, nonetheless. His contributions included both direly needed technological innovation and the brave decision to move the factory to Shenzhen City. After a period of five years, private ownership rights had slightly changed. New opportunities were thereby developing alongside the shifts in the political system. The retired father then founded a new business in Yunhe County in 1985, that region's first private enterprise, Zhenpeng Handicraft Factory. He brought his second son, He Bin, into the business, thus formally starting the He Family business. The father gave a warning to his son emphasizing that while he could become a shareholder, only competence and skill would make him a Managing Director. He Bin, reflecting on this start, described the basis and idea of autonomy in taking over this second business of the family:

> I am his son. Why did he say that? Without any hesitation I responded that I wanted to be the Managing Director, and I would use all means to run this company well. I said to him, I have been trained to be independent, but I am not a replica of you. My thoughts are independent and you have to support me.

Managing the family as a conglomerate in a cluster of companies contained rivalry tensions so that each role-taker had his or her own territory and autonomy. This increased the complexity of the ownership as several members owned different companies. In this way, they had stronger autonomy as leaders within the business. This is more limited if the family owns only one company as the roles of the family within the business have to be closely aligned and one has to compromise with other family members. The overlap through co-ownership still created a need for dialogue within the family unit. When He Bin's mother did not understand the way the new generation used their autonomy in their roles or why her son invested so much in marketing and exhibition, his sister explained to her: 'If you don't advertise yourself, people will think that your brand is gone. It's an advertising era. New things can replace the old quickly. If you are good at leading, you will keep leading the industry.'

Individual and family autonomy in Sweden

This case shows the tensions, and sometimes hard choices and priorities, a family has to tackle when they negotiate roles and autonomy in a business. The roles of the three siblings are today well defined as they were aligned and negotiated in relation to each other. Their history tells of how they have negotiated and balanced individual and family autonomy in the current division of roles. One brother is in the role of Managing Director and CEO, another is Head of Production and the sister is in the role of Chair. While from the outside, these differences might look hierarchical, in reality, the power among the siblings is evenly distributed since they are co-owners. In addition to loyalty, cooperation and autonomy, the values that are at the heart of the firm are about quality and focus on technological innovation. The Chair can do nothing, not even sack the others, without ruining the business. In the same way, the CEO cannot do much without approval from the Chair or from the brother in the managerial role at the core of business production.

The founding grandfather and grandmother had worked for financial survival but also focused on a concern for the local community when generating their business idea. It was a response to what the founding patriarch had seen of breathing and lung diseases among miners in the mining town where he was an engineer. The couple started producing safety breathing devices in their home. Family and business values, continuous technological innovation, and the integration of these in the business, are the basis for the task the siblings are committed to. Most family businesses wish to be independent and protect their unit autonomy *in relation to the capital market*. They prefer to stay free in relation to financial institutions and hold the principle that profits should be invested in the business. They are not seeking to put the business on the stock market as the family would then have limited autonomy in pursuing what they think is a long-term strategy – to reinvest profit into technological development. In this case, there was a discussion about how to keep resources available for research and technological development.

This *stability in ownership and leadership* gives continuity for employees and owners alike. According to Leif Melin (Brundin et al., 2012), it is common that a family member/part owner holds the CEO position for at least 15–20 years. This Swedish family business follows the general pattern in Sweden where the same person stays CEO for about 3–4 times longer than is usual in traditional corporate business.

The task of a healthy community and a healthy family

The last case shows how a family is seeking to create family autonomy within a local context. The second generation made the business a political tool, daring to be strategically proactive after the founders had started the business with a need for financial survival. A family commitment made them seek political autonomy by addressing political issues in their local community and business context. The autonomy the family is seeking is not only financial survival with income and employment for themselves and their children; as family of traditionally Lutheran Arabs, they are also seeking a place in society without threats from other religious groups. Such tolerance for difference and family autonomy should be a part of any healthy community. Since this was not, in their view the case they, negotiated this within the business.

> I try to put my political ideas in action here, in our business. That we don't work exclusively. You know, I have people working here: Israelis, Arabs, Jews, Palestinians, Muslims, Christians. So you try to translate your political opinion into the business by example, by what you are doing. And, frankly

speaking, in business when you generate employment, it is much better than politics because you control what you have got. To a large extent, you control it, so you can do the work that fits your political thinking. Politically, I never thought some sort of solution within the state would work. I don't think a Palestinian state will work. I never did, never will. You have to find a way in which you share and celebrate the differences in our society and… and with being financially successful, and using the company this way, we are proving it.

Second generation, older brother

This type of leadership includes linking individual, family and business autonomy. The third generation is taking part in expanding the business to other cities in the region: Athens, Rome, Istanbul and Damascus. This strengthens the autonomy for the family as it reduces the overall political risk for the business. Spreading the business offices into other regions does not only give the family more freedom and financial security, it also manages the business system so that the family can generate business from groups initially coming to one place such as Jerusalem. In this, the business increases its ability to determine its success. The role of cooperating partners such as agents the business relies on is also taken into account.

That is why we thought to have those offices outside. To keep our agents. To keep in touch with our agents so that when business comes back here, we still have them; they'd not gone to others. And of course we can make money.

Co-founder and mother

For the next generation, there is a price to pay for choosing to work for the family and in Jerusalem. One is to live with the political risk of working in the business. The other is the personal choice of working and living in Jerusalem rather than leaving Israel and finding employment elsewhere which could lead to their citizenship being revoked. There are some job opportunities for Arabs, but this is limited to quotas set by the Israeli government. In this way, the different choices at the individual, family and business level are linked. They constantly create conflicting needs and paradoxes that cannot be solved. The leadership task is therefore to negotiate the needs and the design of roles while taking into account all the levels of autonomy.

Afterthoughts and reflections

Negotiating role and learning

Managing both change and development of roles involves three major factors: the individual, the role and the system. This is true also for the family business. Theories that are associated with psychoanalysis deal with questions such as

'Who am I?', 'How do I fit in?' and 'Where am I going in life?' The psychologist/ psychoanalyst Erik Erikson (Erikson, 1993) believed that if parents allowed their children to develop freely, they would hopefully endeavour to find their own identity. This perspective on healthy endeavour is optimistic, and we saw examples where parents permitted their offspring to strive freely in our healthy and successful family businesses. Assisting the younger generation in developing and leading useful lives is a major concern for the elder generation according to Erikson. He also suggested that successfully resolved crises that are social in nature make us develop as human beings. Establishing a sense of trust in others, a sense of identity in society, and helping the next generation prepare for the future is what we all have to work on. A possible paradox might occur when negotiating one's own desires within existing roles in a family business as the psychological needs of the individual sometimes conflict with the needs of the family and the business. In addition, if parents continually push their children to conform, teens may face identity confusion which can become a problem later in life. Erikson emphasized that the individual way of resolving conflicts in the early stages may provide both opportunities and limitations in patterns of reaction during later stages. An integrative approach suggested in *Family Business on the Couch* by Kets de Vries, Carlock and Florent-Treacy (2010) demonstrates how using both a psychodynamic and a systems approach can help families prepare for both life-cycle transitions and the psychological issues that family businesses face.

Emotional climate and projections

The degree of positive emotion in the relationship between family and firm influences the managerial and governance practices (Poza, Hanlon and Kishida, 2004). The feeling a certain business (as an object) arouses in its members, owners and employees – good or bad – will usually affect task commitment. Keeping an eye on the emotional climate including one's defence mechanisms and having a systems approach suits both family and business. We discuss projections and other unconscious processes in the final chapter, chapter 18, and Box 11.1 shows some advice useful in keeping the discussion at a less emotional level.

Box 11.1 Advice and guidelines

1 *Engage in dialogue on psychological needs.*
   Engaging in dialogue is the best trust-maintaining survival strategy. When it comes to difficulties connected to family business, the significance of the two roles as owner and leader is important. As described, they are often interwoven. A lack of awareness and acknowledgement of tension can lead to conflict and scant expansion and positive development.

2   *Do not be too preoccupied by the 'top-leader' role.*
The entrepreneur role and active ownership are important. The two research fields of entrepreneurship and family business have long been kept apart. One has mostly studied pure business development while the other has focused on questions of succession, conflict resolution and survival linked to business leadership.

3   *Analyse the roles continuously, be creative and task-oriented, not bureaucratic.*
Good leadership is a matter of coming to an agreement *on values that are to be upheld in the family as well as in the business.* This calls for good communication channels where questions concerning leadership, roles, family influence, growth and the like can be discussed.

4   *Define and agree on the family and individual financial saturation level without being moralistic.*
With an individual financial saturation agreement in place, the leaders can bring to the fore a continuous and long-term agreement on long-term strategies and long-term thinking.

References

Borwick, I. (2006). Organizational role analysis: Managing strategic change in business settings. In Newton, J., Long, S. and Sievers, B. (eds.), *Coaching in Depth: The organizational role analysis approach,* 3–28. London: Karnac.

Brundin, E., Johansson, A. W., Johannison, B., Melin, L. and Nordqvist, M. (2012). *Familjeföretagande: affärer och känslor.* Malmö: Studentlitteratur, SNS förlag.

Davis, P. and Stern, D. (1988). Adaption, survival and growth of the family business: An integrated systems perspective. *Family Business Review, 1*(1), 69–85.

Erikson, E. (1995). *Childhood and Society.* London: Vintage.

Kepner, E. (2004). The family and the firm: A co-evolutionary perspective. *Family Business Review, 4*(4), 445–461.

Kets de Vries, M. F. R., Carlock, R. S. and Florent-Treacy, E. (2010). *Family Business on the Couch: A psychological perspective.* London: John Wiley & Sons.

Obholzer, A. and Roberts, V.Z . (1994). *The Unconscious at Work: Individual and organizational stress in the human sciences.* London: Routledge.

Öquist, O. (2010). *Framgångsrikt ledarskap med systemteori: mönster, sammanhang och nya möjligheter.* Stockholm: Gothia.

Poza, E. J., Hanlon, S. and Kishida, R. (2004). Does the family business interaction factor represent a resource or a cost? *Family Business Review, 17*(2), 99–118.

Reed, B. and Bazalgette, J. (2006). Organizational role analysis at the Grubb Institute of Behavioral Studies: origins and development. In Newton, J., Long, S. and Sievers, B. *Coaching in Depth: The organizational role analysis approach,* 43–61. London: Karnac.

Schröder, E. and Schmitt-Rodermund, E. (2013). Antecedents and consequences of adolescents' motivations to join the family business. *Journal of Vocational Behavior, 83*(3), 476–485.

Senge, P. M. (2010). *The Fifth Discipline: The art and practice of the learning organization.* New York: Doubleday.

Sharma, P., Chrisman, J. J. and Chua, J. H. (1997). Strategic management of the family business: Past research and future challenges. *Family Business Review*, *10*(1), 1–35.

Von Bertalanffy, L. (1975). Perspectives on General Systems Theory. In Taschdjian, E. (ed.) *Scientific-Philosophical Studies*. New York: George Braziller.

12 "Letting go" and "moving on"

Mourning and strategic capacity

Victoria Grady and James Grady

[A healthy response to loss] is defined as the successful effort of an individual to accept both that a change has occurred in his external world and that he is required to make corresponding changes in his internal, representational world and to reorganize, and perhaps to reorient, his attachment behavior accordingly.

Bowlby, 1980, p. 18

Introduction

The inherent forces that drove our ancestors to form into groups are the biological product of qualities necessary for our survival. These drives persist with us today and remain "…among the absolute universals of human nature" (Wilson, 2012). John Bowlby (1969) contributed with insights regarding the mental mechanisms of attachments in adults as well as in children. He thought the drive to form attachments to groups is inherent to our nature, and functions unconsciously when we do not respond to this drive by forming them consciously.

Most adults spend a large proportion of their time within the context of their employing organization, deriving much of their daily routine, social interaction and confidence from this setting. The human instinct to form attachments to groups that provide security and comfort is just as robust today as it was in our distant past. For this reason, attachment behavior is often directed to the employing organization. The extent to which these efforts are not supported or reciprocated by today's organizations, and their leaders, influences the extent to which employees seek out other aspects of the organization for security and support. These alternate attachments can be tangible organizational objects, or relationships, as well as abstract ones.

In this chapter the consequences of the loss of an attachment is described with the use of excerpts from previously described case studies. When these substitute attachment objects are removed or replaced, the sense of loss can come on unexpectedly. The loss is experienced as a result of the modifications that employees must make in their living and/or working arrangements, and is

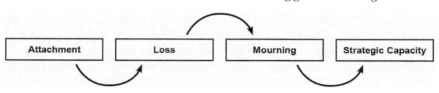

Figure 12.1 Loss, mourning and strategic capacity

associated with symptoms of depression. It is these symptoms of depression following a loss that lead to a period of mourning. While this period of mourning is painful, and often filled with uncertainty, it is an essential part of healing. It is out of the need to make readjustments in our ways of doing things, the need to adapt, reorient ourselves and accept the inevitable, that we are able to recover.

The period of mourning leads us into new territory; it is through a healthy grieving process that we find the type of renewal and growth that increases our capacity to think in new ways – to problem-solve more confidently and move in new directions, increasing strategic capacity. Because of the inclusive and familiar relationships in successful family businesses, they are often in the best position to take advantage of this leadership opportunity. See Figure 12.1.

This chapter focuses on these issues in several successful family businesses and attempts to provide some insights on which to base efforts to improve less successful business entities – both public and private. In this respect we will examine how successful family businesses deal with their difficulties, and relate them as important factors that can be used by any business. We will, in the rest of the chapter, go through this model and describe each part with illustrations from the cases.

From attachment to strategic capacity; mourning of loss

Attachments

Much of the initial understanding of the significance of Attachment Theory in adults comes from Bowlby. Our need for attachments is deeply embedded in our nature, and over-determined to the extent that it persists as a compelling part of our heritage. In a manner similar to the intensity of the infant's desire to maintain a relationship with the mother, attachment behavior in adults causes one to strive to remain committed in significant relationships (Bowlby, 1969).

Our need to form attachments is of special interest since it is the driving force for much of our behavior. It is this drive that facilitates the ability to find others willing to organize into a group. Remaining in the group, however, requires the building of relationships that extend beyond the purposes of security. Once attached as part of a group, behaviors are re-directed toward purposes supportive of the group – finding food, shelter, reciprocal behavior, etc. These behaviors are re-directed toward the provision of a secure base which further enhances our ability to overcome obstacles that confront us (Crowell & Treboux, 1995). The combination of these qualities serves to direct the efforts of the members toward the formation of more cohesive and productive groups, which in turn becomes a more secure container. The group's members are then better able to thrive and persist (Panksepp & Biven, 2012). As a substitute for our ancestral groups, employees have an inclination to attach to their employing organization, and/or to what it symbolizes. Originally a survival function, this gives today's groups the responsibility of serving as a containing, or protective, function in order to enhance and support the security needs of its members. In fact it has been shown that when organizations fail to provide this function it "...is often associated with the subjective feeling of insecurity" (Parkes, 2001, p. 10) within the organization.

The success of many family businesses today arises out of this sense of unity and loyalty that remains as a relic from the past. The strongest attachments exist when they are directed to the products as well as to the business family itself. It seems that the family business may often be in a better position to respond to our inner forces to belong than non-family businesses; the leadership and sense of community that surfaces is an attraction to, and is attracted by, that sense of belonging. This may occur more often when the family leadership is compassionate and inclusive in nature. It is in this manner that a strong sense of loyalty has developed in the Swedish family business (discussed in Chapter 7).

The Swedish family business started out of the charitable dedication and concern of the early leadership. This business was built on the shoulders of the founder who was determined to improve the safety equipment used in local mining operations. Later this cause was championed by his son who worked to improve the products, and a grandson who has expanded into international markets. During this time the underlying principle has always remained the same – service to others.

The hiring philosophy over the years has remained one that revolves around finding steady workers who appreciate the purposes and importance of producing quality products. These workers have proven themselves to be conscientious and reliable; they have a long-term commitment, and they have developed an affinity for their work identities. From this a strong vision has emerged that has captured the loyalty and devotion of employees. Because they are never asked to sell a product that does not meet the highest standards, those in sales have become missionaries for the company. A feeling of pride extends from their conviction that their company produces products that are really that good, compelling them to live up to the same standard of quality inherent in their company's products. This level of dedication shows that many employees are attached to the business model itself. For most employees, it seems to serve as a safe container. However, even when this is not the case, the symbols and artifacts provided by the quality of the products are profound, and make good substitute attachment objects. As a result, most employees are engaged and become an important part of the success of this venture.

While purposes may have differed for each of the family leaders, and certainly among employees, it is likely that the strength of the vision generated, and the values and products, by the founders, generates the affection of family members and employees. These symbols can provide attachment objects for employees and family members. The theory of the nature and importance of such substitute representations, or objects, comes from the work of Winnicott (1971). A part of their value comes from the way in which they represent or symbolize the purposes of the group and individuals (Ibid.). Individuals who have lost one source of emotional security are likely to look for, or remain near, other havens of safety, be they people, places or things, which can provide a feeling of attachment similar in emotional quality to that found in the concept of "home". With such strong attachments to real objects, and representations, one can easily develop a problem with letting go. What we found is that most of the families would go through, or even initiate, a loss of strong attachments. They would create new businesses and as a family unit help other family members go through mourning processes. New business plans and new products would create safety, or the family would transition employees and other family members through a loss process. The feelings caused by the loss of an attachment are an issue that is not quickly resolved.

Loss

Loss may be a less well recognized or considered aspect of Attachment Theory. Grady and Grady (2012) observed that the loss or removal of those objects familiar to organizational life leads to activation of attachment behaviors. When a loss is perceived, it will be resisted. This resistance is "…the reluctance to give up possessions, people, status, expectations" (Parkes 2001, p. 11). The response differs only in intensity as determined by the nature of what is lost. Most studies of loss portray the response to the death of a beloved person; however, studies of other types of loss reveal a response that is in many ways similar. Although not extensive, these studies have included: divorce, unemployment, forced relocation, death of the domestic pet, childlessness, losses involving a home and losses involving a limb (Parkes, 2001). Grady and Grady (2012) also showed that attachment behaviors can result from all types of loss, including not only concrete, but also abstract objects.

Resistance to change is a much explored issue. There is the expectation among many change practitioners that "resistance to change" is about the introduction of something new. The efforts of leadership suggest that they believe employees are more accepting when they understand how and why the change is needed – so they try to "sell" the change. In our experience this is the wrong approach. In fact our research suggests that this resistance is much more directed at what is lost than at what is newly introduced (Grady & Grady, 2012).

We find an example of loss in the USA family business case described in Chapter 3. After nearly 40 years in the barbeque (BBQ) business, the Fosters were faced with a big decision – they owned two very successful restaurants, but their abilities were stretched very thin as they attempted to manage both. The reality was that they could keep their flagship but labor-intensive BBQ restaurant business – the one that had served them exceedingly well for the past 25 years – or they could redirect all their efforts to their relatively new restaurant business. This new venture would not only allow them an earlier retirement, it would also serve to provide their son and his family with a unique opportunity. This opportunity was not only less demanding, but had prospects for more future growth. It was a straightforward decision strategically, but a difficult one emotionally. On paper there was an element of risk, but the real difficulty lay in the problem of identity. Charlie was well known and respected throughout the region for the quality of his BBQ. He identified himself with the image of BBQ – he was deeply attached to this image. But after a few years of successfully managing both restaurants, it finally became obvious to all; it was time to sell the BBQ restaurant.

To understand the nature of their loss we should review a brief history. Over a period of about 10 years, and after leaving a minimum wage job in a cotton mill, the Fosters had risen from a very meager standard of living to a rather comfortable one. By the time 40 years had passed their success in the restaurant business had far exceeded their wildest expectations. They had transitioned through four ever-larger and more successful BBQ business ventures. But now the time had come for them concentrate all of their efforts into furthering the opportunities in the newer venture.

> We had run first one then another BBQ restaurant for 40 years, so we had a lot of conversations leading up to selling our most recent one. BBQ was so much a part of my life that when we sold that restaurant I felt like I had lost my identity.
>
> Charlie

Charlie's loss of identity may have been personal for him, but it also had an impact on his family. His daughter Gail recounted an experience she had soon after they sold the BBQ restaurant. She was visiting her mother when she heard her father coming in from work. She met him at the door giving him a big hug. Then she stepped back puzzled – there was something seriously wrong. Then she burst into tears – he had lost that friendly hickory smoke smell. In that moment it felt as if she had lost her real dad, the one she had known and loved all of her life. She felt devastated and was afraid.

In humans, anxiety is caused by fear and is distorted by "our capacity to look forward and backward in our mind's eye and … create phantoms of the imagination" (Panksepp & Biven, 2012, l. 4473). It is a "fear of the unknown" that adds to the unsettled nature caused by a loss and imposes upon the leadership in an organization an obligation. Any planned change should take full account of the effect the decisions will have and everything possible should be done "…to anticipate and provide for the psychosocial effects of the [loss]" (Parkes, 2001, p. 210). In some families, those which have spent their years together building closeness and expressing empathy, these skills may prove more natural than in others. Businesses led by these families will have an advantage. It is one of the reasons for success in many of the family-owned businesses we are profiling in this book.

In successful family businesses there are often leaders with a sense of responsibility toward the issues that are of concern to employees. There is often a more familiar or inclusive feeling about the work space, office protocols and artifacts – and other objects, both physical and abstract. All these attachments provide an employee with a level of security on which they have come to depend. The loss or threatened loss of any of these attachments should be expected to lead to a series of symptoms that include anxiety and fear and have negative implications for the purposes of the organization. It comes in the form of employee grief and the period of mourning that follows.

Mourning

The grieving or mourning process is a natural one and results whenever we face a significant loss. Our assumptions about the world around us are altered. When the old assumptions become invalid, our internal world is in conflict with the external world. It is the disruption of these mental models that causes a period of instability and insecurity that we call mourning. Since our internal models of the world are revised much more slowly than are changes in the outside world, it produces within us a sense of longing (Parkes, 2001).

> [A]n individual responds to separation or loss with various mixtures of protest, anger, anxiety or despair... it is likely that the behavior is the natural... response of any human being in that type of situation.
>
> Bowlby, 1969, p. 375

It is the anxiety generated by separation and distress, or loss, in the mammalian brain that is believed to be the origin of human grief (Freed & Mann, 2007), and can lead to depressive despair (Bowlby, 1980; Panksepp & Biven, 2012, 1. 6664). This was observed after the Fosters sold their flagship BBQ restaurant. Gail described how she and her mother would cry a lot – and when the crying slowed they avoided eye contact to keep from starting all over again. Even after several years her mother is still unable to go back into that restaurant, and Gail admits "...I get a lump in my throat when I go up to the register to place my order and pay. It is like – wait a minute, this is just not the way it is supposed to be."

Bowlby (citing Marris, 1958) claimed that grief and the associated mourning processes result when the loss of an attachment object activates attachment behaviors (Bretherton, 1992, p. 12). It is a normal and healthy response to most significant losses; it triggers sadness when we lose a person, a friendship but also a job, the connection to a place or a role. If not mourned properly it can lead to more enduring depression (Bowlby, 1980). Parkes (2001) points out that grief is a process and not a state, and it is more similar to a physical injury than other types of psychologically painful events as the change in the brain is physical and unpleasant. After experiencing loss, we mourn and endure a period that seems disconnected from reality; it is as if life has lost all meaning. But to recover we must replace once comfortable habits or thoughts with new and more unfamiliar and uncomfortable ones.

Early in the previously described USA case study there came a time when the Foster's daughter Gail came to her parents for advice – she wanted to open a restaurant of her own. Would they assist her in this venture? They were resistant at first, but Gail's reasoning was sound and the thought strangely appealed to them. With their involvement, Gail was very successful. Fifteen years later, however, Gail's abilities and responsibilities expanded; she did not have time to properly manage the restaurant. Even with pressure from her family and friends, she found herself continually putting off the decision to sell. "I really had a hard time letting go of it; I guess it was that whole attachment and loss thing."

The period of mourning began when Gail realized with some finality that the restaurant was holding her back, and compensating for her occasional absences was becoming a burden for her family. In many ways she was forced to learn many difficult and stressful lessons; now it was time to let go. While it was really hard – there were so many memories – she had also grown from the experience of ownership and matured through the process of mourning.

The process of grieving can in many cases be drawn out, and in some ways may never be settled. But in all cases of healthy mourning the essentials are dealt with, the disruptive nature of the grief is resolved, and there is the return to an improved ability to function. This growth in the ability to function is the unexpected benefit of the recovery from mourning.

Strategic capacity

Bowlby confirms that grief and mourning are normal and form part of healthy responses to loss. While the most intense forms of sadness are elicited in healthy people, the response will later result in some sort of growth. A healthy process can have sadness, and a shorter period of depression and a sense of disorganization. The thoughts and feelings will reorganize from new bonds and interactions (Bowlby, 1980). In this way one can recover and start a new process.

This was characterized by Grady (2005) as a type of instability that leads to a period of disruption or "loss of effectiveness". However, this mourning period, if understood and supported by management, can be shortened, and can also lead to a time of growth.

Returning to the USA case, for several years Charlie managed to run both the flagship BBQ restaurant and the much larger new one. But he was getting older, and he had always said that "the more restaurants you own, the more they own you." But even Charlie realized at some level that they were not yet ready to make such a big transition. It made sense intellectually, but none of them were ready emotionally. BBQ had been their life, and a very good one, for nearly 40 years – so the conversations went back and forth for over several years. Finally, the decision was made. As a result, there may have been a sense of relief that they could now focus on the future, but there were no celebrations. They had dealt appropriately through the mourning phases, they had learned to exercise restraint when restraint was needed, and were ready to innovate and to embrace the challenge with a new level of confidence. They were now able to concentrate on managing and taking advantage of the inherent flexibility of the new restaurant. Their strategic capacity for making these decisions had increased.

> Even after we had made the decision and the papers were signed it was still painful for a long time. It is harder for Betty probably than for me. It was so very emotional for Betty. It was really hard for me for maybe two or three years – I felt as if I had sold my identity. I still do sometimes, but not so much anymore. The decision proved to be a really good one for all of us, and we have benefited from it.
>
> Charlie

The Tanzania family business (Chapter 4) evolved from the founder couple who built up a safari camp. Their first venture was a cattle ranch that proved unsuccessful. Their opportunity to serve as occasional hosts for friends and family led to the idea of a guest resort. As this resort business began to grow, competitiveness developed among the four sons. Trying to share the management responsibilities equitably was not working, but as expatriates the only way for them to remain in Africa was to work together for that common cause. The issue of competitiveness and mistrust resolved itself as three of the sons developed satellite businesses. Each of these businesses allowed that son to work independently, and also allowed the operation of the resort to benefit from the increased strategic capacity. Trusting that each had the common desire to do what it took to remain in Africa, and trusting that they could each work better toward this common cause independently, they branched out, as limbs on a common trunk. A more subtle benefit of the attachment/loss/mourning/growth sequence is the emergence of new levels of trust. Trust is one of the key components of successful family businesses. When it has become a natural attribute within the family over the years, trust can find a way to overcome the competitiveness within families that emerges from time to time.

Afterthoughts and reflections

Out of projects conceived at a kitchen table, by hanging out in an uncle's restaurant, from building counterfeit tool handles, while driving a taxi-cab and in an effort to remain in a foreign land, some flourishing family businesses have emerged. In this chapter we have reviewed a few of the cases from around the world that are contained in this book. Each has been remarkably successful and has met and even exceeded the needs and original intentions of their founders. In these cases there are consistent themes that emerge. Drawing attention to these provides examples of best business practices both for family businesses and traditional business models.

This chapter has looked at Attachment Theory from a historical and organizational perspective. It reviews the importance of attachments to our well-being, and describes how attachments may play an enabling role in family businesses. When the family dynamics make a business an attractive attachment object, or provide other objects and symbols that serve that purpose, it can establish a sense of belonging and provide for a secure base and more engaged employees.

The loss of an attachment object in an organization causes a type of instability (Grady, 2005). And a sequence of instability or unsettledness caused by loss leads to a period of mourning. This can impact the effectiveness of the organization. With family support and new interesting "objects" to attach to a mourning period can be shortened. The process can lead to growth and re-commitment. This is the message to take home from this chapter – that, if healthily and properly handled, grief can lead to substantial benefits for family owners and their employees.

It should be noted that, nearly 50 years after Bowlby's first book (1969), current research on this area has begun to confirm many if not all of his expectations. Advances in magnetic resonance "x-rays" now allow scientists to examine the inner workings of the brain stem – an ancient structure between the brain and the spinal cord. It is the area of origin for the drives that cause us to form those attachments that bind us and keep us committed to the security and companionship provided by the group (Panksepp & Biven, 2012). It is this area that is also involved in the grieving process that occurs after we are separated from our attachments. This is the area that collects the first data we receive from those nerves that monitor the world within us, and around us; all of humanity responds to it in the same way. We are driven by this area to seek attachments to others and to love, care for and enjoy their company. It is from this area that fear arises when our attachments are threatened, and that promotes our grief when they are lost. We have much more to learn about our human nature from this research, past and present, and with time we may find that it revolutionizes the way we treat and think about others.

Box 12.1 Checklist on good mourning processes

1   *What are primary attachment family members and employees?*
    Do the employees respect the leadership within the organization? If not, why
    not? Can one communicate on emotional ties and a sense of loss?

2   *Do the family members or employees focus their attachments more on secondary, or
    transitional, attachment objects?*

3   *Carefully and honestly consider the nature of the family and employee reaction to radical
    changes.*
    Is the organizational culture and leadership as supportive of change as it should
    be? Has there been change that has been particularly difficult? How difficult was
    the transition? How long did it take? Did the family or employees become
    noticeably less effective during the readjustment period? Did the family members
    or employees benefit from the process? If not, why not?

4   *Does the organization expect or desire increases in strategic capacity?*
    Is the organization interested in a plan that will improve the response to change?
    Is the organization interested in improving and increasing the capacity of family
    members and employees?

References

Bowlby, J. (1969). *Attachment and Loss, vol. 1: Attachment.* New York, NY: Basic Books.

Bowlby, J. (1980). *Attachment and Loss, vol. 3: Loss.* New York, NY: Basic Books.

Bretherton, I. (1992). The origins of Attachment Theory: John Bowlby and Mary Ainsworth. *Developmental Psychology*, 28(5), 759–775.

Crowell, J., and Treboux, D. (1995). A review of adult attachment measures: Implications for theory and research. *Social Development*, 4(3), 294–327.

Freed, P.J. and Mann, J.J. (2007). Sadness and loss: Toward a neurobiopsychosocial model. *American Journal of Psychiatry*. 164(1), 28–34.

Grady, V. (2005). Studying the effect of loss of stability on organizational behavior: A perspective of technological change (Unpublished doctoral dissertation). The George Washington University, Washington, DC.

Grady, V. and Grady, J. (2012). The relationship of Bowlby's Attachment Theory to the persistent failure of organizational change initiatives, *Journal of Change Management*, DOI :10.1080/14697017.2012.728534.

Panksepp, J and Biven, L (2012). The archaeology of mind: Neuroevolutionary origins of human emotions. New York: W.W. Norton and Co.

Parkes, C. (2001). *Bereavement: Studies of grief in adult life*, 3rd Edn. Philadelphia, PA, US: Taylor and Francis.

Wilson, E. (2012). *The Social Conquest of Earth*. New York: Liveright Publishing.

Winnicott, D. (1971). *Playing and Reality*. New York: Basic Books.

13 Selling the business

A UK founder

Gry Osnes and Victoria Grady

Introduction

When a family decides to sell its business it is often experienced as a loss for the family and/or founder. A sale of the business is, by far, the most frequent exit choice for owners of smaller to mid-sized businesses (Coad, 2013). While selling a business often can trigger a perception of failure, it can equally be the result of a careful strategic process. The family may be selling the business to an employee, or revenues from the sale of one family-owned business may be used to invest in a bigger enterprise. If the business continues to thrive under new owners, and the family profited from the sale, it is hardly accurate to categorize this as failure. Options include putting the company on the stock-market, selling the business to other family members and a management buyout. At the same time disagreement within the family over whether to sell or not can cause family tension, ruptures and unhappiness. Family members will feel this more strongly than others involved in the firm; some may support the sale while others may be opposed, resulting in painful conflicts.

A sense of failure might originate from the loss on behalf of the owner and family. Loss and a need to mourn it, will often be a part of a strategic process regardless of how profitable the outcome is. Sometimes the family does not have children who can, or who want to, take over the business. The reason for the family choosing to sell the business is often attributed to this "succession failure". But there are other factors to be considered when strategizing a transfer to the next generation. The suitability of the business to be owned by a family can depend on future challenges and the competitive context. A third variable is what the family could gain, financially and otherwise, by selling the business.

The sale of a family business represents a complex and challenging dynamic for the loss process. Not only will the loss be experienced by the family but also a significant number of employees will be impacted by the sale of the organization. These loss and recovery processes can be experienced very differently by the people involved. Grady and Grady (2012) showed that significant instability develops from loss of both tangible and intangible objects, here the family connection to the business, in radical change processes. This is the case for both owners and employees. The connection between family and business is not the only such "object". Objects can be people, places, ideas and concepts, both tangible and intangible. Family business examples include the loss of a leader, a change in business process, the relocation of physical space, the cessation of production of a cherished product or the selling of a business. With the loss of an object, the mourning process for both the owner family and the employees becomes an integrated part of the transition.

The grieving or mourning process is a natural one and results whenever we face a significant loss (see Chapter 12). Our assumptions about the world around us are altered. When the old assumptions become invalid our internal world is in conflict with the external world. It is the disruption of these mental models that causes a period of instability and insecurity that we call mourning. Successful evolution through a healthy mourning process supports the intellectual achievement of growth and recovery. The process is challenging for the most prepared – which in this case is likely the owner family – and even more challenging for those not directly involved in the decision process, the employees. With that said, there are ways to provide direct support to the employees.

The introduction of a transitional object (Winnicott, 1971) as a support mechanism can potentially reduce the intensity. The nature and importance of substitute representations or objects is central in Winnicott and this tradition's thinking about change and adaptability. These "transitional" objects do not necessarily have intrinsic value in themselves. Rather, their value comes from the way in which they represent or symbolize a new direction, or transition, giving some comfort to the individual and/or the group.

Individuals who have lost one source of emotional security are likely to look for or remain near other objects of safety, be they people, places or things, which can provide a feeling of attachment similar in emotional quality to that found in the concept of "safety". The transitional object supports the individuals in the organization experiencing the challenge of the loss. In this case, the employees are likely experiencing a more acute loss, as they were not directly involved in the decision to sell. Both planned and unplanned loss need to be supported. But particularly in the case of a business sale, the employees often experience a very potent response. The introduction of the transitional object for the employees provides the support necessary to successfully complete the mourning process and achieve recovery.

A best practice process

In this best practice example the owners had a good understanding of the future demand in a sector that had transformed itself more than once over 40 years. The founder did not wish to expose the business and family to an escalation of commitments, and the timing of the sale was well judged. To have family members and children involved, but letting them choose other careers was important. A process of disengagement and loss, followed by recovery and engagement in other activities was developed. The owner had

---

Box 13.1 Commitment escalation

A capacity for taking decisions leading to radical strategic change is critically important for any business, and is a necessary prerequisite to competitive advantage. It can be difficult to accept and implement. As family owner there is the overlap of emotional attachment (as family members) and rational judgment (as business managers) that can make this more difficult. Typically they are often willing to make personal sacrifices in order to keep the business running (Salvato, Chirico and Sharma, 2010).

This personal commitment can lead to path dependency, in which practices and policies, or "routines", are used repeatedly, despite failing to address the strategic challenges facing the business. Such path dependency, or irrational commitment, can prevent change in, for instance, the strategy, the product or the entire business activity (Ibid.). *Commitment escalation* can prevent necessary change or a rational decision that the family or business would benefit from. This paradox caused Randall (1987) to suggest that commitment has two sides: a motivating element that enables the family to overcome obstacles and achieve ambitious goals, or visions for the family; but also an inhibiting tendency towards narrow thinking, where the commitment causes the firm to remain stuck on certain paths regarding product, a type of ownership structure or business process/model. Lack of flexibility and a capacity to *detach* can evolve into entrapment such that resources are wasted in what would, from the outside, look like a lost cause. Including non-family members in the family decision making, sometimes at the board level, can prevent such commitment escalation (Woods, Dalziel and Barton, 2012).

---

built up a very strong internal work-force and this was one of the particular challenges when selling the business. He took into consideration processes of loss and mourning for employees who had been employed for decades and had been a part of the texture of the business.

The publisher's case of loss and recovery

The case featured in this chapter concerns a founder who wanted to avoid commitment escalation and decided to sell. Family members had worked for the company at various stages but had chosen to pursue other careers that were closer to their own interests and needs. The sale of the business involved a process of disengagement and loss for the owner-founder, followed by recovery and engagement in other activities. In negotiating the sale of the company, considerable consideration was given to the position of employees who had been employed for decades and there were strong friendships and a high degree of commitment and identity involved. In the selling there was a consideration of loss and mourning processes for employees who had worked for the business for 20–30 years.

The founder had owned a group of companies for 48 years, including publishing and information distribution ventures in the UK, the USA, Asia and elsewhere. When discussing and planning the future of the business, the founder consulted his immediate family – a wife and three daughters, two of whom had worked in the business in senior roles in the past. Even though there was agreement on the decision to sell, it involved feelings of loss: loss of social identity, loss of a role and activity and loss of relationships with long standing colleagues.

Suitability of private ownership

Throughout the years of the company's operation, the digital revolution in information distribution had been born and matured, causing a radical transformation of the publishing industry in the years leading up to the sale. Competitive pressures and the growing power in the distribution of information by global digital giants such as Google, Apple and Amazon had led to defensive mergers and acquisitions among the publishers of content. Big publishing houses grew bigger in order to acquire more content and strengthen their position in negotiating with these new digital platforms.

The company was founded in 1967 as a specialist publisher of practical books on business management under the A-Publishing Press Imprint. During the 1970s and 1980s the company not only expanded into other business information and education media such as the organization of seminars and conferences and the production of training films but also started to publish academic research monographs. The academic publishing programmes grew through internal development, the acquisitions of smaller businesses and the launching of joint ventures and expanded rapidly. Its publications had a far larger international market than the UK-oriented business publishing side and this was re-enforced by the establishment of subsidiary companies in the USA, Singapore and Australia. The various academic imprints were consolidated under the B-Publish name in 1996.

During these first 30 years of the company's existence the book or journal in its printed form remained the pre-eminent and most prestigious form of communicating academic research and professional practice. The channels of distribution – through bookshops, library suppliers, and mail order – were open and established and their ownership diverse. A privately-owned company such as B-Publish could grow in this environment without let or hindrance from larger commercial interests. In this case the growth was facilitated financially not just by the company's own trading success but by the owner's financial and managerial involvement in other companies. His earnings from these activities meant that he and his family did not have to take money from the business and were free to reinvest all the profits in expansion.

In the last 20 years, however, the digital revolution has produced major changes in the publishing environment: the advent of ebooks, the decline of bookshops, the global reach of Amazon and Apple and the "free" information sources that are accessible through the search engines of Google and others. All these factors have led to a massive consolidation of both general "trade" publishing and academic and professional publishing. The founder comments:

> Even the big publishing houses have a challenge with being invited to a negotiation table with the big digital giants. This is where prices and margins are squeezed, both for the publisher and the author.

The future challenges for the privately-owned B-Publish were formidable. In addition the large international publishing companies wanted and needed to get bigger. Opportunities for acquiring the few independent medium-sized companies were getting scarcer and this was important for the fortunate timing of the sale. Therefore, the price fully reflected the company's value, enabling effective estate planning for the family, providing a significant financial bonus for the employees and benefitting the charitable trust which the founder had established some years earlier.

Loss and recovery in relation to employees

A main strategy for the business had been the loyalty and long-term employment of the publishing staff as a critical factor for success. Many authors would stay loyal and want to make a deal with "their" editor rather than with a particular publishing house. This relationship would sometimes last three to four years before the book was published, and if an editor left, the publisher would not only lose good authors but also the time that had been invested in developing the author and the concept of the author's book. The company's success owed much to a team of editors, marketing executives, managers and support staff, who were connected to the business beyond a salary and coming to the office. The location of the business outside London helped to create an intimate atmosphere, where everyone knew everyone. The founder's long-term involvement with the company and the employment of two of his daughters created an atmosphere where private ownership, strong friendships among employees sometimes leading to marriage, and a connection to a small town, resulted in a "family" culture and a lower employee turnover than the company's main competitors.

This human resource strategy was successful, but would result in a sense of loss, both for the owners and employees, when the decision to sell the company was made. To mitigate the impact, the owner adopted two main policies. First, when negotiating the deal, he sought to optimize the conditions for employees. All employees received a "thank you bonus" that depended on the length of their service. In many cases this amounted to the equivalent of one year's salary. Many of the editors moved over to be employed by the new owners of the company and the staff who did not transfer were given time to consider their future employment options as well as their full redundancy entitlements.

Loss and recovery of a role

In the sale, the art books' publisher unit was excluded, with ownership being retained by the founder. This had formerly represented less than 10 per cent of the total revenues generated by the business. The exclusion was agreed with the buyers partly for commercial reasons. As a publisher of illustrated books it was a very different form of book publishing and did not really fit into the buyer's publishing activities. This also meant the founder could continue in his role as a publisher. It fitted well with some of his earlier business ventures as the owner of a small art gallery and a collector of paintings.

In common with most owners in our cases, he did not see himself retiring into a non-working role. From the start of his career he had been involved with the publishing of books. Although art book publishing is a challenging activity from a commercial viewpoint, it remains a sector where the printed book continues to enjoy many advantages. Another form of continuing occupation for the owner and continuity with the past was represented by the charitable trust that the owner had founded eight years earlier. Additional contributions had, over the years, come from the businesses profits and staff and members of the family had been involved in its activities. The trust would fund educational projects in Zambia and employees had been active in fund raising. Two of the company's directors continued as trustees of the trust after the sale of the company.

Loss and recovery of a private company's "family" culture

The businesses had several family members involved and with provided an added element of cohesion or embeddedness (Sharma, 2004) for the family. Two daughters had worked in the company – one in editorial management and one in marketing management – but had left due to their own family priorities. In this case the link between the founder-owner and the business was moderately strong. In this case the founder had a stronger degree of involvement and identification than other family members. At the same time the business was in a sector that posed huge challenges for smaller independent businesses. As he expressed it himself:

> Of course it has been a great pleasure to have two of my daughters work in the company. Apart from any other consideration, it was a way of ensuring that if I passed away they would be informed about the nature of the business and the people in it. They would have been better able to work with company's management and determine the future for the company in my absence. But I don't think that I or they ever considered that they would want to take over the running of the company in the future. Nor do I think that this situation would have been very different if I had a son, who might have had less domestic commitments than my daughters. And what certainly has changed is the technology and structure

of the publishing market. I'm not sure that a medium-size independent company with an international reach can achieve the growth rates required to survive in the long term.

Afterthoughts and reflections

Successor intention

Successor intention then becomes crucial in the calculation for whether the family should maintain the ownership of the business or move on and develop other types of activities from the profit a sale would give. Handler (1990) completed a sequence of studies that explored the succession dynamic from the perspective of successor intention to join the business. This was then analysed in context, taking into account the intention of the predecessor, and the relationship between the predecessor, or family member as owner or leader, and the successor. Handler calls this a "delicate dance" where the needs of the predecessor and the successor are adjusted to each other during a shorter or longer time period. One of the difficult parts for the predecessor is the letting go of a role. "Letting go" is a process of acknowledgement of a loss, mourning and recovery, as explored in Chapter 12. This is further exemplified in the ladder entrepreneurship chapter, Chapter 3, and in the French succession chapter, Chapter 5.

Employees

Of particular concern to the owner was the effect of the aftermath of the sale for his employees. A group of dedicated editors had been critical to the long-term success of the organization. The notion of family and friendship stretched far beyond the founder's immediate family. It included the dedicated employees who ultimately became part of the owner's extended family. He had created a human resource policy of generating a comfortable environment, where everyone knew everyone. The focus of the organization was based on establishing long-term relations between the family and the employees to create a "family of employees" which led to low turnover and a passionate commitment by the employees to the organization. While this intense success helped the business flourish, it also made the sale of the business even more painful.

Of significant note in the case study is the consideration the owner gave to the employees through his art collection. He had built up a significant collection of art, and many of the paintings had hung in the company's different offices. All the employees who had worked there for more than five years were allowed to choose one painting. As highlighted previously, one primary challenge of loss is the ability to successfully transition through the mourning process with the goal of achieving recovery and subsequent growth. The pain of the transition and the mourning process can be minimized by introducing a transitional object. According to Winnicott (1971) transitional objects, by definition, provide support and comfort during times of challenge and stress. There is no more significant stress than loss. He provided the perfect transitional object for his employees through the selfless distribution of his art works. This provided the employees with a gentle reminder of the greatness of the organization as well as a demonstrating the monumental appreciation of the owner for the dedication and commitment of the employees.

References

Coad, A. (2013). Death is not a success: Reflections on business exit. *International Small Business Journal, 32*(7), pp. 721–732.

Grady, V, and Grady, J (2012). The relationship of Bowlby's Attachment Theory to the persistent failure of organizational change initiatives. *Journal of Change Management*, DOI: 10.1080/14697017.2012.728534.

Handler, W.C. (1990). Succession in family firms: a mutual role adjustment between entrepreneur and next generation family members. *Entrepreneurship Theory and Practice 15*, pp. 37–51.

Randall, D.M. (1987). Commitment and the organization: The organization man revisited. *Academy of management review, 12*(3), pp. 460–471.

Salvato, C., Chirico, F. and Sharma, P. (2010). A farewell to the business: Championing exit and continuity in entrepreneurial family firms. *Entrepreneurship and Regional Development, 22*(3–4), pp. 321–348.

Sharma, P. (2004). An overview of the field of family business studies: Current status and directions for the future. *Family Business Review, 17*(1), pp. 1–36.

Winnicott, D.W. (1971). *Playing and Reality*. London: Tavistock Publications Ltd.

Woods, J.A., Dalziel, T. and Barton, S.L. (2012). Escalation of commitment in private family businesses: The influence of outside board members. *Journal of Family Business Strategy, 3*(1), pp. 18–27.

14 Having power or strategizing authority?

Gry Osnes

If you want to know who controls you, see who you may not criticize.

Tacitus

Oh, how hard it is to part with power! This, one has to understand.

Aleksandr Solzhenitsyn

Introduction

In family business research the link between family business and conflict has been explored in dèpth. It often focuses on tensions between the generations (e.g., Handler, 1990; Lansberg, 1999) and rivalry, envy between siblings and/ or conflicts of Oedipal origin (Kets de Vries, 1996). These are often seen as inherent to inter-generational (Salvato and Melin, 2008) and intra-generational relationships. We found these problematic dynamics in what were otherwise very successful family-owned businesses. They included rivalry that could have led to the collapse of a collaborative ownership and the undermining of the leadership; founders reluctant to let the next generation have control; and tension and family conflict originating in not giving sisters or daughters equal rights. All these are threats to the family cohesion and a successful succession outcome.

We found one common denominator that prevented these dynamics spiralling out of control and by this stagnate or destroy the business. All the families would spend time thinking through and negotiating the authority individuals or the family would have. It would be an ongoing process and would be monitored. This chapter focuses on how strategizing authority prevented negative succession dynamics, further rivalry and conflict. Such negotiation was also the source of innovative and win-win arrangements, and new entrepreneurship. We found that, when conflicts and tensions arose, the family would generate an intervention or action that focused on the tasks for ownership and the business. Strategizing the tension between individuals' drive, family ownership goals and business goals would lead to new entrepreneurship as a solution. Further, this proved to be a healthy mechanism for managing what can be, in successful family ownership, a concentration of prestige, wealth and power that can have a detrimental effect on the human mind. In this way they would rework the authority arrangements (Hirschhorn, 1998) within the family in relation to ownership goals and business goals. This would be the basis for balancing and aligning a sense of entitlement with the reality principle of business needs and goals.

The strategizing of authority creates a safety net on three levels:

1   At the individual level, the dialogue with and consideration of others creates internal voices that points out complexities and interdependencies between family members and others. This counteracts hubris and egocentricity.
2   At the group level the family explores successes and mistakes, and individual members' strengths and weaknesses, in order to find complementarities and identify gaps in their abilities. This would often lead to a distribution of power within the family. In this way control and a sense of entitlement would not be taken for granted by any member. The distribution of power would be thought about regarding what it would be used for, what the task was and the influence that would be wielded. The power is the negotiated and strategized, not unconditionally held.
3   At the organizational level, this strategizing of authority identified active owners and gave clarity to their role; likewise to family members as leaders, who had insight into their own strengths and weaknesses. They would not necessarily be more competent or skilled than competing non-family members, but they would be committed.

The strategizing and distribution of authority at these three levels would in our cases prevent commitment escalation (Salvato, Chirico, and Sharma, 2010) and group-think (Kahneman, 2003). Commitment escalation and group-think can lead a group or business down a strategic course that, for an outsider, increasingly seems doomed while the insiders, here the family or management team, seem unable to change to another course.

Power and authority

In the public arena, news media, films and plays the family owner is often depicted as a system with a centralized power structure around one person. This might often be the reality of how many family ownerships function but we found this rarely to be the case. When the family started, openly, to describe how influence was managed another picture emerged. We do not know how representative this picture is. Media and/or tradition might shape a taken-for-granted assumption of what we came to call *monolithic control*, one person controlling the business ownership. An illustration of this is the famous industrial owner, the Wallenberg family in Sweden. They control a substantial part of the companies on the Swedish stock market and have been family owners, and a dynasty, since the early nineteenth century. Over several generations power has been distributed between two brothers or two cousins (Lindgren, 2002) in addition to having powerful CEO and non-family leaders. Other recent research findings, covering a big selection of cases, supports this. Family firms that share management between several family members perform better than those who centralize management in the hands of one family member (Kellermanns et al., 2012). Kellermanns also found that family firms did better when ownership was concentrated in a single generation, rather than spread out between two or more generations. The conclusion being that while dispersed management control within a generation can be an advantage, the sharing of ownership across generations can cause problems. We found the same and will explore how strategizing of authority lead to solutions of a paradox between power and authority.

Differentiation of power and authority

We build on an intellectual tradition that regards authority as the influence that has been negotiated within a system (e.g., Clegg, 2010). This system can be in an organization of any type where there are boundaries, roles and interconnections. Based on this, we define 'power' as influence that has *not* been negotiated. Power within an organization can be used with both good or bad intentions and outcomes. There is also a differentiation between an individual's power and authority and a system's power and authority.

Table 14.1 shows the difference we apply to power and authority. In cell (a) influence is in the form of system power consisting of a legal structure and sovereignty in ownership. Legal structures, such as private ownership, are socially constructed and managed differently within different regions. Within the legal framework a person, such as a member of an owning family, need not negotiate when they exercise these ownership rights. This power can be internalized and give people, correctly or not, an experience of someone being powerful. The mind is slippery in this regard. We are often acutely aware of the social hierarchy we are surrounded by and attribute power as inevitable when the reality is that it is constructed in our minds. In this way we might relinquish the right to question or critique where power has become a habit, not a reality bounded in legal rights. It can be regarded as inevitable or 'true' and a part of an unchanging reality. Questioning it can often be taboo and will be sanctioned, seen as a lack of respect and/or ignored. In cell (b) we see system authority. This is the negotiated organizational assignment of roles. Ideally this is the negotiated organization with interconnection of roles and boundaries created for task accomplishment. When negotiated and focusing on task it is system authority, when taken for grated and based on entitlement it is system power.

Within family ownership the tension between power and authority is unique compared to other types of businesses. The family, depending on the legal structures and local customs, has a legal claim of ownership. There are many regulatory variations that can limit this, such as employee rights of representation at the board in Scandinavia and Germany. An extreme case was the Chinese

Table 14.1 Differentiating between power and authority

	Type of influence	
	Not negotiated: *Power*	*Negotiated in relation to task:* *Authority*
System level	(a) System power Individual or collective sovereignty in membership or ownership. Legal structures as private ownership. Others are norms taken for granted or unexplored assumptions about organization.	(b) System authority The assigned roles and boundaries of an organization or a business. The influence or roles are created and negotiated in relationship to tasks for the organization or the family.
Individual level	(c) Individual power The will and capacity for self-creation and to promote self-interest, also in relation to collective interest. Safeguarded by individual rights or based in the emotional and intellectual resources of the individual. Limited by power structures at the systemic level (a) and 'as if'.	(d) Individual authority Created in interpersonal relationships when in work roles and can be informal. Negotiation in entering a role and negotiations in developing the role.
Dynamics	A focus on entitlement as based in legal rights or in a sense of justice. Can be pathological as a focus on one's own, hubristic entitlement.	A focus on task, where tasks are defined as contributing to the overall goal of the business or the family. Influence is measured in terms of the importance for task accomplishment and the capacity the individual has for accomplishment.

case where the founder established the business as an employee of the commune and no private ownership existed in China at that time. In a commune system the founder's successor was to be elected by the employees, who in this instance chose his son as the next leader. After this succession the political climate and economic policies changed so that the family could own several companies as described in Chapter 6.

Within the regulatory limitations, if they exist, the family themselves has to manage the power and authority dynamics otherwise regulated by the governance systems of publicly quotes companies. The tension between having power, at the system level, and creating authority is significant and creates complicated dynamics. We will show how different families, when encountering family and business conflicts and problematic issues, shifted from having power to strategizing authority. In some cases this involved creating new entrepreneurship that would alter the distribution of system power within the family or the strategizing of authority within the business. The focus in strategizing authority is not entitlement but on the tasks the family set for themselves in their ownership, furthering the business goals. Analysing the task, and the challenges involved in achieving them, is the reference point for how influence within the family and with other leaders is aligned.

Succession as construction of authority

Different elements of authority are managed through the succession. It defines and creates the connection between individuals, the family and the business. The succession can be seen as a process where one can renegotiate, and also transform the top leadership role. It is reliant on those involved being able to imagine new possibilities and contain and negotiate difficult issues. Creating a dialogue so as to negotiate the authority within the family has in general been advocated in the family business literature: either as corporate governance structures (Lansberg, 1999) or a family council (Carlock, 2001). While formalizing such dialogues certainly helps, some of the families were able to do this informally. Whatever type of structure the family use, the negotiation and alignment of authority is a process both about individual drive and about family and business tasks. It will lead to different decisions that will influence renewal of entrepreneurship and the decision making structure within the family and within the business.

Succession is discussed in more detail in Chapters 5 and 16. In Chapter 5 we focus on succession and the individual transition, and personal relationships, and how it was managed very well in a case that had all the potential to be a very destructive process. In Chapter 16 we describe the particular elements, or building blocks, in strategizing a succession process. Further it explores succession as a construction of authority and leadership that manages personal issues, rivalry and competition between family members. In this chapter we will explore issues around the individual having unconditional power in terms of personal development.

The strategizing of authority

The different types of power and authority are dynamic in nature and shifts can occur due to events or be created as part of a strategic process. A mind-state of power and a sense of entitlement as owners can be handled within the family as it strategizes to assign authority, defining roles linked to tasks. The main anchor for authority, and how it is strategized, is to focus on the ownership tasks for the family business and for the business. We had only one case where a family member had sovereign power for a long period of time and it eventually created a problem for the family and the business. Another case had a founder couple that clung to the power they had. In the first case the family member was dismissed and a distribution of influence between the remaining siblings developed. Both these two cases had a sibling group that negotiated authority in accordance with the values and goals of the family business. Hubris or a sense of entitlement was then not allowed to put the business as risk. Roles they then created for themselves reflected their respective talents covering the main leadership tasks of the company. The strategizing of authority would resolve a threat without the conflict spiralling out of control.

Managing the threat of hubris

Hubris is associated with an absence of humility and a sense of being 'intoxicated by power'. It has common elements with narcissistic personality traits which feature, for example, poor decision making or impulse control, weak modulation of aggression and lack of appropriate empathy (Russell, 2011). When a family member acts as owner, and has important roles within the business, groups and non-family employees can feel inhibited from criticizing them or articulating counter arguments. Other external stakeholders might also not have available channels for concern or critique. Strategies on dispersing leadership, within the family and with non-family leaders, counteract this. This is not only a risk for the business but also for the individual involved. It is a challenge to manage oneself if one has power and absolute control. Over time one rarely notices how it slowly erodes one's judgement and empathy. Hubris develops over time, starts with initial success and then confidence, becoming overconfidence, impaired judgement and excessive risk taking. This is famously illustrated in the Greek myth about Icarus, the son of Daedalus, who dared to fly too near the sun on wings of feathers and wax (Petit and Bollaert, 2012).

Box 14.1 Routes in strategizing authority

In our cases, we found two routes for how authority could be negotiated or created (see Figure 14.1):

1   Negotiation route: The individual family members can negotiate among themselves, and clarify the authority they would have within the family. This would determine how the family would authorize itself to act within the business. It includes negotiating within the business, with employees and non-family leaders. While the family has a strong hand within the business, they will seek to retain loyal leaders and talented people by giving space for their roles and aspirations for interesting careers. This route is the individual and family group creating roles and authority where autonomy, entitlement and influence is negotiated within the family.

2   *Entrepreneurship route*: Individual members or sub-groups in the family, or, indeed, the family acting as a whole, can seek new opportunities. With more entrepreneurial achievements one can increase individual authority without having to negotiate the ownership of an existing business in the family ownership group. Success with new ventures or innovation (new product, process and/or market) can be developed within the existing business or as a co-investment and

later be integrated into the established business or a family-owned business. We found cases of both new ventures that were integrated into the family business and the establishment of new ventures that lead to cluster ownership.

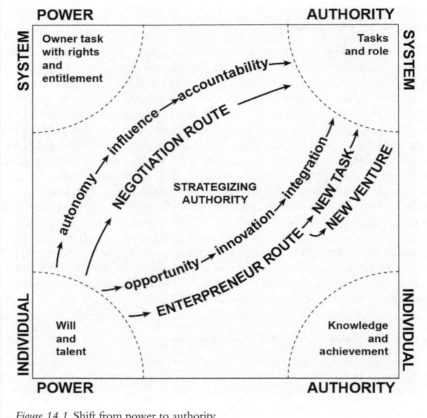

Figure 14.1 Shift from power to authority

Cluster ownership

Cluster ownership (see Chapter 6) seems to be a very efficient way of avoiding rivalry between siblings and between generations (Michael-Tsabari, Labaki and Zachary, 2014). It features separation of assets while retaining sufficiently close cooperation that the businesses still operate as a unit. The way authority was strategized and created followed different paths in the two cases we are considering. In the Chinese case the owner retired, handed over the executive leadership to a son, and started a new business with his second son. The father would not be a rival to his son but instead gained new power and authority with his second son. The power shift consisted of relinquishing system power, while building on individual power, and establishing and implementing individual authority through entrepreneurship. In this case such initiatives resulted in a cluster of companies that would cooperate. Family ownership and entrepreneurship thereby expanded a domain, and in so doing diminished rivalry and envy between and within generations.

In the Israeli case, the brothers who took over their parents' business in Jerusalem divided the business into three parts. It prevented rivalry and tension between them, as they had different attitudes towards risk. One brother who was entrepreneurial and liked risk took over the hotel part of the business. New entrepreneurship allowed him, with external financing, to increase this part of the business into a chain of hotels. The other brother took over the tour-agency and a bus company. To the outside observer, and to customers, the three companies would operate as one unit. In this way, in the businesses as a domain of power and legal entitlement, system power was divided. At the same time they built an organization of operation that together used these three assets and by this authorized themselves into positions of leadership, employed other non-family leaders and gave their children access to employment in the organization. The family distributed authority between the brother and other non-family leaders. They would only act as owners in a coordinated way to maintain the family's principles; for example, if they had employees who were intolerant and did not accept the necessity of working with people of different religions, they would have to leave.

Inclusion of gender diversity

With social change and women becoming more empowered, a shift seems to have taken place in family owners who had traditionally preferred male leaders. The strategizing of authority so as to include sisters was achieved in two different ways in our cases. In the German case, Chapter 15, the family revisited the patriarchal family tradition and acknowledged that a female co-founder, and her daughter, had been in informal but crucial roles. By dividing up the roles and giving a sister a role on the executive board the authority the daughter had developed was acknowledged and led to a distribution of control within the family.

A more entrepreneurial path was developed in China where a mother coached her daughter to start her own business. She started up an internet-based business that sold goods from the main family business that her parents owned and which was headed by her brother. She would be highly selective in the goods she selected from the family business and she would supplement it with wares from other suppliers. In this way she developed her small business that she would later sell to her brother. This contributed to the start of a distribution channel for the business within China. Her entrepreneurship led to her having more authority within the family and a supporting role to her brother. Through entrepreneurship she increased her individual authority and this had implications for her influence in the ownership forum.

Use of non-family based authority and competence

In all the cases a non-family leader had, over a long time period, sometimes as much as 20–30 years, a crucial and influential role beyond the actual job they were hired to do. In two of the cases a top leader the family trusted mentored a successor groomed for the top leadership role or already in the top leadership role. In the Israeli and French cases, a non-family managing director had both management and strategic responsibilities. Later, in Chapter 17, we will discuss the role of a non-family Chair of Board in two family-owned businesses. These leaders were trusted to align with the family's interests and uphold family values. Non-family leaders would also respect, and work with the family, in strategizing how commercial success was linked to the social identity of the family. These leaders would have individual and system authority based on strategizing, in partnership with the family.

Another dimension of non-family authority is when the younger generation gain work experience away from their family business. Externally developed competence and skills enhances the family member's individual authority and, if they later work for the family firm, they more easily fit into the organizational structure. It increases their status within the family when competing, in a good way, or when power and entitlement is distributed within the family. Many of our next generation had done this for shorter periods. In the French business the children had very successful careers outside the family. Importantly it enabled them to tackle a difficult situation with their parents and to be tolerant, and not too power-greedy.

Storytelling and politics

The difficulty of acknowledging the reality of who has power and authority was shown in how one of our families, in its family narrative, excluded important aspects of the founder story. When the researcher asked in depth about the early years and the founding it transpired that the children were very much co-founders with their parents. As a teenager a son had spotted the possibility of buying a small shop, which was later expanded into a chain of shops. Both the children were actively working with the parents in the early days, something that was not reflected in the founder narrative. The established parental narrative, in which they were the sole founders, would in this case maintain a boundary between the generations in order to conform to a conventional family structure. Excluding their offspring's crucial role in the founding created tension between the generations as it was used to emphasize that they did not to have any entitlement to the business. Eventually, a good strategy in any case, the children would work and have leadership roles outside the business with stellar careers. The brother became a CEO in his in-laws' business that he grew to a global business. The sister became an entrepreneur of what is now a global luxury brand. When they returned to the family firm they had the authority to manage difficult parents and take on leadership and active ownership roles.

Use of exit roles

We have, in several of the cases and other chapters, illustrated the use of exit roles for the founder or former owners. It involves a relinquishing of the power of ownership. The former owner might start a new business, as in the Chinese case, or start in another middle management role as in the Israeli and French cases. In the US case there was little opportunity for retirement for a series of family founders, as they needed the income, and new entrepreneurship left the owner with the original business while the second and third generations built up new businesses. In this way the owner or leader did not lose an active work life but stayed involved. The founders had to accept relinquishing control they had had and, as they would be active in exit roles, the new owners would have to accept the former generation was watching them.

The need to have total control can be driven by a need for acknowledgement and to be in the centre of things. It can feel intrusive to have others questioning and being able to criticize or question one's actions. Between the two positions of either the former or the new generation having total control is a period of transition that can take years and will require tensions and ego-needs to be managed carefully. The second generation Israeli owner who, with his brother, is planning to create exit roles and hand over the top leadership roles to the third generation described such tension. With humour the tension, affection and accountability between generations is tolerated. Their mother and founder, now 90 years old, are still active and working in the business. As he, now planning his own exit role, explains:

> My mother is head of accounts, and she still finds these mistakes, I do not know how she does it! She then wants to explain to whomever has done it what the mistake was. She gets someone to come and fetch you. This happens to everyone, family members and employees. If one of my children or their cousins is told to get me – I know what it is before it's said. It's a glow in how they move or their voice – 'Tata wants to see you!!'

> I'm now 70 years old. I do not want to be in such an operational owner and leadership role anymore. My brother and I have discussed this and I

took two of our children aside and talked to them. We want to hand over the operational leadership roles. They asked me 'What about Tata?'

I told them 'Do not draw the wrong conclusion, I will not retire, I want a role where I can do more of the things I like, developing other things. I will also sit and comment on the mistakes you make.'

Transferring control of ownership

Sibling ownership groups and control

When founders have relinquished ownership control, the next generation develop their own system for how control and power should be exercised. In the Israeli case they divided the business they inherited into three companies that operated as one business unit. The ownership of separate parts was arranged so that each brother owned a part of the business that suited their appetites for risk and need for profit. It worked extremely well, and their children would have the opportunity to take up roles, and develop new business units, within a business run by an uncle or their own father.

Sometimes an owner generation constructs the ownership so that one individual in the next generation will have full ownership control. In our research this practice was only used in the Swedish case and it was changed in the third generation. For the third generation the business would be controlled and lead by three siblings. Family cohesion made it possible to take fast and forceful decisions, which is one of the competitive advantages for a family business. Ward (2004) discusses another option: the use of a golden share as another strategy for control that can be used by a sibling group. One of the owners is then able to act on behalf of other passive owners. This can be created through consent between the siblings, or by transferring the shares, with one member inheriting control of the company. Another option for siblings is that they are co-managing partners, an option chosen in many of our cases. An investment partnership in which the siblings do not have leadership roles within a company is an alternative. We did not have any such cases, but cluster ownership with family members leading different companies would be an alternative model.

Cousin ownership groups

Among cousins the control and voting on ownership strategies has to be different. Ward (2004) showed how more sophisticated voting arrangements and systems of influence have to be developed in a cousin consortium so as to maintain good ownership of complex businesses. A golden share, as described above, is not recommended for a cousin consortium; in such a dispersed group it is likely to lead to conflict and a lack of real authority on the part of the holder of the golden share. Ward suggests a family holding company, or cluster ownership, entrepreneurial venture fund and/or organizing the company as if it were a public company. When a family-owned business increases in size and complexity, with an increase in profit, establishing a family office for the third or fourth generation is a practice that is increasing in popularity. Family members choosing careers outside the family business can have their wealth managed by the family office employees. A family office enables the family to create a support system of employees who can help owners to develop new entrepreneurship or philanthropic activities.

Warning: the construction of power in a golden share

We will use a case from the USA to illustrate the downside of using a golden share system. A founder together with the second generation of the family had created a very successful business and the profit had been channeled into new businesses. The third generation took over a big and relatively diversified business in oil–related activities, transport and property. Two sibling groups, related as cousins to each other, owned the business. Sibling group A controlled a small majority of the shares. In this controlling sibling group one of the siblings had, on loan from his father, a golden share. In this way the controlling owner in sibling group A would control his siblings' and cousins' ownership. While this monolithic control was intended to prevented passive ownership. It created conflicts and, rather ironically, also passivity. At some point one of the cousins in sibling group B wanted to have more control of the risk he was exposed to and/or be bought out. Between such a diverse group of cousins there were differing notions and levels of willingness to take risks, but the minority owners had little influence. Hostile personal relationships made negotiations impossible. The arrangement involving the use of a golden share was also humiliating for the sibling group as it assumed incompetence when considering risk willingness. Years of court battles led to a gradual and partial process of dis-investment for one cousin. With such a public family conflict, including press coverage, the family spent resources on lawyers and family time on the conflict. The use of a golden share can, under certain circumstances, work for sibling collaborations (Ward, 2004). In this case, however, it created conflict as the cousins had not been given the opportunity to negotiate and agree on the how the controls were to be constructed. The following is a description of how both the negotiation route and the new entrepreneurship route were obstructed by this golden share and its rigid and dysfunctional application.

Development of hubris

The controlling owner in sibling group A had mixed success in the business ventures he controlled, and in the investments he made, on behalf of the siblings and cousins. He built up one company, followed by a very profitable sale, but later there was a very badly judged investment. Despite this, his brothers had never posed a threat to him, nor challenged his role as active owner. For the controlling sibling the combination of an initial spectacular success, then an equally spectacular failure. It followed the classic pattern of success leading to overconfidence, poor risk-assessment and partly blaming others for the failures. With no-one, except an ageing father, to rein in the power in the golden share, it became a classic display of hubris developing. After huge losses on investment more senior and experienced non-executive board members were added to the board. The controlling owner was Chair of the Board and with this he kept the final control. At the same time he had, due to the failed investment, lost prestige in the business context. This loss triggered him to compensate by wielding his power within the sibling group and included attempts to control the inheritance from the other brothers to their children. As there was no safety net or balance of his power within the sibling group strong emotions and bullying, rooted in childhood relationships, were re-enacted.

Unconscious dynamics and power

A mind-set of hubris and narcissism is unconscious, and features an oscillation between overconfidence and a sense of inferiority. Hubris and overconfidence compensate for a sense of inferiority or vulnerability. The person harboring these tendencies is at best marginally aware of the emotions, and how they guide their thoughts and strategizing. When there are weak, or absent, checks and balances on the power person a capacity for good judgement deteriorates. Hubris includes increased arrogance and a focus on finding faults and limitations in others issues. It is difficult for employees to raise such sensitive subjects in discussion. Friends or colleagues might hint at these dynamics. If prominent hubris is displayed it requires quite robust interventions to prevent them spiralling out of control. The force necessary, and pain involved, increases when there is a lot of power and status involved. It will be all-but impossible for employees, and both difficult and high-risk for close friends to address or correct this dynamic.

Transferring dysfunctions to the next generation

In this USA case the controlling owner developed a wish to transfer the golden share to one of his children, a member of the fourth generation. Again hubris, accompanied by an undercurrent of inferiority, creates wishful thinking. In this way the fourth generation was planned to have an owner that would not need to negotiate and control his siblings', cousin' and distant cousins' wealth. He would have a shareholding of only 10 per cent, but a golden share that would give him control of the wealth of cousins with a larger shareholding. Implemented in this way a golden share is a poisoned chalice both for the family member with the control and for the cousins, and for family cohesion.

It could prevent both the controlling family member and the other owners from developing and establishing their own authority and accountability among themselves. It further prevents developing arrangements independent from those of former generations.

Autonomy and influence over own wealth

When issues of autonomy is not negotiated it will almost certainly lead to conflict. The lack of strategized authority allows for interpersonal tensions, and irrational and unconscious emotions, to spill over and ruin family relationships. Such destructive spirals divert attention from more constructive strategies and the opportunities of creating new types of family activities. As occurred with the third generation in this case, the lack of family cohesion could obstruct innovation and cooperation around experimenting with new entrepreneurship. Handing over power in this way intrinsically obstructs the delicate and slow process of building and maintaining trust within the next generation. It undermines the efforts of owners in the succeeding generation to build their own authority, and with this, collectively, a system that allocates authority with a focus on business challenges and tasks.

Afterthoughts and reflections

Reality orientation: business and ownership tasks

A part of the process of strategizing authority is to focus on tasks beyond one's own wishes and needs. It enables the group and individual to develop a good understanding of reality, and to understand complexity. It also creates a safety net for the individual so they do not become hubristic, narcissistic and egocentric. Such dynamics are famously shown in Shakespeare's plays about how power affects the mind-set of kings, or contenders for powerful positions, when power is concentrated. The contenders display hubris and lack of empathy for others. In the golden share case in the USA, a dynamic emerged in which childhood drama and relationships would be re-enacted and played out. The price for the family was high. It led to conflict and break down of a relationship between cousins and lack of cohesion between siblings. An individual or a group that for a while acts in a hubristic manner can be corrected and learn from mistakes. This process would lead to greater capacity for reality orientation and strategic capacity. Hubris and lack of strategic capacity has often been witnessed in family businesses, but not exclusively so; analysis of the financial crisis, and its causes in the culture and leadership in the financial sector, shows that any concentration of power can encourage hubris and narcissism. When not corrected or challenged these features become the habits of dominant individuals and groups. At this stage the process is not easily reversible, unless the individuals are willing to commit to processes that improve self-awareness, such as extensive coaching or therapy.

Flexibility in the balancing of authority and power

A note on what is often referred to as maintaining family harmony: we think that phrase can idealize a state of affairs. We prefer to use family cohesion. There will be rivalries and conflict in families; with sufficient scrutiny one might struggle to say that any family is harmonious, or at least always harmonious. In addition, ownership of a family business will increase the stakes for what the family is engaged in; any underlying, or unconscious conflict and tension might erupt and be triggered by the ownership. In this way the family owner, particularly in relation to influence and power, has to struggle with issues that families seek to resolve in counselling.

In balancing of use of power and creation of authority, the family is again confronted with conflicting options and scenarios. To have and act from power, rather than negotiating, is efficient in the short term but is seductive, even addictive. It can trigger, not solve, issues of destructive competition, envy and jealousies. These are well-known threats to good judgement, not only in family businesses but within leadership and strategy in general.

The investment in creating and strategizing authority can be significant: the process can be slow and include long and elaborate discussions, examining the contextual reality, negotiating of influence or authority given to a role and person. It is a long-term strategy that will build family cohesion. It can enable the family to acknowledge things about themselves as a family and as individuals that in other families are kept hidden and never explored. As such, strategizing authority is a development process for the individuals and the family.

References

Carlock, R. and Ward, J.L. (2001). *Strategic Planning for the Family Business: Parallel planning to unify the family and business*. Basingstoke, Hampshire, UK: Palgrave.

Clegg, S. (2010). The state, power and agency: missing in action in institutional theory? *Journal of Management Inquiry, 19*, 4–12.

Handler, W.C. (1990). Succession in family firms: a mutual role adjustment between entrepreneur and next generation family members. *Entrepreneurship Theory and Practice, 15*, 37–51.

Hirschhorn, L., 1998. *Reworking Authority: Leading and following in the post-modern organization* (Vol. 12). Cambridge, MA, US: MIT Press.

Kets de Vries, M.F. (1994). The leadership mystique. *The Academy of Management Executive, 8*, 73–89, doi: 10.5465/AME.1994.9503101181.

Lansberg, I. (1999). *Succeeding Generations: Realizing the dream of families in business*. Boston, MA, US: Harvard Business School Press.

Lindgren, H. (2002). Succession strategies in a large family businesses group: the case of the Swedish Wallenberg family. Paper, Sixth European Business History Association Annual Congress in Helsinki, August 22–24.

Kahneman, D. (2003). A perspective on judgment and choice: mapping bounded rationality. *American Psychologist, 58*(9), 697.

Kellermanns, F.W., Eddleston, K.A., Sarathy, R. and Murphy, F. (2012). Innovativeness in family firms: a family influence perspective. *Small Business Economics, 38*, 85–101.

Michael-Tsabari, N., Labaki, R., and Zachary, R.K. (2014). Toward the Cluster Model: the family firm's entrepreneurial behaviour over generations. *Family Business Review*, *27*(2), 163.

Petit, V. and Bollaert, H. (2012). Flying too close to the sun? Hubris among CEOs and how to prevent it. *Journal of Business Ethics*, *108*(3), 265–283.

Russell, G. (2011). Psychiatry and politicians: the 'hubris syndrome'. *The Psychiatrist*, *35*(4), 140–145.

Salvato, C. and Melin, L. (2008). Creating value across generations in family-controlled businesses: the role of family social capital. *Family Business Review*, *21*, 259–276, doi:10.1177/08944865080210030107.

Salvato, C., Chirico, F. and Sharma, P. (2010). A farewell to the business: championing exit and continuity in entrepreneurial family firms. *Entrepreneurship and Regional Development*, *22*(3–4), 321–348.

Ward, J.L. (2004). *Perpetuating the Family Business: 50 lessons learned from long lasting, successful families in business*. New York: Palgrave Macmillan.

15 Gender in family entrepreneurship

Mona Haug

She is an undercover boss, because she has close contacts with the workforce and knows how they tick.

In this family women power has always been there, but it was covert at the beginning; now it is overt.

Third-generation family members

Introduction

In this chapter we look at how some unique aspects of gender in family-owned businesses (Casperz and Thomas, 2015) set them apart from other types of organizations. We give a brief overview of the mainstream theories of leadership and gender. Some of these, including the 'great man' theory, lie at the heart of leadership and management theory and represent different schools of thought (Bolden et al., 2003). The great man theory, which conjures up an image of a western male military hero, has strongly influenced leadership thinking (Collinson, 2011). This influence was demonstrated by research at Colombia Business School in New York, the Howard/Heidi research study. Students were asked to evaluate a non-existing person, 'Howard's' résumé'. They considered it impressive and pronounced Howard a leader they would like to work for. A peer group was given the same résumé with a slight change in name – the non-existent Howard became Heidi. Students evaluated her as equally effective but rather selfish and someone they would be less eager to work for (Muir, 2012). The stereotypes demonstrated in this study are that we align our perception of certain characteristics, competences and associations with male and female leaders (Collinson, 2011), regardless of their effectiveness.

Traditional western male leadership thinking is embedded in manifold ways. Communal traits, such as caring and a relationship orientation, are associated with women, while agentic traits, such as decisiveness and straightforwardness, are more likely to be associated with men. A female leader may receive positive feedback on the way she fulfils her leadership role by giving clear, strategic and goal-oriented objectives (Eagly and Karau, 2002). However, at the same time she might score negatively, and be perceived to be too dominant and aggressive.

Gender in family businesses

In the same way that traditional and mainstream leadership and management theory focuses on the (male) individual as the sole source of leadership, the early family business literature focuses on male entrepreneurship (Brush, 2006). Even though entrepreneurship itself is clearly defined as gender-neutral, it often leads to a neglect of the role of female co-founders in family-owned companies (Barrett and Moores, 2009). Despite this, several studies report that women are increasingly taking on powerful roles as owners or family business leaders (Karataş-Özkan, Erdoğan and Nicolopoulou, 2011). Feminine characteristics, such as being more trustful, listening and inquiring more, enhance a family business when they are related to information sharing, developing relationships and empowering employees (Vera and Dean, 2005). Some new research indicates that, as owners, women take choices that align themselves to such sharing, development and empowerment (Remery, Matser and Flören, 2014). Women in Dutch family businesses preferred shared ownership while men preferred full ownership. Women's preferred transformational leadership styles make them more open to other people's opinions and encourage them to make collective decisions. According to Vera and Dean (2005), women prefer to take their time to make decisions that will benefit their people and not just their business.

Jimenesz (2009) reviewed research on woman and their roles in family businesses, focusing on the obstacles they face and the positive aspects of their presence. She argues that daughters received greater recognition of their skills and competences when they joined the family business after previously gaining work experience outside the firm. Also, their leadership roles were strengthened when they were officially supported by their father. One example is the takeover of the medium-sized machine tools construction company Trumpf in Ditzingen, Germany, which was passed from father to daughter. The owner of this well-established company published a book in which he set down his reasons for passing the torch to his daughter and not to his son (Leibinger, 2010).

Surprises in our best practice cases

In all our best practice cases a couple had founded the company and worked together in the business over a lifetime. Male and female co-founders were united by a shared dream that strengthened the families' determination to achieve and sustain their objectives. This trust and collaboration was the glue that held them together and the basis for how they transferred the company, their management style and the company philosophy to the next generation.

Among our cases were co-founders of then-new ventures that dated back to the beginning of the nineteenth century. Over the last 10 years many women, members of the third and fourth generations of these families, have assumed powerful positions alongside or in the place of their brothers. One Swedish case features a couple who started the business, a second generation of male leadership with little female involvement and a third generation in which a sister acts as co-owner and chair of the board. In the cases observed in Tanzania, Israel, the US and the UK, a founder couple started the business with the wife active in key operational roles, back-office functions such as accounts and finance, developing the business model or as the main entrepreneur. The roles of these women developed differently but were often flexible, so they could work from home. In two of the cases the woman was the sole owner.

These women took part in the decision-making that has traditionally been seen as a male domain (the responsibility of their husbands or brothers). In contrast to what is often assumed, the role of the women in these cases is not that of 'Chief Emotional Officer'. Recent research supports the notion of hidden female champions (Boulouta, 2013) and suggests that they are now stepping into the limelight (Koenig et al., 2011). It seems that women also continue to take on leadership roles that are more culturally aligned with female characteristics. One of these is the strategic use of communication channels. This can be observed in the Swedish case, where the CEO's sister communicated the company's philosophy by sharing it with the staff. In the German case it was also the CEO's sister who created a bond between management and staff by greeting employees personally and remembering and asking about their family events and issues. She also communicated the management's intentions to the workforce to find out what they thought about them and whether they would be supported by the staff. She would share her knowledge with her brother, who acted upon it.

Female leadership in family ownership

The co-founder couple

Although in all our cases a founding couple started the business together, the most striking example was a business started in the early 1930s in what was then Palestine, a region with little institutional development, for example in the educational sector, and where women had few rights and roles beyond getting married and producing children. As in other cases, this couple came from a lower middle-class or working-class background, but unusually for this time and location, the wife was instrumental in starting the business. The following quote shows her reflection on making an unusual choice for a woman. At the beginning she started to develop a support function for their guide business:

> My family, you know, still old-fashioned, they said, girls, why does she have to finish her education? She will be a housewife. And whatever she learned now, that is enough. So they told me either you stay at home, no more and you do nothing, or you get married. And when my husband came to ask for my hand, and there was such a difference between ages…. Just sitting there and having more and more kids. But marrying my husband it has great influence on me. He really helped me a lot. And encouraged me.

There [was no] woman here that did what I did. No one. It wasn't easy for a woman here, in Arab culture. To go to the airport with groups and to bring groups to the house. It wasn't easy.

And our clients who used to come home, I used to take them here, to my home, give them tea. And every tourist who comes would like to go to a native home and see how people live. And this way we built a name.

This female co-founder states that, thanks to her husband's open-mindedness, she was able to contribute to the business. Unlike other men, her husband did not follow the traditional rules and guidelines of a culture that discouraged women from working. If he had, they would not have been as successful as they are now. For them it was a win-win situation. The husband supported the wife's personal development in spite of cultural circumstances. She in turn accelerated the business turnover by offering a unique experience to the customers whom she invited into their home.

A woman working as equal partner can be a new concept within many cultures. In West Germany, for example, until 1958 men had sole authority over their wives and children. A husband could allow his wife to work but he was in charge of her salary. It was not until 1969 that women were considered legally competent and until 1977 wives still needed the permission of their husbands to be able to work outside the home. However, the women in our case studies had always considered themselves valuable partners. It is remarkable that these founder couples stayed together for decades. The women knew that the family business was a pathway to increased wealth for themselves and their children. Their focus was on ensuring stable business growth, securing financial resources, increasing loyalty among employees by creating solid relationships and preparing their children for a future succession. The flexibility in a co-founder couple and in the context of social norms in the local environment is again described by the wife and co-founder from then Palestine:

Oh yes. Oh yes. Lots of gossip. I didn't care, I didn't mind. I did, I am not from Jerusalem. I am from Bethlehem, from Beit Jala, I was born in Beit Jala, so I didn't care. I didn't know anybody and until now I don't know. I don't visit people and nobody visits me because I didn't have time. First with the kids and then with the office. So I didn't care what people say. As long as I am satisfied and I know myself.

When my children were young until 10, 11 years old I wasn't working. My husband was doing the guide job and this is it. But after three of them were in university and the first one got married so young. I had nothing to do, I just had to do something.

Women as business developers and entrepreneurs

When something new is created, it is often difficult to pinpoint where and how the idea originated. It may have been a result of exchanges in dialogue, experimentation and testing ideas. In some of our cases it was unclear whether it was the husband or the wife who developed the business model and concept for the business. In some cases the founding couple contributed equally. In the case study of the Swedish entrepreneurial couple who developed breathing apparatus in their kitchen during the depression in the 1930s, it is not possible to make out who contributed what to the creative process, which involved discussion, experimentation, sewing together prototypes, testing facial fit on various members of the family and getting feedback from the miners who tested the equipment. In two of the cases it was the wife who had a deeply felt need to fill a gap or solve a problem that posed a great and intriguing challenge. In the Tanzanian case the wife established a safari camp in the bush, working with her husband. In the UK case the wife started what would become a prestigious French retail fashion business. In these cases the husbands were involved in financial and operational work. Again, the closeness of the couples in these cases meant that business models and business development grew out of dialogue rather than being one individual's brainchild.

Back-office roles

Most of the women in our studies held powerful roles as financial controllers or business developers. Crucially, the first role could be done from home and these women had little actual presence in the business. However, being able to leave and re-enter the business arena as they wanted or needed made it easier for women to hold on to their influential positions and balance family and work priorities. This would not only be the case for female co-founders (wives). In other cases women looked after the accounts, moving formally into a finance role as the business developed. This was work they could do at home and fit around the children's schedules. This meant that they were simultaneously in charge of the financial health of the family and the business. This often gave them the power to veto large expansions and investments, so they were also responsible for the risk management and economics of both the family and the business. We also found female co-founders who were instrumental in developing business models and business technology. In the US case the co-founder's daughter describes her mother as 'the brain behind the financial part of it', which is to address issues as they arise and communicate them openly and clearly.

Sisters and daughters

For the last 10 years the women in these businesses – sisters and daughters – have been contending for top leadership, or similarly powerful, positions. In the US, Chinese and Israeli cases, this was negotiated allowing for an absence of several years to have and raise children. This was not seen as a bar or disadvantage to re-entering the business or having a role as the future owner. This trend is part of social changes over the last 40 years that have benefited women, such as equal opportunities and possibilities for education. Women today have much more freedom to combine work and family roles.

In our cases it was seen as perfectly normal and acceptable for daughters to leave their roles in the company for shorter or longer periods of time to look after their children. In most of the businesses the daughters had been raised in the knowledge that they would be able to combine career and family. The strong links between power, trust and gender cleared the way for the successful relationship processes in the different case studies. In the American case (Chapter 3) the daughter had different ideas as to how to run her own business. It was an independent venture, owned solely by her, but supported by an investment from her parents, who helped her run it. This gave the daughter a head start, and the venture was only one of several businesses the family controlled. They had their different views and disagreements but were able to talk them through. Conflicting opinions about how to run the business were resolved through effective discussion. All parties had the same objective: to accumulate wealth by drawing on their individual strengths and synergies. As a daughter in one of the businesses expressed it:

> I had the children, stopped working for a while and came back again. It was only logical for my father that I would come back and I would always be present somehow. It was my objective too and we had outlined my path right at the beginning.

In the American case study, the daughter did the same demanding jobs as other employees, just as she had observed her parents doing. All the daughters in our cases experienced strong family bonding and the transparent value-driven leadership ethos by which their parents lived. Their preparation for the roles they would one day take up, if they wanted to, was a long-term strategy. In these case studies women profited from a balanced relationship with the founders that increased their sphere of influence (Jimenesz, 2009). As daughters they were treated equally with their brothers as part of the next generation of leaders, and given the same access to resources, knowledge and business acumen.

Female intergenerational transmission

There are several cases where women from different generations were involved in the business and encouraged a new dynamic, one which is, perhaps, often ignored. It was shown most markedly in the French case where the female owner was also the business developer and held the main competitive knowledge. She trained her daughter, taking her along on buying trips for the next season's fashion collections. Her daughter later developed another lifestyle business with her husband that was sold when they divorced. In this company the daughter's role as the innovator of scents and related beauty products was adapted to her role as a mother and she worked partly from home. (This company is now a global events business.) After this business was sold, she re-joined her mother's business, and she and her mother would then go on to help her daughter also come into the business, beginning with a modest role that her grandmother gave her in the storehouse of the flagship store. The granddaughter later joined her mother on the buying team for a new shop she had developed. After some years she was moved to the flagship-store purchasing team. In the US and Israeli cases we observed similar transitions between women of different generations.

Radical change in a German case

The German case study is a four-generation, medium-sized family business founded in 1952, with approximately 140 employees, which sells bottled mineral water from springs. It is currently in a long and well-prepared transition phase from the third to the fourth generation. Traditionally passed down from father to son, the business is now preparing for a shift to a gender-balanced leadership that will be continued by the next generation. The family that had originally owned the land on which the springs were found had left to make a living elsewhere when their house was damaged by bombing in April 1945. The founder of the company tested the water, bought the land and started his business on a shoestring. He had the water analysed and quickly understood that its high concentrations of magnesium and calcium were excellent properties for promoting sport and good health.

In this case the current leader realized that it was time to accentuate the transition to the fourth generation and finalize it within five or six years. The company had been passed down by his grandfather without debts and he sees it as his responsibility to do the same for the next generation. The current leader will be joined by one of his female cousins on the executive board in recognition of the accumulated power bases. Her younger cousin comments on her entry into the (so far) male-dominated patriarchal leadership system: 'It is sure to change, there is a new authorized signatory, she is sure to bring change and rock the boat a little, simply because I believe a woman does things differently.'

Intergenerational transmission

The son, the descendant of three generations of male leaders, exposed to a male leadership style and used to his father having the final say, has to share power and authority with his cousin. The young female leader comes from generations of women exercising power backstage and cannot draw on established role models. However, her mother predicted: 'In this family women power has always been there, but it was covert at the beginning; now it is overt'.

This female leader, the niece of the CEO, has still not entered the company as a major decision-maker, and for now remains in the background. Her female cousin, by contrast, is becoming CFO. Her mother considers this as smoothing the pathway for her daughter, who will have the chance to lead the company within the next 10 years, along with her male cousin – if that is what she decides to do. In this particular company women have never held an official position of power. The male oriented leader-follower dynamic in the subject of this case study had been passed on through the generations.

Distributed leadership

The German company had a 40-year history of strong decision-making by the current leader, who enjoyed a high level of trust and positive visibility (Gordon, 2011). The leadership was in reality divided between the CEO and his sister as they had both to sign major contracts and agreements. A sister and cousins who were members of the board had high impact and influence. The collective leadership decisions made by the current leader are built upon the trust relationship between the five female and two male members of the board. This kind of exchange of authority and power of ownership can be seen over the lifespan of a family business. This system will be extended when another female fourth-generation owner follows in a few years' time. In the Israeli case, a third-generation female entrepreneur has started other businesses in the region.

The checks and balances of power dynamics between siblings and cousins often goes unnoticed beneath the superficial perception of male-dominated leadership. As our cases show, trust relationships guide decision-making. Family members discuss decisions among themselves, so that their synergies and values are integrated into the decision-making process. Contrary to what is often assumed, and often seen in other businesses, the female owners in our study were not bought out but remained active as owners. As a strategic unit they managed the control and execution, security and risk, innovation and consolidation. If and when family members are bought out, due to tensions and disagreements about strategy and operations, or other differences, the family reduces the complexity it can deal with. This reduces the range of perspectives they can access and negatively affects the quality of decision-making.

Afterthoughts and reflections

Our discussion in this chapter has centred on the growing significance of female leadership (Ely et al., 2011) and how it features in family business and family ownership. Leadership is still often equated with masculine qualities in a corporate environment, representing obstacles to women's career development (Koenig et al., 2011). Our surprising finding, however, is that the family business environment enables women to combine powerful corporate roles with motherhood. Being able to do both has been part of the long-term strategic approach of the co-founders and subsequent generations. This raises interesting considerations as to the successful family business concepts other companies can draw on and emulate to counteract the patriarchal leadership style that has defined them until now (Collinson, 2011).

From monolithic to distributed leadership

Trust relationships and shared responsibilities within the family business are key aspects for shortening decision-making processes and communication paths, and accelerating outcomes. In all the family case studies that we observed, power was dispersed between female and male leaders. The families embrace complex, ambiguous and interconnected leadership dynamics that in the past have been undervalued and unexplored (Gordon, 2011).

What we discovered in our case studies is very distinct. The view taken in all these cases was a long-term strategic approach encompassing prospective leaders. The family businesses attempt to learn from their mistakes and adapt their course of direction. They might pass over the role and responsibility of leader to someone else within the family, but they still consider each other as part of one big family that shares one vision. It is a process of trial and error, and learning from experience and reflection. The female co-founders and their husbands created for themselves complementary roles depending on their talents and interests, and their own unique leadership style. They listened to employees and customers, and tried to integrate other people's opinions wherever possible.

Social change

Developments in the socio-political landscape after the 1940s and 1950s have enhanced the sense of entitlement experienced by the daughters in these family businesses. After the Second World War several authors noted a backlash against the idealistic image of women as home-makers and mothers, and employment outside the home was seen as both an ideal and the norm.

Since then, the feminist movement, bringing with it the benefits of widely available birth control and opportunities for women in higher education, started a slow revolution that is still evolving. But is something unique happening on a larger, even international, scale? Over the last 10–20 years, female co-founders, and subsequent generations of daughters and granddaughters, have moved forward little by little, step by step, gaining ground in family firms by occupying powerful professional and leadership roles. They can be no longer be considered hidden champions. They have entered the limelight and can be seen performing on a national, regional and maybe even global stage.

Quota regulation and gender issues: a European perspective

Following regulation, in Norway women must make up 40 per cent of all companies' boards of directors. This has now become the norm in several

European countries. These regulations were initially put in place to give employees a say in the running of the company. Employee or union representatives have the right to vote on the board. This is never a majority vote but, when there are several owners represented on the board, their presence can tip the balance between such ownership interests.

The increase of legally binding quotas is intended to overcome the lack of women in board positions in general, but it will affect the dynamics of family business ownership to a great extent. It will have further implications for leadership styles both at the board and at the top executive level. Our European best practice cases show that changes in societal perceptions have prompted companies to mirror these political changes by including female representatives on the board. The question now arises as to whether the impact of new female leaders within family businesses will influence the traditional perception of the heroic male leader on a larger scale.

References

Barrett, M. and Moores, K. (2009). Spotlights and shadows: Preliminary findings about the experiences of women in family business leadership roles. *Journal of Management & Organization*, *15*(3), pp. 363–377.

Bolden, R., Gosling, J., Marturano, A. and Dennison, P. (2003). *A Review of Leadership Theory and Competency Frameworks*. A report for Chase Consulting and the Management Standards Centre. University of Exeter, UK: Centre for Leadership Studies.

Boulouta, I. (2013). Hidden connections: the link between board gender diversity and corporate social performance. *Journal of Business Ethics*, *113*(2), pp. 185–197.

Brush, C.G. (2006). Women entrepreneurs: A research overview. *The Oxford Handbook of Entrepreneurship*, Oxford, UK: Oxford University Press, pp. 611–628.

Casperz, D. and Thomas, J. (2015). Developing positivity in family business leaders. *Family Business Review*, *28*(1), pp. 60–75.

Collinson, D. (2011). Critical leadership studies. In A. Bryman, D. Collinson, K. Grint, B. Jackson and M. Uhl-Bien (Eds.). *The Sage Handbook of Leadership*. London: Sage.

Eagly, A.H. and Karau, S.J. (2002). Role congruity theory of prejudice toward female leaders. *Psychological Review*, *109*(3), p. 573.

Ely, R.J., Ibarra, H. and Kolb, D.M. (2011). Taking gender into account: theory and design for women's leadership development programs. *Academy of Management Learning & Education*, *10*(3), pp. 474–493.

Gordon, R.D. (2011). Leadership and power. In: A. Bryman, D. Collinson, K. Grint, B. Jackson and M. Uhl-Bien (Eds.), *The Sage Handbook of Leadership*. London: Sage.

Jimenesz, R.M. (2009). Research on women in family firms: current status and future directions. *Family Business Review*, *22*(1), pp. 53–64.

Karataş-Özkan, M., Erdoğan, A. and Nicolopoulou, K. (2011). Women in Turkish family businesses: drivers, contributions and challenges. *International Journal of Cross Cultural Management*, *11*(2), pp. 203–219.

Koenig, A.M., Eagly, A.H., Mitchell, A. and Ristikari, T. (2011). Are leader stereotypes masculine? A meta-analysis of three research paradigms. *Psychological Bulletin*. *137*(4), pp. 616–642.

Leibinger, B. (2010). *Wer wollte eine andere Zeit als diese. Ein Lebensbericht.* Hamburg, Germany: Murrmann Verlag.

Muir, S. (2012). Heidi versus Howard – perception barrier to be hurdled. *Agriculture Today* [online]. Available at: http://www.dpi.nsw.gov.au/archive/agriculture-today-stories/ag-today-archive/march-2012/heidi-versus-howard-perception-barrier-to-be-hurdled-commissioner

Remery, C., Matser, I. and Flören, R.H. (2014). Successors in Dutch family businesses: gender differences. *Journal of Family Business Management, 4*(1), pp. 79–91.

Vera, C.F. and Dean, M.A. (2005). An examination of the challenges daughters face in family business succession. *Family Business Review, 22*(4), pp. 366–369.

16 Strategic avenues for succession

Gry Osnes

BRUTUS:
What means this shouting? I do fear the people
choose Caesar for their king.
CASSIUS:
Ay, do you fear it?
Then must I think you would not have it so.
BRUTUS;
I would not, Cassius, yet I love him well.

Shakespeare, *Julius Caesar*, 1.2.85–89

Introduction

Succession is one of the most difficult processes for any organization to address strategically. It triggers strong group and individual dynamics. It involves the ambitions of a group, a family, employees or other stakeholders. The main issue triggering strong emotions is whether their stake, assets or employment in the business, are safe. At the individual level, succession will trigger competition among candidates for the top role. In a family business it can provoke sensitive and powerful emotions around issues such as favouritism and love.

Succession is crucial for any type of organization. In the case of family-owned businesses, it is often seen as the weakness, the argument being that the succession pool is severely limited through restriction to family members. Typically the pool is the sons and daughters of the founders or current owners. There is much research, and many theories, on the sources and nature of conflict and problems in family succession. Whether or not a succession is of a family member – and a family-owned firm is not obliged to appoint a family chief executive – is but one part of a complex dynamic. It is still commonly perceived that 'succession' is a single event, transferring control from one leader, or one generation, to the next, relating to just one company. This 'baton-passing' concept is an unhelpful, mono-dimensional perspective. Experience and research reveal seven strategic tasks to be solved for an effective succession. An important point to note is that most of these tasks are similar to family and non-family firms alike. This next section describes this strategic approach to succession, with most dimensions relevant to any organization.

Strategy practice or conflict

We position succession strategizing as a way of avoiding or managing conflicts, or strong feelings and emotional behaviour. The purpose is to optimize the succession outcome for the business, family and individual members. In family business research there has been a preoccupation with succession as disturbance or as being synonymous with conflict (Rowe et al., 2005; Kets de Vries, 2001). In contrast, succession can also assist strategic reorientation (Kesner and Sebora, 1994), adaptation to context (White, Smith and Barnett, 1997), and renewal of entrepreneurship (e.g. Wasserman, 2003). With a focus on the succession as role phenomena (e.g. Boethius, 2007; Handler, 1990) the study positions itself in a neutral position, as a succession can involve both constructive and destructive processes.

There is a strong link between governance and succession. A governance structure's most important tasks are to monitor the leader and ensure an effective succession. Where the family is the main owner, it may choose to govern directly or use different types of hybrid structures or a traditional board. In some countries, for example Germany and Scandinavia, regulations prescribe a certain size of board. They also specify that the role of Chair of the Board and CEO are separate. Often the family creates hybrid structures involving an ownership meeting or eventually a board. Regardless of the structure, there will be an implicit or explicit procedure for selecting the next leader. In a family this might be the oldest son. The family, or owner, may have an idea about the significance of the knowledge, commitment and connection between family and business success. It might choose the oldest son due to ideas about the superiority of necessity of male leadership, or reflecting a society with such a culture. It is also often implicit that the determination of birth order avoids uncertainty and destructive conflict.

Best practices

We have found that business-owning families use one of the three succession avenues: the first is where a family member or several family members are recruited into one of several top leadership roles. A second involves appointment of an external non-family member to the top leadership role. The third option is the entrepreneurship route, where setting up a new venture creates the succession strategy – for example, the successor family member heads a spin-off company. A new business may become the main activity. Another version of this latter option is to divide the business or create new ventures so that several family members own companies in a cluster ownership.

Managing the succession transition

What is a succession?

In research, succession is sometimes operationalized at the *individual level*: the leader's entry into and/or exit out of a role (Boalt Boethius, 2007; Handler, 1994). We call this a leadership transition. At the system level a 'succession' or 'succession planning' has been used for a diverse group of succession events; for example, the whole process, the procedure for recruitment or the preparation process for a particular successor. It is also used for building of a pool of candidates, a particular successor's immersion into the role or the management of the relationship between an incumbent and successor.

Three strategic avenues in family business succession

Several different strategic avenues are open to family businesses planning a succession. The two main ones – strategizing a family member and strategizing a non-family member into the top leadership role – have several sub-categories. We identify these as seven tasks that need to be addressed so as to develop a succession practice. The process of strategizing enables the strong competitive forces triggered by succession to be managed, including issues such as conflict and rivalry. It will often stretch over time, and different outcomes of different strategic tasks will be revisited. When the hand-over occurs, the strategizing comes into effect. Selecting the best-fit top leader constitutes just a part of this process. The key processes and disciplines for a non-family and family succession are discussed in more detail in Boxes 16.1 and 16.2, respectively.

At certain points in an organization's development, it may be necessary to create a new organizational structure, or reform an existing one. Family and non-family succession is *resetting, renewing or transforming governance* (see Figures 16.1 and 16.2). We will describe how one family switched from an oldest son succession strategy to a distributed leadership for the owners. In the future they are planning, with the transfer to the fourth generation, to hire a non-family CEO.

Box 16.1 Strategizing a non-family CEO into the family business

The successful strategizing process of recruiting a non-family member into the top leadership role in a family business has some of the similar, and some different, strategic tasks to be solved as other types of organization. Any succession consists of a complex process with several tasks that need to be thought about, or strategized. They are not necessarily completed in a sequential manner, but they do have to be orchestrated as the outcome of each needs to be aligned. The different subsections are strategized and developed, and may be adjusted in light of the outcomes of the other elements.

When recruiting a non-family leader, some hybrid governance structure, such as an ownership or board meeting will manage the relationship between the owners and the leader and establish some procedure for accountability.

(i)   **The strategy implicit in the governing structure**
This first strategy element can be an ownership forum or advisory board, and it can help establish trust, appropriate for the type of ownership and business (e.g. Kenyon-Rouvinez, Koeberle Schmid and Poza, 2014). If there is no formal structure in place, we regard the family unit as the governing body managing the succession and accountability. In itself this is a strategy and shifting it to a more formal hybrid version is in itself a strategy practice that determines the following building blocks for succession strategizing.

(ii)   **Reviewing past leadership tenure and future needs**
This process is described as *leadership tenure strategizing* (see Figure 16.1). It involves analysing past achievements, mistakes and so on; creating a shared narrative about what was or was not effective in a past leadership tenure, with the aim of creating an understanding of what will be needed in the future. There should be discussion of the competitive context and threats in the future. This establishes a mandate for leadership.

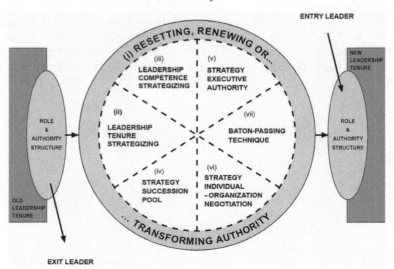

Figure 16.1 Succession strategizing wheel: a non-family member succession

(iii) Individual leader competence strategy

This determines what type of leader will be able to execute the mandate. This process (Phase iii in Figure 16.1) creates a wish list of personal qualities, matched to the mandate. It will include statements on qualifications and personal qualities, such as emotional maturity, focus, resilience, work experience and networks. There will be a process for evaluation of the individual under these headings. Consideration should be given to analysing the complementarities between and within leadership tenures; between incumbent and successor and the management team.

(iv) Creating a succession pool

This is important even if the succession is likely to be from within the family. When one chooses to recruit a non-family managing director, or CEO, or reviewing this option while also looking at the leadership potential within the family, the family is designing the succession pool and managing resource dependencies. There is a significant reduction of risk if there is more than one option for the top leader. For all firms it helps to develop a cadre of potential leaders internally and not be over-reliant on head-hunters. Consideration needs to be given to the criteria for the leadership pool, as well as for training, coaching and other forms of development.

(v) Establishing the executive authority

This is extremely important as too much or too little autonomy for the top leader can have wide ramifications. We found that when the families recruited a non-family leader they chose to call the role 'managing director' as the leader would have less discretion on long-term strategies. In our cases family members would create active ownership roles where they would focus on different long-term strategic development or work. The executive authority given to a top leader will also depend upon the phase in the organization's development.

(vi) Matching organizational need and individual drive

This is the *negotiation* between the owners and the successor-leader. It will only be able to proceed effectively if the mandate and executive authority phases have been conscientiously completed. The appointing board needs to identify and encourage the candidate's drive and ambition for the post, as well as their suitability in other respects.

(vii) Baton-passing technique

This is the hand-over, a complicated process that can only partly be planned. It also is a process of testing out and starting on the process of establishing and maintaining trust between the owner and the leader.

Transmission of knowledge and values

It is helpful to carry out analysis for the hand-over as to what information or knowledge is necessary for the new leader to have at once. This is important as overwhelming a new leader can, in the immersion process, obstruct them from forming an independent analysis of what can be important issues to address. An advantage in recruiting someone from outside, depending on the mandate and how much new thinking is necessary, is that, for a while, the new leader can have valuable outside perspectives. For a while she or he can balance this outside perspective with high inside access and dialogue that can enable the building of trust for necessary changes in strategies. Another knowledge transmission is the acknowledgement of any 'skeletons in the closet' in the business: embarrassing mistakes or personnel issues that eventually will emerge. As a process the immersion of a leader is when the family and employees are a 'reservoirs of knowledge and values'. It is a delicate dance of offering and holding back information or knowledge, so that the leader can balance acquiring knowledge and independence of thinking. Holding back important information might be as obstructive as offering too much.

Interpersonal relationships

The relationship between incumbent and successor is of great significance in determining an effective succession and will mostly be present in the hand-over process.

Transmission of values

When a family chooses to recruit a family member, see Box 16.2, they have started the process differently, with a transmission of values and knowledge. If they recruit a non-family leader who has not worked in the business before, the transmission of values is also a part of the hand-over process.

Box 16.2 Strategizing a family member as the top leader

There are seven tasks to this process as well. Six are essentially the same as for the non-family succession described in Box 16.1. The main difference with a family succession lies in the mandate, Phase ii. Instead of this phase being 'leadership tenure strategizing', the family strategizes the knowledge, skills or values they want to transmit to and develop in a successor or a group of potential successors in the family. It might be that a designated successor did not possess the personal qualities necessary. The succession pool can then be expanded with siblings and cousins.

(i) **Resetting, renewing and transforming the governing body**
    The family may be the forum that decides on the succession. In such succession processes the family system might develop a more formal ownership group or ownership council. This might involve the creation of hybrid governance structures. Reforming the structure in itself can become a part of strategizing a succession.

(ii) **Knowledge, skill and value transmission**
    A family firm will typically have, as a first or obvious option, the appointment of an individual from the next generation to take over from a retiring current leader. This involves slow immersion of the next generation into the business, often from a young age, which goes in parallel with the other strategic elements.

The mandate is usually focused on values, though of course family firms have to ensure that a successor has sufficient knowledge and skills. See Box 16.1.

(iii) Individual leader competence strategy

A family firm may make a team, or adjust the ownership structure and involvement of other members, to compensate for more limited leadership capacities. This also influences executive authority. See the Swedish case descriptions.

(iv) Creating a succession pool

To create a succession pool the family may include cousins or in-laws, or benchmark with external candidates. If the latter is the case the family is switching between strategizing a family member and a non-family member into the leadership role.

(v) Establishing the executive authority

This determines the autonomy the leader will have. Active owners and family may focus on business development or innovation. By contrast, in a corporation, all areas would fall to the CEO. This difference carries implications for the types of leaders the family appoints. The *strategizing of the business need and drive to the leaders* is where the parties involved often have to compromise.

(vii) Baton-passing technique

This is the final, seventh, stage of the process. As described in Chapter 5, the family in the French case found that this would be an almost impossible process and chose to recruit a non-family CEO so as to buffer the relationship between the children and parents in the hand-over.

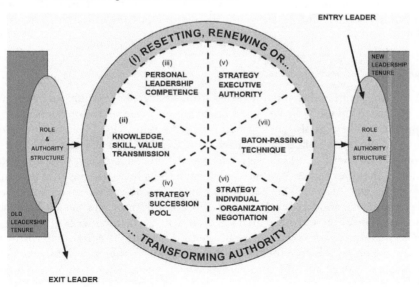

Figure 16.2 Succession strategizing wheel: a family member succession

Strategizing successions

We uncovered many examples of best practice in succession strategies that mitigate or prevent classic family business succession problems. The families would, over the course of the history of the company, use either: (i) A family member succession strategy, (ii) A non-family succession strategy or (iii) new entrepreneurship. While the first option is seen as typical, use of the other strategies is widespread. Many companies switch between these three avenues. Only one of the six best practice cases had not, in the past, switched between these, and it was planning to do so in the next succession.

The new entrepreneurship avenue contains two main strategic options: either expanding the business through designating the next generation to develop new ventures within the established business, or supporting and co-starting new businesses. Switching, often using several of these avenues at the same time, enables the family to exercise a strategic hyper-flexibility in succession not available to other types of organizations.

Strategizing a family member succession

In a family-owned business, a parent's life very much centres on the business, and the children spend much of their time at the workplace, in some cases working for some pocket money. They may make educational choices that are useful for the business. This is not always the case, and we met many who chose different educational paths. When they do enter the business, they start in very operational roles, though in many cases are later exposed to a wider range of experiences. Many say that some years of work outside the family business was very valuable. Below we discuss different dimensions of strategizing the succession:

Succession as constructing authority

We found that families often diverted from strategizing a family member into a top leadership job. The weakness of having only one successor candidate was apparent in the Swedish case. Traditionally the reins were given to the oldest son. In this case a sibling had to leave the CEO role, and the new CEO was a younger brother but a leadership trio was designated between him, the sister and another brother. A distributed leadership model was developed where one of them was head of the production unit and, formally, of technological developments, another brother was CEO and the sister was the Chair of the Board. They did not plan for their children, who at the time were in their teens or younger, to become or aspire to be the top leader of the company. However, as the generations before them had, they would have the opportunity to work in the company part time and earn pocket money. Their parents envisaged them in future roles as active owners or board members, and expected to be recruiting a non-family manager or CEO. Strategizing was concerned with planning the next leadership tenures (see Figure 16.1). The company was growing in size and complexity, it was competing at a global level and they were not expecting that one of their children would have the specialized competence that would be needed.

CEO or managing director

Several families switched from having a family member in the formal top leadership role to someone recruited from outside. In these cases the leader was most often called the managing director and not the CEO, reflecting how the executive authority was strategized. The families in the Israeli and Swedish cases both did this, while carving out active ownership roles for themselves. A distribution of authority between the family members would be balanced out with the competence and authority of a non-family leader, and they could reduce the burden on the family of many administrative tasks. Managing director roles would be more operational and would not have overall strategic responsibility. Strategic tasks would be shared by the active owners, involving discussions in informal decision-making meetings or at board level. The leadership structure is not very hierarchical or formal, three to four family members, sometimes with a non-family member included as leader, would be in continuous discussion and take decisions and create strategies in a fluid and efficient way. A mix between fluidity and structure can create competitive advantages for the family business.

Expanding the pool

Traditionally, it has often been decided that the pool consisted only of the oldest son. In others it would include nieces and nephews. Both the Chinese and Israeli case expanded the pool with third and fourth generation members. Complementary strategizing technique was used for matching a designated successor with other family members with different skill sets or personal talents. Non-family employees would also be used in this way.

Making the deal

A part of the succession process is to negotiate the package, and match the leader's drive to the needs of the organization. In some cases, a family member had taken out too many benefits, causing conflict. Negotiating the salary of a family member as an executive is a sensitive area, in addition to the increase in shares that all the family members will enjoy. In a family there can also be a situation where there are plenty of candidates but none has a wish, or drive, for joining the business. Or, as in some of the cases we researched, someone was involved in the business as leader, but with certain ambivalence as they did not feel the choice was taken freely. A succession also *includes strategizing the kind of executive authority* a CEO should have. In a family business, with active owners, this can be less than a CEO in a non-family business. It is a difficult area that can cause tension. The carving out of executive authority depends on the effectiveness of other succession strategies for optimizing the succession, and how much trust there is between the stakeholders, owners and employees, and the leader. To assign and delegate executive authority, is also about accepting followership.

Baton-passing technique

We found that most of the succession hand-overs were reported to have gone smoothly. This is contrary to what is often discussed as a problem with a founder or owner/leader having problems with letting go of the role. It was a problem in the case discussed in Chapter 5 but this was solved in an ingenious way by the French siblings: they switched over to recruiting a non-family CEO as a temporary leader with a contract of four years. This is described in more detail below.

What we found, to our great surprise, was that in most of the cases the founder/owner did not retire but continued to work in the business in a different role. In three of the businesses female founders worked in leadership roles until their mid 80s. They had flexible work but no wish to retire; one was managing a farm supplying food for a chain of safari camps. Her retired husband was running charities linked to the safari business. In the US case the original founder was still, at an advanced age, managing the original barbeque restaurant. In Israel the female founder, now 90 years old, was head of accounts. While it can cause friction, the involvement of several generations may have benefits such as family cohesion, knowledge and value transfer, and social identity. This is discussed in depth in the chapter on gender, Chapter 15.

With such flexibility the hand-over of control does not trigger a loss of social identity in the incumbent; social networks are not lost and the continuation of an active older life is enabled. This might be crucial as most, if not all, of these founders and owners are highly driven and not very well suited to a sedate retirement. In the Chinese case, discussed further below, an owner's retirement and boredom led to new entrepreneurship for the family cluster of businesses.

A non-family leadership succession

The French family in our case studies decided to employ a leader from outside, and the Swedish family was planning a non-family leader for their next succession. The Israeli family had for a long time had a non-family managing director managing their business. We will give a detailed description of the strategizing process that the French owners followed. Two siblings found the business needed to be professionalized, some marketing needed to be modernized and the business needed to grow. To effect this they *strategized the former tenure* of their parents' leadership, found the gaps and, together with analysing their business challenges and how they saw the sector developing, carved out a mandate. Instead of recruiting themselves they used a head-hunter to identify and *strategize the succession pool*. Required *personal qualities and leadership capacity* included marketing experience from another luxury brand, and the emotional tolerance and flexibility to work and manage change despite obstruction from the parents. The chosen candidate had a strong *executive authority* from siblings who felt that mistakes were allowed; they supported risk and change, and would support her. They would themselves be involved in the major strategic decisions about the market they were in.

The deal resulted in a good package and a six-year contract for her. Her drive was to go from being a middle manager in another luxury brand to taking on larger role in a smaller business, where she would gain top leadership experience. The risk for her was high, but she knew that success would qualify her for CEO roles in bigger companies. In this way the needs of the organization and her drive were well matched. In the *baton-passing technique* phase the father was side-lined, he was in his early 90s. The siblings would act as active owners on behalf of the parents and support the CEO when she entered the role. Such support would prevent scapegoating and isolation. The siblings *strategized multiple successions concurrently*; by the start of the hiring of a professional CEO they had already thought, and strategized, the next leadership tenure. Already then it was planned for the brother to be the CEO, the sister head of innovation and business development as the siblings felt they complemented each other. A third succession would be a third generation family member.

The biggest difference between the two strategies seems to be the first step, the choice between having a big pool of candidates that are not family members or restricting the pool to the family. If the family pool is large, it enables a hybrid approach. By constructing active ownership roles, the family can recruit both family members with commitment and tacit knowledge and external leaders with complementary competences. A strategy in Israel was that the family members would not to have administrative roles. They would be strategists, entrepreneurs and change agents. For the family business it offers a mix of two succession strategies.

We found that women, in most of the cases, had powerful roles in founding and continuing the business and is explored in the chapter on gender issues, Chapter 15. In the Israeli case the family used, in a flexible way, elements from all the avenues, demonstrating how, when one does not have a monolithic mind-set about ownership and control, succession can be the source of innovation and a win-win event for the whole family, the business and its development. Gender issues were also solved in the succession process in most of the cases.

Entrepreneurship as a succession avenue

We were surprised to find how often new business ventures have been used to leapfrog the succession problem. In the US case the family supported their children to start new businesses, which means that the original business is not contested territory. It reduces the sibling rivalry when there is just the one primary role, at the top of the company. By creating something new one builds one's own authority. If a family promotes and supports a new business, the rewards are not at the expense of someone else in the family. We saw this in most of the cases; even if there had been a buy-out of the family member, the individual who left often started a new business. The next section will feature a case that shows how this approach dealt with issues of gender and succession.

One of the most unusual examples of entrepreneurship and succession was seen in the Chinese case. A second generation owner had been elected by the employees to the role as managing director for a business making wooden toys. His father had started the business as the community leader of the village and the business was at that time owned by the commune. The commune, the locally elected representatives from the village, demanded that the employees chose the leader. A short time after the founder retired he became bored. With his son safely in the role of the top leader, he started a new business with a nephew in the same line of business.

The village had begun winning many orders from major toy producers abroad. Later a change in laws would permit private ownership of businesses. Some years later a disastrous flood wiped out the first commune-owned business. The second generation that was running this business started another, closer to Shanghai. It was less successful than the first and they moved it back to a neighbour region. By this time several employees from the commune-owned business had started their own smaller businesses, still within wooden toy production. At this time the local level the village had several competing, but also collaborating businesses, supplying about 40 per cent of all the wooden toys in the world. The founder ran his business in an old-fashioned way with his nephew. His son, on the other hand, was more adventurous, starting specialist design companies, and increasing margins by developing a China-based distribution, attracting the interest of global companies.

Afterthoughts and reflections

Collapse of succession strategizing

Succession is fundamentally a system that constructs leadership, and what one believes is necessary leadership. Succession is a transition and a decision-making event; new possibilities can be explored, discovered, created and acted on. Families can be prone to habits or precedence that reduce the strategic capacity by precluding exploration of the business and its context and informing the succession. Such weaknesses contribute to a collapse, or partial collapse, of strategic capacity. An equally dysfunctional but individual process is rivalry. Rivalry in succession commonly occurs, and can lead to the choice of the wrong leader and misplaced, or lack of, strategic thinking and vision. This can occur not only among siblings but between a former leader and a successor. It's caused or intensified by a narrow focus on having some role, or prestige, love or achievement that someone else has or can give. Such path dependency or group think causes one to miss seeing the wider context and the long-term future, making a review of individual capacities or visions less likely. In this way remaining a legacy, not reviewing it, prevents exploration of new possibilities. It is healthier to discuss and explore the past and future in a measured way.

Other threats in succession are scapegoating or idealization of a leader, which may occur in either family or non-family businesses. Scapegoating is a group mechanism where a group turns against a member or the leader of the group. All problems and mistakes are attributed or associated with the scapegoat, typically forcing the individual to leave the role. It is a very powerful dynamic, the victim of scapegoating is almost defenceless and the group usually feels self-righteous, and deliberately avoid exploring other problems, own hubris and the context. The group or family may harbour wishful thinking that the ideal leader exists and just has to be found. Such wishful thinking can lead to idealization of a leader preventing the proper monitoring of performance, often providing excuses for early warnings signals or bad performance. It is a serious threat in a succession.

Moving from a monolithic to distributed leadership.

Nepotism is a potential weakness in a family-owned business. Our cases indicate that this can be exacerbated by a monolithic mind-set that views a succession as being about one person and one company. The cases in this book illustrate an imaginative and intelligent range of other options. Recent research has focused on family owners owning clusters of companies and this fits with our findings on best practice. It does not mean that difficult group and family dynamics cease to exist but they get more diluted and more manageable. What we call the 'monolithic ownership/succession pattern' will inevitably trigger strong rivalry in any group.

References

Boalt Boethius, S., (2007). Succession and managing the transition from predecessor to successor. In *Det enkla är det sköna. En vänbok till Kjell Granström*, Einarsson, I.C., Hammar Chiriac, E. (eds). Linköping, Sweden: Skapande Vetande, 185–200.

Handler, W.C., (1990). Succession in family firms: a mutual role adjustment between entrepreneur and next generation family members. *Entrepreneurship Theory and Practice* 15, 37–51.

Handler, W.C., (1994). Succession in family business: a review of the research. *Family Business Review* 7(2), 133–157.

Kenyon-Rouvinez, D., Koeberle Schmid, A. and Poza, E., (2014). *Governance in Family Enterprises: Maximizing economic and emotional success*, New York: Palgrave Macmillan.

Kesner, I.F. and Sebora, T.C., (1994). Executive succession: past, present and future. *Journal of Management* 20(2), 327–372.

Kets de Vries, M.F., (2001). *The Leadership Mystique: An owner's manual*. London: Financial Times Prentice Hall.

Rowe, W.G., Cannella Jr., A.A., Rankin, D. and Gorman, D., (2005). Leader succession and organizational performance: integrating the common-sense, ritual scapegoating, and vicious-circle succession theories. *The Leadership Quarterly* 16(2), 197–219.

Wasserman, N., (2003). Founder-CEO succession and the paradox of entrepreneurial success. *Organization Science*, 14(2), 149–172.

White, M.C., Smith, M. and Barnett, T., (1997). CEO succession: Overcoming forces of inertia. *Human Relations*, 50(7), 805–828.

17 Developing healthy ownership

A non-family Chair of board in Norway

Gry Osnes

My task is to align capacity and willingness within the family, and align it with the risk, opportunity and challenges in their business

Eivind Reiten

Introduction

This chapter is the result of conversations with an experienced Chair of Boards, Eivind Reiten, in Norway. It focuses on two family companies for which he has served as Chair. Both families are significant business owners, each with several different companies held within one structure. We will show how a Chair of a family-owned business has to manage the overlap of two systems, family and business, and respect and work with the owners' wishes, including succession, and the social identity invested in the business. A task managing this system overlap, shapes the role as Chair and is in addition to the over-arching duties of ensuring the business is profitable and has recruited the right people. As such a Chair can contribute to the health of the business and family dynamics. A non-family executive or Chair has to accept this context, and help strategize when they operate on the boundary between the family and the business. We will discuss the concept of socio-emotional wealth, describing factors other than the financial profit of the company that the family will take into account. Further we discuss some findings and suggestions for governance in family firms.

Socio-emotional wealth and family control

In recent years a theoretical perspective has been developed on how family business and family owners preserve what is known as their socio-emotional wealth (Gómez-Mejía, et al., 2007). Family owners will not only wish to optimize the financial return, they will also take into consideration the social identity, or socio-emotional wealth, they have invested in the business. They are prepared to make choices that might be less optimal for profit so as to maintain this link and social identity with the business. Socio-emotional wealth encompasses invested prestige in a wider context, social identity within the family and a wider network, the business as a symbolic artifact and the opportunities that this creates, both financially and personally.

Succession, stewardship and developing social capital, as described earlier in this book, show how the family uses its emotional ties to build and grow the business (Ibid.). They may at times prioritize social identity or the need for control and autonomy ahead of short-term profits. Such priorities also influence the way they choose to use a governing body or board. This enables them to make strategic choices that are not only based on economic considerations, and to avoid financial risk. They might even seek financial risk to align the activities with their current or aspirational socio-emotional wealth. Non-family executives and board members would be expected to take this into consideration.

Governance of the family business

In public companies the board's main function is to safeguard shareholders' interests (Monks and Minnow 2011). The board is often seen as the cornerstone of the governance elements aiming to align the interests of managers and shareholders. The primary tasks are control and advice for the top leader and his or her management team. In addition the board can have an additional strategic board function. The way a family recruit non-family board members can ensure the appointment is a source of intellectual and social capital (Sirmon and Hitt 2003).

Family firms are often reluctant to install independent board structures as they fear losing decision-making ability (Voordeckers *et al.* 2007) and in particular the social identity invested within the business. Research on the practice of governance is fragmented, the governance dynamic is a complex one, and actual practice is very diverse. In the USA the Chair of the Board and the CEO is often the same person; this is called role duality. In Europe these roles, directed by regulations or tradition, are held by different people. There are different regulatory regimes in European countries. In Norway, where the cases for this chapter operate, each company that employs more than 50 staff has to have a board. The board is led by a Chair and a CEO is appointed by the board. In most of the Nordic countries the employees also have a right, or duty, to elect a representative as a board member.

In addition to different regulatory systems there is further variation in the actual practice of how a family board functions. It can vary with frequency of board meetings, member commitment and their experience, company culture, and type of firm or industry. All these aspects affect the board's ability to fulfill its tasks (Corbetta and Salvato 2004; Minichilli *et al.* 2009). An additional factor is the ownership structure. It can be one owner with a controlling share, a sibling partnership, a cousin consortium or a public family firm (Gersick 1997). These different types of ownership groups will operate different structures for establishing trust and leadership.

The management structure will vary according to whether the arrangement is a sole owner, a sibling partnership or a cousin consortium. In the example of a sole owner, the firm is owner-managed, with a fairly simple structure comprising a board of directors responsible for strategic management and succession. In the case of a sibling partnership, there is management by the broader family, with additional procedures in place to handle differences of view within the family. The cousin consortium requires more features, including family meetings and probably a Chief Family Officer (Kenyon-Rouvinez et al. 2014).

A Family Council convenes meetings where family members talk through issues. It makes what are often informal discussions within the family more structured and open. It can organize and structure the interests of the family, establish trust within family members, and manage its relationship with the business. Such a hybrid governance model can reduce conflict by facilitating dialogue and face-to-face discussion. The Family Council can determine the selection of the board of directors and influence, if not decide, the management succession (Gallo and Kenyon-Rouvinez 2005; Lansberg 1999).

The role of Chair

The role of Chair of the Board is increasingly being recognized as a specialist professional role, including non-executive directors with relevant expertise. Within this, the role of the Chair is crucial: she or he directs the board's work and is a pivotal contact for both executives and owners. It has been advised (Kenyon-Rouvinez et al. 2014, page 95) that, if the Chief Executive is a family member, that the Chair is not, and vice-versa. The Chair should be capable of some distance from the executive team, to maintain a certain distance and be able to challenge, in a healthy and democratic spirit, the plans of the executive. He or she should encourage non-executive board members to speak up, and to foster open discussions.

In this chapter we explore what the strategic choice of tasks so as to balance the business and family system set by this Chair and the board. The use of a board with a non-family Chair becomes the vehicle where a family system and business system overlap. It implies that someone other than a family member is involved in the sensitive issue of balancing the relationship between the family and the business. That includes the issue of socio-emotional wealth, or the family's invested social identity within the business. A family has, as priorities, security and well-being of the family and increasing autonomy and independence for the offspring. A business seeks risk and growth, but also needs stability so as to be able to work towards long-term strategic goals. Some of the drives and needs of the family and business are in conflict. This means that managing on the boundary can be paradoxical and complex.

Box 17.1 Overlapping system of attachment and transitions

The family unit is a system that features very strong attachment, in part as a biological instinct, between parents and their children. The main functions of the family are to provide emotional safety, protected-ness and trust for the children and between the parents. Drive for safety and trust is an indication of health, but there will also be a drive for autonomy for the offspring. A family has to balance these two paradoxical drives.

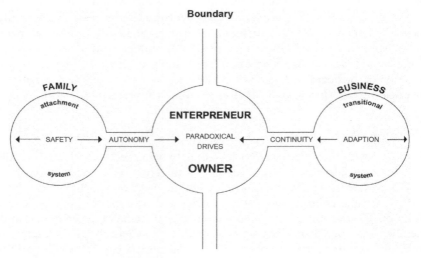

Figure 17.1 Attachment and transition in family ownership

One of the main tasks of the business is to be in transition, in exchange with the external reality, so as to adapt, create and increase value. It seeks adaptation and risk, a drive that is contrary to a family need for feeling secure. The family also seeks autonomy for its members, and family owners can often create a unique sense of autonomy. In this way a board for a family business has to maneuver an unusually high degree of paradox resulting from needs that can be in conflict, both within the family and between the family and business.

Alignment of attachment, risk, capacity and opportunity

Distribution of leadership between generations

We will explore a family ownership that originated from a large, renowned business that earlier had control shared between two brothers. Both brothers had worked in the business for a long period. They decided, with some sadness, to divide the business and other assets, which comprised property and cash. The oil and construction business interests consisted of different businesses. To keep the integrity and synergy of these, the brothers decided that splitting them up would be too difficult. The business was high-risk, in a volatile market with complicated risk assessments. While such a move can feel like a defeat and a loss, the brothers judged that it would prevent a destructive spiral featuring underperformance of the companies.

A family branch ended up with cash and a property portfolio. The third generation brother who took over this part was an expert in the oil industry, not in broader asset management, as he had worked most of his professional life in the business his grandfather had started. Major decisions on business investments and the associated risk profile would have to be taken to build up a new business for the family. The owner opened up a process that also took into consideration the interests of the fourth generation, reflecting their needs, wishes and risk appetite. He and his daughters decided to recruit a non-family member to Chair the board. The following is how the Chair, Eivind Reiten, approached the request:

> I wanted to be an independent Chair with more non-family members at the board than family members. Otherwise we are only an advisory board. They chose two more, one expert on property and one on compliance. But it is about trust. We would not vote against a block of family members on an issue of major importance.

Loss and new opportunities

While there was a sense of loss in having to part from the original business, there was also a unique opportunity. This owner had gained a high degree of freedom as regards the way in which the family could construct their investments, choose the level of risk and develop what type of businesses they wanted to be involved in. In this way they could choose to change the type of social identity the business would provide for them. It could be more diversified than the old business. They could choose to build on this legacy or start anew. Questions arose over whether they should make oil sector and technology related investments, and what other assets and investments this should be combined with. The father had his inheritance and legacy from his father and his own work over many years.

A part of the work of the Chair was to explore the risk appetite, and the talent, in the family group. One of the daughters was identified as a future active owner. Her sister had other, non-family business interests but would, with her father, be one of the family members sitting on the board. Her cousin, who worked in the business, was sitting on other boards of smaller businesses the group owned. The family decided to appoint a non-family CEO. Two generations of owners would in this way distribute the leadership of the company, and of the succession, with two non-family members. One of the tasks of the non-family Chair and CEO would be facilitating the training of the third generation active owner:

> We will prepare and organize it for her, as the future leading owner. But she is not exempted from the ordinary demands professionally and on

discipline. She has to submit herself to those. She has to accept another authority system than ownership.

Eivind Reiten

Re-establishing the link between family and business

The second case concerns a family who had several businesses in property development and construction. The owner, from the second generation, passed away after a short period of illness. His children were in their teens. The business had for years been managed by this second generation owner. While he was alive, the rest of the family had little to do with the business.

> During what was a short period of illness he set it all up legally with the inheritance and a trustee board. They are now acting as owner until his children are older for now they are the 'owner' I report to.
>
> Eivind Reiten

The Chair had to, once the children had grown up and finished higher education, start the discussion with them of what engagement, if any, they wanted to have in the business. It was important to establish, through sensitive discussions, where the interests of the children lay. Should the children wish to become involved in the management of the business, it would be necessary to create roles for them. Further, the training for those roles, while at the same time equipping them to take on the ownership, had to be planned. There were several companies of different sizes within the group. The smaller boards could serve as a training ground for family members. Reiten commented:

> I had to start the dialogues in the family about the assets, the structure, etc. The dialogue is about future interest and capacity for each of his now young adult offspring.

The link between the business and the family is most often established by the family members active in the business and this process had been interrupted by the too early death of the owner. The family members would have to learn about the business, should they wish to be involved. First, they would be learning about the business as employees. This would involve professional roles where they would be expected to follow the normal rules of employees. If they wanted to continue to be active as owners, the business would need to have a plan for preparing them for succession into the ownership role.

The tie and link between family and business

In the dialogues the Chair has with the family a crucial discussion should be brought into the open: the risk profile or risk willingness that the family wants to have. In both the above cases the task of the Chair was to make sure that the risk the family took on would be the basis for healthy ownership; that it reflected the interest, the knowledge and capacity and the tolerance for risk within the family. As Reiten stated:

> What is important is the concept of risk within the family, where they are both intellectually and emotionally in their willingness.

A task of the Chair is to align the family's willingness for risk with their talents and aspirations. It possesses its own momentum, life stages and events influencing it. Momentum in the business is different; events and business opportunities will arise and there will be a window where an opportunity is open. The board is there to oversee these dimensions, and align differing dynamics so to healthy ownership and a sustainable business. A non-family Chair is positioned on the boundary between the two systems and their dynamics. This is still the case where there are family members who work within the business.

Box 17.2 The tasks of a non-family Chair

In this example, the Chair was operating in a regulated jurisdiction, where companies are required to have a board, so establishment of the boundary was already completed. Within some parts of Europe and the world there are no such regulations in place.

Establishing the boundary

Tasks establishing a boundary is shown in (1) in Figure 17.2 and can be a difficult task, as some family members lose control with the establishment of a board, and

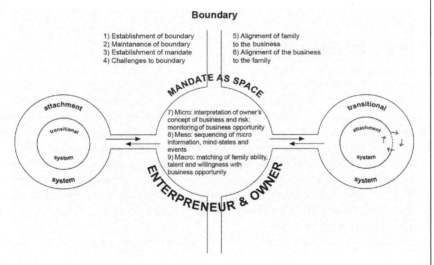

Figure 17.2 The tasks of a non-family Chair in family ownership

others might gain control. Throughout the work the boundary has to be maintained. It needs to have a mandate that is not undermined by non-family managers taking major decisions without the influence of the family; or family members taking decisions without at least consulting the board. In most businesses, not only family businesses, there can be different types of challenges where the interests of different groups do not coincide.

Space for dialogue

Within the Chair's mandate there is space for dialogue where the family interests and the needs of the family are aligned with the context and how it influences the strategic options for the business. Issues of the family's appetite for risk are aligned with their talents, capacity and other life choices. A review at the board level, and consequent disinvestment or investment would then be agreed on. Balance between ownership and continuity and new entrepreneurship would be created. At the micro level (7) the Chair and board maintain continual dialogue with family and business as to where the family and business are in their understanding and willingness for risk and opportunities. Since both systems, family and business, have momentums that are not necessarily moving in the same way, these investments and decisions have to be synchronized. Some discussions or decisions (8) might move the family a little forward while the company is held back a little. Opportunities that need to responded to within a short time frame will force a dialogue where the family has to speed up and take fast decisions. Time for digestion is, in this way, created and managed so that each system can adjust and align their internal processes. As Chair and board they then need the trust not only to be advisory, but also to make interpretations and arrive at conclusions as to where things are moving. This manages and aligns business decision-making with the risk willingness and talent of the family, as indicated in (9).

Afterthoughts and reflections

Even in family ownership where relationships are healthy, the family and the business will have conflicting interests and contradictory drives. A healthy approach to governance is to ensure that no major conflicts of interest are overlooked. Capable Chairs will acknowledge that differences of interest, and differences of points of view, will inevitably occur. The bigger problems arise from failing to acknowledge and discuss them. Strategic goals for the governance system – the board, a Chair or an eventual Family Council – is to align the capacity (talent) and willingness (risk) of the family with the strategic business decisions, taking into account the opportunities that present themselves and the structure of ownership. The family should not be exposed to risks that do not suit their temperament.

A Chair of the Board who is non-family can work perfectly well – and is often recommended where the Chief Executive is from the family. Many of the key factors for success are more qualitative than structural: to do with the quality of the dialogue between key stakeholders, and of the discussions held at board level. An imperfect structure with good communication and relationships is likely to outperform the 'ideal' governance structure where open dialogue struggles because the key players are not making sufficient effort, or because they are holding superficial conversations that overlook or downplay important issues such as appetite for risk and strategic direction.

References

Corbetta, G. and Salvato, C.A. (2004). The board of directors in family firms: one size fits all? *Family Business Review, 17*(2), pp. 119–134.

Gallo, M.A. and Kenyon-Rouvinez, D. (2005). The importance of family and business governance. In *Family Business* (pp. 45–57). London: Palgrave Macmillan UK.

Gersick, K.E. (1997). *Generation to Generation: Life cycles of the family business.* Boston, MA, US: Harvard Business Press.

Gómez-Mejía, L.R., Haynes, K.T., Núñez-Nickel, M., Jacobson, K.J. and Moyano-Fuentes, J. (2007). Socioemotional wealth and business risks in family-controlled firms: Evidence from Spanish olive oil mills. *Administrative Science Quarterly, 52*(1), pp. 106–137.

Kenyon-Rouvinez, D., Koeberle Schmid, A. and Poza, E. (2014). *Governance in Family Enterprises: Maximizing economic and emotional success.* New York: Palgrave Macmillan.

Lansberg, I. (1999). *Succeeding Generations: Realizing the dream of families in business.* Boston, MA, US: Harvard Business Press.

Minichilli, A., Zattoni, A. and Zona, F. (2009). Making boards effective: An empirical examination of board task performance. *British Journal of Management, 20*(1), pp. 55–74.

Monks, R.A.G. and Minnow, N. (2011). *Corporate Governance* (5th ed.). West Sussex, NJ, US: John Wiley & Sons.

Sirmon, D.G. and Hitt, M.A. (2003). Managing resources: Linking unique resources, management, and wealth creation in family firms. *Entrepreneurship Theory and Practice, 27*(4), pp. 339–358.

Voordeckers, W., Van Gils, A. and Van den Heuvel, J. (2007). Board composition in small and medium-sized family firms. *Journal of Small Business Management, 45*(1), pp. 137–156.

18 Drive in family capitalism

Integration of emotions and strategizing

Gry Osnes, James Grady, Victoria Grady, Mona Haug, Liv Hök and Olive Yanli Hou

In discussion with successful family owners that have overcome painful processes and conflicts, a question that occurs is 'What makes these people tick?' This chapter focuses on an elusive but central aspect of family capitalism: drive. One can safely conclude that a strong drive is involved in establishing and running a family firm. We easily assume we understand what we talk about with 'drive' or someone being 'driven'. But what does it mean? With this as a starting point this chapter serves as a summary of the book. We point out how each chapter explicitly or implicitly explores drive. We try to answer that question by drawing attention to the connection between the complexity of drive, strategy practices and leadership.

Examples of desires prominent in family ownership are connected to financial safety and survival, ambitions. It is about for a particular kind of engagement with the world or having a particular place in society and communities. There will be bumps in the road and painful events, and longer periods of tension. *Emotional effort is necessary. Risk is taken financially, emotionally and socially and is a part of family ownership. Family owners' drive, their strategizing, enables them to mobilize substantial resources in creating strong purposeful action to maximize their chance of success.* We offer some perspectives on how a family is driven in its role as family owner, how they tolerate the financial and personal risk and sustain a mind-set of long-term thinking. The family owner will know these things 'in their gut', and the chapter offers some theory to explain these experiences. Family executive coaches, consultants and advisers can benefit from understanding the owning family as a dynamic group. So will researchers with an interest in practice.

We suggest that family capitalism captures something different from the focus on individual 'self-interest' and 'greed' within agency theory and other economic theories. We describe how socio–emotional wealth (Gomez–Mejia *et al.*, 2007), the tie or attachment between the family and the business, is an important dimension of family group dynamics and the basis for different strategies, both in ownership and leadership. The family acts as owners through different strategies, including stewardship, serial entrepreneurship, switching of succession strategy avenues, negotiating autonomy and long-term commitment within the family. This is a complex set of drives, and forms of strategy execution, that go far beyond a quest for financial profitability. The book therefore questions the traditional premise that self-interest and greed are the only drivers for growth and innovation in our economy.

We complement this notion of socio-emotional drive within the family group with other individual drive theories. Socio-emotional drive theory captures part of the family group drive, but we found it does not cover the notions, and crucial aspects, of individual drive. Individual drive is important as both innovative and destructive forces often can come into play. Four perspectives building on different strands of psychoanalytic theory to explore how individual constructs drive. We also mention some of the fallacies, or threats, that reduce drive. We briefly illustrate how parts of psychoanalytic theory building on Sigmund Freud (1914, 1937) are relevant. Further we introduce attachment theory building on the findings of John Bowlby (1969) and elaborate on affect and instincts and a biological perspective on how drives are a feature of our biology (Panksepp and Biven, 2012). Lastly, we introduce a drive perspective building on Donald Winnicott (1971) that puts an emphasis on our drive for authenticity, being an active agent in the external reality in a playful and innovative way.

Socio-emotional wealth preservation

Socio-emotional wealth explains the rationale of family owners, in particular when they make choices that might reduce profits. It focuses on how the family as a group strategizes their social identity, prestige and social cohesion within the family. Socio-emotional wealth includes the invested prestige in a wider context, social identity within the family and a wider network, the business as a symbolic artefact and the opportunities this involves both for financial and personal gain. A threat is that the family may put excessive focus on these aspects and neglect profitability. Gomez- Mejia *et al.* (2007) suggest that socio-emotional preservation has five constructs that together capture the ways families strategize the business and that are unique to family businesses. These are called FIBER which stands for:

> **F**amily control and influence,
> **I**dentification of family members with the firm,
> **B**inding social ties,
> **E**motional attachment of family members,
> **R**enewal of family bonds to the firm in succession.
>
> Gomez–Mejia *et al.* (2007)

Family control and influence

A family group's drive for socio-emotional wealth and how to manage this is illustrated in Chapter 17, through how a non-family Chair works on the boundary between the family and the business. It is further explored in how a family uses, for an interim period, a non-family CEO for the business in Chapter 5. We found that the issue of control is not as straightforward as having a controlling ownership stake, but involves distributing the power within the family, while acting as a unit using that control. It can further be distributed with non-family leaders, and the process of power distribution within the family, and strategizing authority, is described in Chapter 14. It enables the family to manage their dependency on others' knowledge and skills.

Identification of family members with the firm

The aspiration the family has for the business, how it provides for financial safety, the link with social networks and prestige or a role in the community, combine to create the social identity for the family. In the stewardship chapter (Chapter 8), and in the ladder entrepreneurship chapter (Chapter 3) the families studied developed this identity together. The way the family and business are interwoven in the respective strategies, the family involvement and gains they have from the business create a unique identity within a family firm (e.g., Berrone, Cruz and Gomez-Mejia, 2012).

Binding social ties

Berrone *et al.* (2012) suggest that family owners often are deeply embedded in their communities. Business strategies are influenced by such emotional and social ties. Effort and strategizing builds social capital and relational trust, closeness and interpersonal solidarity. In Chapter 4 we showed how a family's emigration to Tanzania accentuated the use of social capital as a strategy for the business. In the succession chapter about the French family (Chapter 5), we saw how social ties between different family owners through marriage benefitted the business. Within the Chinese case (Chapter 6), as in the Tanzanian one, the issue of social ties within the business and within the local community is explored, as is the practice of cluster ownership. While much of the drive theory we describe here is based on 'western thinking' we also found a more collective notion of drive exercised in this case (see Box 18.1).

Box 18.1 Confucianism and the family business

Cultural setting is another important factor that may influence the family's personal and group drives and decision-making processes. Although family businesses from Protestant, Quaker, Catholic, Jewish or Muslim backgrounds may share some similarities in family values despite their religious differences, the international differences in family businesses' culture (national culture) could not be underestimated (Denison, Lief and Ward, 2004) and is crucial in understanding the subtlety of the individual family business drives. In our Chinese case (Chapter 6), Confucianism (or

---

Confucian values) as a specific cultural influence merits a closer look. Different from any other region, Confucianism is rather a pragmatic lifestyle philosophy that incorporates a series of social codes which have existed in Chinese society over centuries. Confucianism encourages collective thinking and ethical yet orderly behaviours, which influence the subconscious and dynamics of Chinese family businesses. Confucius' social philosophy stresses the cultivation of *ren* by every individual in a community. The term *ren* is used to describe an extremely general and all-encompassing state of virtue, which no living person has attained completely (Waley, 1938). It is similar to the words 'humane', 'altruistic', or 'benevolent' yet not exactly the same. The concept of *ren* determines that Chinese family business owners would be reluctant to pursue profit-making as the only goal, as it might conflict with such a strong social norm.

Confucianism places family business in a social context, in which the interpersonal relationships inside and outside of a business family are subject to a variety of environmental influences (Yan and Sorenson, 2006). All the core thoughts advocated by the Confucian culture such as 'humanity, righteousness, harmony, loyalty, courtesy, honesty and cleanness' are thereby cultural aspects directing behaviour or making drives acceptable. These values are more collectivist than the individualist Western societies (Hofstede, 1980). In the *Book of Rites*, one of the Confucian classics, there is a saying: 'Cultivate yourself, pacify/regulate your family, manage the nation, [then/in order to] bring peace to the world.' This further explains why Chinese family business owners would be more willing to take the responsibility of reviving the glory of family, community and nation as a natural choice from an early stage, or sometimes even as a starting point for their entrepreneurship practice.

A focus on social ties within the culture, and our Chinese family business, responds to the Confucian values placed on them. Some argue that Confucian values might hinder innovation as they focus on interpersonal relationships and social harmony instead of individualism. However, the social awareness, reputation and trust that Confucianism emphasizes constitute the cornerstone of the family businesses in the cluster region, and the social ties become social capital, from which family owners benefit over the generations.

Emotional attachment of family members

We found, as suggested by socio-emotional theory, that attachment, and the emotions connected to this process, are hugely important to how the family business owners strategize. Emotional attachment is a distinctive attribute of family ownership. We discuss this in depth in Chapter 12 covering emotional attachment, how losses occur and how families recover and expand their strategic capacity. Attachment can be to a social identity, a product, or a knowledge base, and the recovery process from loss of this, for the owner and employees, is also explored in Chapter 13. Attachment and entitlement is discussed in the chapter on strategizing authority (Chapter 14). Importantly, the attachment and issues of gender, and a sense of entitlement between women and men – as wives and husbands, sisters and brothers – are explored in Chapter 15.

Renewal of family bonds in succession

Unsurprisingly we found that the families in all the cases aimed to keep the business for future generations and would take into account a time horizon of 10–20 years. Rarely is a succession plan clear, as the process is too complex and conditioned on individual family members' trajectory, events in the family and external events influencing the business. A succession is a state of mind where certain tasks, or parts of the succession complexity, are strategized. Succession strategizing is described in Chapter 16; the implications of power balances within the family in Chapter 14 and discussion of succession of the role of Chair in Chapter 17.

Psychoanalysis and family drive

Sigmund Freud, neurologist and the father of psychoanalysis, proposed a developed psychodynamic theory (Freud, 1914). He proposed that human life evolves in a complex dynamic of being partly in the past, partly in the present and partly in a dream and fantasy about the future. Personalities, and the complex interaction between personalities in the family, shape the family business. Freud's theory also matches well with how we see the families, living partly in the past, in the current situation and in the future. As such the business connects different generations and is a vehicle for the thoughts and feelings of family members. This is illustrated, in particular, in the Swedish case, where the challenge of tough global competition is linked to what the founders thought and felt, and the current generation's understanding of this.

Psychoanalysis has a developed theory based on the clinical practice of therapy for individual clients. This has resulted in many strands of different theories, offering several perspectives on how people think and act in ways that are destructive for their life. The aim for a therapeutic process is to increase the individual autonomy and we explore how family ownership and healthy family dynamics allowed for such autonomy in Chapter 9 and Chapter 11.

Larry Hirschhorn (1998) explores the experience of working with one's unconscious and reworking and exploring how to develop genuine authority within the organization, and, furthermore, how this is not only an individual issue but also a group process. We build on this in Chapter 14 but apply it so that one can explore the reworking of authority within the family and the business. Kets de Vries (Kets de Vries and Carlock, 2010) has been one of the major contributors in applying psychoanalytic theory to leadership and organizations. He has focused on how the intra-psychological dynamics of an owner or founder has implications for the group dynamic, identity and collective mind-sets in the organization. We found his description of the compensatory needs of the founder particularly useful. The succession case in French fashion is a classic example (Chapter 5) of such compensatory needs, over-involvement of the founders managed in a constructive way by their children.

In developing best practices, families had been able to understand their business context; to take reality into consideration as they make successful strategies. In this process family members challenge each other's understanding of reality, autonomy in their roles (Boalt Boethius, 1983), and develop and strategize authority. It is important not to overuse a pathological perspective when one is analysing healthy systems and individuals. The families we studied had been forced to deal with hard realities in their contexts, in the reality about themselves and the family. While successful, there are always threats to such reality orientation. In certain circumstances, people display anxiety and defences, including a particular type of defence called projection, or projective identification. These dynamics can distort the perception of reality by one family member or the family as a whole.

Not always conscious: defences

In the psychoanalytic understanding, defences (Freud, 1937) are a part of reducing how accurately we perceive. We put a lot of energy into constructing and maintaining these. The reality has to be distorted for a version of it to be accepted. We all do this to some degree. When someone says 'you are so defensive' it means that someone has heard something they see as an attack and they deny it or explain it away by referring to something that does not relate to themselves as person. It defends against feelings that are painful, sad or other strong unpleasant feelings such as guilt. They are kept unconscious by the defences.

There are several defence mechanisms against unpleasant emotions: rationalization, repression, rejection and hiding through displacement and regression. Object relations theory (Klein, 2002) relates to psyche in relation to important people during one's childhood. In this theory, objects are usually internalized images of primary caregivers. Some objects continue to exert a strong influence throughout life, and later experiences will in different ways reshape those early patterns. These internalized objects are immersed with emotions that can be sad or pleasant; some are helpful; while others can be anxiety-provoking. Is one unaware of objects and the emotions they are infused with, they will shape our perceptions and strategies. They can distort and flaw reality orientation and threaten the family-owned firm. One response to the challenges is through splitting: a simplified reaction where one solution is looked upon as all good or all bad with no middle ground. When one is occupied by this mind-set, any alternative is likely to be rejected as dangerous and unacceptable without adequate reality testing.

Anxiety as drive

We usually think of anxiety as an unpleasant inner state that we seek to avoid, if possible, as it acts as a signal that things are not going well. Consequently, we search for any defence mechanism to reduce anxiety. But our anxiety can be helpful; a certain dose is often needed to motivate us to embark on a necessary escape instead of a dangerous fight. Anxiety that is not too paralysing may serve as a drive – it may even be lifesaving. But, if the felt anxiety threatens to be paralysing we need to find ways to cope. The Lutheran Arab case (Chapter 8) illustrates different dimensions of anxiety and how to manage it. The company is challenging political convention in a volatile situation, where violence is common. The stewardship created meaning for the family, a common cause as a shield from the risk of violence. The family members integrated the stewardship into a self-identity, they do not deny or intellectualize the danger and anxiety too much. It is partly defending against a possibly overwhelming worry, but also realizing that the danger is there. As such, in this case as in the US case, the financial safety and anxiety is a major drive.

The theory of defences and defence mechanisms is not very clear or consistent. Most notably, defined by Sigmund Freud in his psychoanalytic theory, is the idea of defence mechanisms. Freud described these as a tactic developed by the ego to protect against anxieties provoked by inappropriate or unwanted thoughts or impulses threatening to enter the mind. When we cannot deal with our desire, the constraints of reality or our own moral standards, we may also find ourselves overwhelmed and controlled by anxiety. In our context drive for autonomy, negotiating individual drive against the drives of others, including collective drives, is powerful and can provoke conflicts. Ownership or a business which can be a vessel for individual and family drive, has an ego function. It is the vessel for negotiating between the drive and outside reality. If the anxiety is too overwhelming family members will become paralysed. If they become hubristic, with too little anxiety or worry, this can jeopardize strategies.

Projection and reality orientation

Tolerating the less favourable parts of oneself, including the collective self – such as a family – is difficult for most of us. A well-known defence phenomenon is projection, also known as blame shifting. It is described as a misattribution of one's undesired feelings, impulses and thoughts onto another person or group. A risk is to develop a narcissistic denial and overvaluation of the self while regarding others as of a lesser breed. This could be the outcome of a personal, or even a shared, lack of insight – an unwillingness to acknowledge one's own difficulties. Projection converts a neurosis or moral anxiety into a real anxiety, which may be easier to deal with. Often forgotten is the opposite of hubris: our reverse tendency to project our own capabilities onto others and to abdicate from responsibility in a role. As such success can be a huge threat for the family. An important thing here is to distinguish between the exercise of power and the taking of authority (see Chapter 14).

The business as opportunity and defence

Within this perspective one has usually seen the family business as serving as a defence, or even compensation, for narcissistic vulnerability, sibling rivalry, envy, hate (Klein and Riviere, 1964) and haunting family myths. Kets de Vries (1989; Kets de Vries and Engellau 2004) has described these aspects and how they can lead to stagnation, destructive rivalry and ,loss of vitality. At an unconscious level an heir may be flooded by ideas about lacking autonomy, insufficient capacity and fear of transition. Unconsciously one may actually be anxious and insecure about having the ability to take over at the same time as struggling with forbidden fantasies on how to replace one's precursor. In family ownership the business might reinforce or trigger such family dynamics. These destructive and painful family dynamics are a part of any family, normally erupting during crises, death and inheritance. While the family business brings high stakes into the family it is not in itself the origin of these unconscious dynamics.

Another useful notion for the complexity of family ownership and defences is what Bowlby called 'defensive exclusion' (Bowlby, 1980). He saw defences as a primary perceptive process; everyone needs to select parts of the world so as to not be overwhelmed. He defined defensive exclusion as similar to, but broader than, traditional defences such as regression, splitting and dissociation in psychoanalysis. The origin and function of defensive exclusion is different. It is a selective exclusion of the information reaching our senses. Some exclusion is necessary to prevent overload, but if certain types of information are excluded over a long period of time it creates a distortion of reality. Exclusion defence describes how we all need to reduce the huge amount of information continuously reaching our senses, so as not to be overloaded. It is an adaptive mechanism ensuring that relevant data is attended to in preference to irrelevant data. But we also exclude information that we dislike, or that disturbs us, and certain types of information might be excluded for long periods of time or even permanently.

Attachment, trust and affect

Attachment theory developed from the premise that the earliest humans found themselves vulnerable as they moved from their earlier homes in the forest into the more open and exposed savannahs. They did not have the speed or the strength to avoid the dangers presented by the more open environment. Their solution was to find security in numbers. Over time the more successful groups developed a very strong connection – a compelling need to maintain the sense of security provided by forming into groups. Eventually this driving need to belong became inherent in our nature and even today is a critical part of our humanness.

The early work of John Bowlby (1969) was based primarily on the attachment relationship between mother and infant. However, he soon discovered that the importance of this relationship extends past the initial survival security of the infant and he was able to relate this drive to our primitive past. In this way he discovered that this naturally based need for attachments generates powerful forces within us, and is also a critical part of our adult life. As such, and when properly established, the attachment objects lay the foundation for much of our future success as productive adults in modern groups – or organizations. In Chapter 12, about mourning and strategic capacity, we describe how a family 'group' serves as an object of attachment. The family is a unit that acts as a secure base, and it is from this base that drives emerge that allow for the exploration of socio-emotional wealth as a worthy venture. Using Bowlby and attachment theory enables one to go into depth on this process that leads to potential benefits, as well as potential harm.

Trust

A propensity to trust others in our lives is based almost exclusively on the development of healthy attachments during infancy. When the infant's efforts are supported by appropriate reciprocal actions and behaviours, a safe and secure base is achieved. If the infant forms the belief that the caregiver is trustworthy it facilitates moving into the next stage of exploratory behaviour. It is these initial and subsequent experiences that build, ultimately in the adult, the capacity to trust. While the experiences with the family are the source of great trust, they can, just as well, be a source of great mistrust. It is a strong sense of trust that is usually at the core of most successful family businesses.

With several members who have established a basic type of trust there is a tight group who will have defences that are exclusive to that group. These can be challenged or sometimes accepted. But a perspective that comes from the collective capacity in such a group can be very high. These groups occasionally become dysfunctional, however, and display group think (Kahneman, 2003). When a group is unable to think outside a particular course of action, a path dependency on a particular strategy, the only way to counteract this is to develop a tolerance to the tension inherent in reviewing alternatives and options. When a stalemate is encountered, advisers or non-family members are important in challenging a collective defensive exclusion. This, and how a change in succession, and a family leader leaving the top leadership role, is strategized, is illustrated in the succession chapter. Further, negotiating and strategizing authority (Chapter 14) and the succession process (Chapter 16) show the process of establishing and maintaining trust within the family, and in relationships with employees and other non-family leaders in the business.

Affect

The concepts of Bowlby's (1969) original attachment theory, based on his 40 years of research, have subsequently been reinforced by functional magnetic resonate imaging; they are, indeed, now seen as a persistent and powerful force in the more primitive parts of our brain (Panksepp and Biven, 2012). The midbrain above our spinal cord is now being carefully studied in this regard. It is an ancient structure that serves to collect data from our senses that monitor the world within us, and around us. Some of these sensory structures tell us how our body is functioning – they tell us whether we are injured, sick or well, and whether we are hungry, thirsty or satiated. Other sensors in this area of the brain serve as the central collection area for data coming from outside our bodies – from those senses monitoring the world in which we live. This is the area that first receives encoded images, sounds, smells, tastes and tactile information that arrives unfiltered from the sensory structures that collect data from outside our body.

As it is first received, this data has not been subjected to any of our filters or our biases, and the initial impression left by this information can often be briefly seen in our various facial expressions. Functional magnetic resonance imaging (fMRI) research and related findings indicate this area may house some of our most basic human survival behaviours. Seven feelings, variously called 'affects' or 'emotions', have been described as a part of our biology. Panksepp and Biven (2012) have described these as affects that have been a part of our nature. They involve our need for the security that is found in our basic urge to form into groups. This need is satisfied through inherent drives that involve SEEKING, CARING, LOVING, and PLAYING relationships that compel us to form and maintain our relationships in groups. They also provide our initial reactions to FEAR, GRIEF/PANIC, and ANGER that describe what happens when our group relationships are threatened.1

The significance of these six affects to the purposes of this chapter is that in this one respect we are all alike – we all use attachments to reinforce our sense of belonging and security. The family, as owner of a business, is as unique as the family is an object, the business, where the family channel this biological drive into an object and strategize it. This becomes a very strong collective driving force. The best practice cases show good enough trust in the family and provide an available functional and adaptable defence system that do not reduce reality orientation too much. They can further add value to the transaction on the market place, and be a transformational system. The drive and ability to go through difficult transitions, to be innovative, is described in the next section.

Transitional drive: reality orientation and play

A transitional approach builds on the work of psychoanalyst Donald Winnicott (1971) and his writings about transitional space and the development of an authentic self, creativity and identity. We explore this in Chapter 11, on autonomy and role, as the family members are negotiating and creating roles they have a wish for, while also taking into consideration the family and its ownership tasks, and the tasks of the business. It is explored in Chapter 9, the Colombian owner's own account of how she developed her role as owner. A notion of the family as a 'transitional space', or an intermediate space where playfulness and reality are a part of the discussion and process, can be helpful.

A crucial ability, concurrently or in sequence, is to have both good reality orientation and playfulness (Amado, 2010). Most of the families, when they managed to have a good reality orientation and were allowed to experiment and play with ideas, would constitute such a transitional space. It contributes a sense of control and creativity in relation to the external reality (Amado and Sharpe, 2001). The capacity to create and to use transitional space is regarded as developing in early childhood and as remaining important throughout life for a sense of subjectivity and a unique self or autonomy.

Shifting between reality orientation and playfulness is fundamental for the capacity to develop new ideas, to innovate and to use the imagination as a tool. Good reality orientation, in the case of organizations such as a family business, includes the capacity to detach and review the family ownership internal dynamic as well as the realities in the business context. Playfulness includes not taking the assumptions, values and structures for granted, but rather possessing a readiness to reconstruct, imagine and explore other possibilities. Transitional space – and also strategic space insofar as the family can strategize a wide range of options – is an intellectual and emotional capacity. It consists of reviewing and playing with possibilities, deconstructing and reconstructing an 'object' (values, products or business) and the meaning or involvement one has with it. The ability to mourn losses is also important for this type of transitional capacity to be used. Transitional space allows for new and adaptive possibilities to be explored, discovered, created and acted on. The polarity to an active strategic space would be bounded rationality (Kahneman, 2003) and a strategy process marked by failure to utilize all available information, group think, limited horizons and tunnel thinking. Different threats contribute to such a collapse, or partial collapse, of strategic space. As explored in this book, a best practice ownership family will use the family as a transitional space.

Note

1   The use of capital letters for these instincts, or affects, is to denote biological circuits in the brain, which are hard-wired. This is to differentiate them from the more daily, common use of such terms denoting emotional states, reflecting a more subjective experience.

References

Amado, G. (2010). Potential space: The threatened source of individual and collective creativity. In B. Sievers (Ed.), *Psychoanalytic Studies of Organizations* (pp. 263–284). London, UK: Karnac.

Amado, G. and Sharpe, J. (2001). Review as a necessary ingredient in transitional change. In G. Amado and A. Ambrose (Eds.), *The Transitional Approach To Change* (pp. 119–136). London, UK: Karnac.

Berrone, P., Cruz, C. and Gomez-Mejia, L.R. (2012). Socioemotional wealth in family firms theoretical dimensions, assessment approaches, and agenda for future research. *Family Business Review, 25*(3), 258–279.

Boalt Boethius, S. (1983). *Autonomy, Coping and Defense in Small Work Groups*. Stockholm: Almqvist & Wiksell International.

Bowlby J. (1969). *Attachment. Attachment and loss: Vol. 1.* New York: Basic Books.

Bowlby, J. (1980). *Loss: Sadness and depression. Attachment and loss: Vol. 3,* (International psycho-analytical library no.109). London: Hogarth Press.

Denison, D., Lief, C. and Ward, J.L. (2004). Culture in family-owned enterprises: Recognizing and leveraging unique strengths. *Family Business Review, 17,* 61–70.

Freud, S. (1914). *Five Lectures on Psycho-Analysis.* Worcestershire, UK: Read Books Ltd.

Freud, A. (1937). *The Ego and the Mechanisms of Defence.* London: Hogarth Press and Institute of Psycho-Analysis.

Gomez-Mejia, L.R., Haynes, K.T., Núñez-Nickel, M., Jacobson, K.J. and Moyano-Fuentes, J. (2007). Socioemotional wealth and business risks in family-controlled firms: Evidence from Spanish olive oil mills. *Administrative Science Quarterly, 52*(1), 106–137.

Hirschhorn, L., (1998). *Reworking Authority: Leading and following in the post-modern organization* (Vol. 12). Philadelphia, PA, US: MIT Press.

Hofstede, G. (1980). Motivation, leadership, and organisation: Do American theories apply abroad?, *Organisational Dynamics*, 1980b, Summer, 42–63.

Kahneman, D. (2003). A perspective on judgment and choice: mapping bounded rationality. *American Psychologist, 58*(9), 697.

Kets de Vries, M.F.R. (1989). *Prisoners of Leadership* (Vol. 36). New York: Wiley.

Kets de Vries, M.F.R. and Engellau, E. (2004). *Are Leaders Born or are They Made?: The case of Alexander the Great.* London: Karnac Books.

Kets de Vries, M.F.R. and Carlock, R.S. (2010). *Family Business On The Couch: A psychological perspective.* Hoboken, NJ, US: John Wiley & Sons.

Klein, M. (2002). *Love, Guilt and Reparation: And other works 1921–1945* (Vol. 1). New York: Simon and Schuster.

Klein, M. and Riviere, J. (1964) *Love, Hate and Reparation.* New York and London: W.W. Norton & Company.

Panksepp, J. and Biven, L. (2012). *The Archaeology of Mind: Neuroevolutionary origins of human emotions (Norton series on interpersonal neurobiology).* New York and London: W.W. Norton & Company.

Waley, A. (1938). *The Analects of Confucius.* New York: Vintage Books.

Winnicott, D.W. (1971). *Playing and Reality.* London, UK: Tavistock Publications Ltd.

Yan, J. and Sorenson, R. (2006). The Effect of Confucian Values on Succession in Family Business, *Family Business Review, 19*(3), 235–250.

Index